Negotiating Conquest

Negotiating Conquest

Gender and Power in California, 1770s to 1880s

Miroslava Chávez-García

The University of Arizona Press

Tucson

The University of Arizona Press
© 2004 The Arizona Board of Regents
All rights reserved

www.uapress.arizona.edu

Library of Congress Cataloging-in-Publication Data
Chávez-García, Miroslava, 1968–
Negotiating conquest : gender and power in California, 1770s to 1880s /
Miroslava Chávez-García.
p. cm.
Includes bibliographical references and index.
ISBN 978-0-8165-2600-0 (pbk. : alk. paper)
1. Mexican American women—California—Social conditions—18th century.
2. Mexican American women—California—Social conditions—19th century.
3. California—Social conditions—18th century. 4. California—Social
conditions—19th century. 5. California—Colonization—Social aspects.
6. California—Ethnic relations. 7. Sex role—California—History. 8. Power
(Social sciences)—California—History. 9. Mexican Americans—California—
Social conditions—18th century. 10. Mexican Americans—California—Social
conditions—19th century. I. Title.
F870.M5C48 2004
305.8'968'720794—dc22   2004006186

Publication of this book is made possible in part by a grant from the University of California, Davis, College of Letters and Science, Division of Humanities, Arts, and Cultural Studies, and the Office of the Vice Chancellor for
Research.

16   15   14   13   12   11   9   8   7   6   5

In loving memory,
María Concepción Alvarado de Chávez (1954–1981)
José Esparza Chávez (1933–1981)

Contents

List of Figures   ix
List of Tables   xi
Preface   xiii
Acknowledgments   xxiii

Part I   **Women in Spanish and Mexican California**

1   Gender and the Conquest and Colonization of
California   3

2   Patriarchs, Power, and Sexuality   25

3   Family, Property, and Economic Independence   52

Part II   **Women in American California**

4   Divorce, Culture, and the Family   89

5   Loss of Property and Economic Independence   123

6   Illegitimacy and Social Dislocation after
the American Conquest   151

Legacies: An Afterword   174

Notes   179
Glossary   217
Bibliography   219
Index   233

Figures

Map of the greater Los Angeles region, ca. 1840   xxvii

1.1   Misión San Gabriel in the 1870s or 1880s   9

1.2   Eulalia Pérez in the 1880s   22

3.1   Native women at Misión San Luis Rey in the 1860s or 1870s   61

3.2   Los Angeles Plaza in 1865   70

4.1   María Antonia Coronel de Godey and Guadalupe Zamorano de
      Dalton in the 1860s or 1870s   105

4.2   Merced Williams, Margarita Bandini, and Francisca Williams,
      ca. 1860s-1870s   112

5.1   An unidentified daughter of Felicita Josefa at Misión
      San Fernando   132

5.2   Los Angeles and surrounding ranchos in 1871   136

5.3   María Merced Tapia de Prudhomme in the 1870s or 1880s   137

5.4   The first official survey of the city of Los Angeles, 1849   141

Tables

5.1   Los Angeles County Property Values, 1851–1880   135

5.2   Los Angeles City Population, 1850–1880   143

5.3   Los Angeles City Property Values by Gender and Ethnicity,
        1857–1874   144

5.4   Los Angeles City Property Holders by Gender and Ethnicity,
        1857–1874   145

5.5   Average Personal Property Values among Californio-Mexicans,
        1857–1874   147

5.6   Personal Property Values by Gender and Ethnicity,
        1855–1874   148

6.1   Illegitimacy Rates at Misión San Gabriel and the Los Angeles
        Plaza Church, 1800s–1870s   160

Preface

In 1519, Chontal Mayans in Acalán, near the base of the present-day Yucatán peninsula, gave fifteen native female slaves to Spanish explorer Hernán Cortés and his men as an inducement for them to leave the Mayan territory. Among the females was a fourteen-year-old slave girl of noble birth and Nahua origins, who was later baptized and known to the Spaniards as "Marina." Marina, or "Malintzin" as the Nahuatl-speaking peoples later identified her, stood out among her female companions for her multilingual abilities. She knew Mayan, which she had learned from her captors, the Chontales; Nahuatl, her native language, as spoken in Tenochtitlán, present-day Mexico City; and several regional dialects of Nahuatl, which were mutually unintelligible to these widely dispersed peoples. On recognizing her linguistic skills, Cortés used her, along with Jerónimo de Aguirre, a Spaniard who had learned Mayan while marooned in Yucatán, to communicate with Nahuatl- and Mayan-speaking peoples. Within a short time, perhaps a month, Malintzin learned rudimentary Spanish, making Aguirre expendable, and she became Cortés's sole translator. Cortés always had her at his side, and she facilitated communication when he befriended the Tlaxcalans, mortal enemies of the Nahuas and Moteuçoma (Montezuma), their leader. She was there when Cortés massacred the Cholulans, allies of the Nahuas, who had planned to kill Cortés and his men. And she was there when he seized, sacked, and plundered Tenochtitlán. Two years after the conquest of Mexico, Malintzin bore Cortés a son and symbolically gave birth to the first generation of mestizos (persons of Spanish and native ancestry, today identified as the Mexican people).[1]

Since Mexican Independence in 1821, most scholars have marginalized and vilified Malintzin, known popularly as as "La Malinche," for her role in the conquest. They have identified her as a traitor to her own race and a highly sexualized native woman, who selfishly consorted with the "white" *conquistadores*. It was she, they argued, who betrayed her people and held ultimate responsibility for the downfall of the Aztec (Mexica) empire and the imposition of three hundred years of colonial rule.[2] In recent years, feminist scholars have reexamined and reinterpreted such depictions of Malintzin and, in the process, have challenged deeply entrenched beliefs about her role in the conquest. Although some feminists see her as a victim of patriarchy—the male domination of women in the family and society—others portray her as an intelligent, strong-willed woman, who not only endured rape, captivity, and the ravages of war but also shaped the course of events leading up to and following the Spanish conquest. As Frances Kartunnen, a scholar of Latin America, has argued, Malintzin was "a gifted woman in impossible circumstances carving out survival one day at a time."[3]

The reinterpretation of Malintzin's role in the Spanish conquest of central Mexico demonstrates the centrality of women, gender, patriarchy, and sexuality in imperial expansion. It also reveals the ways in which ethnicity, culture, and violence informed the policies and practices of war. Since the mid-1970s, scholars have begun to pay attention to native women, mestizas (women of Spanish-Indian ancestry), *mulatas* (women of Spanish-African ancestry), and other *casta* (racially mixed) women of Spanish, Indian, and African ancestry.[4] Despite being bound by specific religious and secular beliefs about marriage, the family, and sexuality, women of all social classes, ethnicities, and regions have played multiple, key roles in the conquest, colonization, and development of Spanish and, later, Mexican society. This book focuses on how Spanish-speaking women—*gente de razón* (literally, people of reason; a term used by the Spanish to identify and distinguish Spanish-speaking colonists from the Native Californians), *neófitas* (Christianized Indian women), and *gentiles* (non-Christian Indian women)—negotiated patriarchal institutions and ideologies as well as the violent transition from Spanish, Mexican, to American rule following the U.S. conquest in 1848.

This study of women of Spanish and Native American ancestry opens in the 1770s, when Spain imposed Catholic, colonial rule in Alta California, and it ends in the 1880s with the ascendancy of a Euro-American,

Protestant, capitalist society. It begins with an examination of how gender and ethnicity shaped the policies and practices of the Spanish conquest and shows that women, marriage, and the family—the basic unit of Spanish society—played a central role in producing a stable society on Mexico's northernmost frontier. It then examines how gender, law, property, and ethnicity shaped social and class relations among Spanish, Mexican, and Native American women and men. It draws special attention to how women dealt with the gendered, class, and ethnic hierarchies that gave elite Spanish and Mexican men patriarchal authority over Spanish-speaking women and over Native American men and women. Despite such power, women of different classes and ethnicities found ways to skirt constraints in the home and larger society.

With the American takeover in 1848, the focus shifts to how the imposition of foreign legal, economic, linguistic, and cultural norms affected the status of Spanish-speaking women, male-female relations, and the family. Among the most significant findings are the manner in which the conquest weakened the economic position of Spanish-speaking men and women yet simultaneously increased the leverage of the latter in their personal and social relationships with men. Women did not assume passive roles during this period, but, rather, they actively adapted their traditional roles and practices to their new social, cultural, and legal environment. In the process, they became agents of cultural change in the Spanish-speaking community, among Californios, that is, early settlers in California and their descendants, and Mexico-born residents. At the same time, they developed new strategies for dealing with their changing circumstances and retaining their ethnic identity.

I begin where Antonia I. Castañeda and Virginia Mayo Bouvier ended their analyses of women of Spanish, African, and Native American ancestry in colonial California. In her groundbreaking work, "*Presidarias y pobladoras*: Spanish-Mexican Women in Frontier Monterey, Alta California, 1770–1821," Castañeda found that women and the ideas about male and female roles and relations—gender—were central to the success of the Spanish conquest and colonization of California.[5] Spanish, mestiza, mulata, and other Spanish-speaking women, she argued, participated in the reproduction and production of patriarchal institutions, such as marriage and the family, and these institutions remained essentially unchanged at the close of California's Spanish epoch. In *Women and the Conquest of California, 1542–1840: Codes of Silence*, Bouvier determined that ideas about sexual differences between males and females—gender ideologies—not only shaped, and were shaped by, the Spanish conquest but also were a powerful element in the "glue" that held the conquest together.[6] My findings confirm their conclusions, but I also build on their work to show that during the Mexican period, women found ways to challenge patriarchs, thereby preparing Californianas (Californio women), *mexicanas*, and *indígenas* (native women) for the even more profound changes in the aftermath of the American conquest.

The U.S.–Mexico war wrought a series of structural and cultural changes that touched nearly every facet of women's lives, even the most intimate aspects of their personal relations. Deena González, in *Refusing the Favor: The Spanish-Mexican Women of Santa Fe, 1820–1880*, has noted the widespread effects of the conquest. In Santa Fe, as my study finds for Los Angeles, "few women escaped the hardships of the conquest."[7] González's book deals with the impact of "economic colonization" on women and argues that the transition from a barter to a trade and then to a capitalist economy "locked [women] into the lowest rung of the wage-based economy." Like González, I demonstrate the deleterious effects of the rapid emergence of a capitalist economy, but my findings also reveal how the American takeover irrevocably altered gender relations and family patterns and created opportunities for women to contest power relationships in marriage and the family. While some women challenged long-held beliefs about those institutions by seeking a divorce, others did so by forming extra-marital unions and having children outside of church- or state-sanctioned matrimony. In the aftermath of the conquest, women engaged in behavior that only a few years earlier was deemed antithetical to the family and the stability of the larger community, but they did so in an effort to carve out a better life for themselves and their families.

The study also sheds light on how the conquest altered Spanish and Mexican law and related institutions that continued into the American era and how those changes affected women's rights, status, and personal relations. Although legal scholars have shown the influence of the Hispanic principle of community property on California common and statutory law, few have studied how women of different ethnicities used the courts to gain equity and justice.[8] I explore those issues as well as the question of how women coped with their familial and personal relationships as well as the changing circumstances in their everyday lives. My work also examines the relationship between law and practice by mining and analyzing thousands of little-studied English- and Spanish-language court cases at the federal, county, and local levels; city council records; private collections; church records; novels; newspapers; memoirs; letters; and scrapbooks from the Spanish, Mexican, and American eras.[9] Despite radical transformations in legal, linguistic, and cultural practices, women resorted to the law to assert their rights to property, children, and support.

Despite what we know about women's experiences, our knowledge is fragmentary. From the surviving records, we can only partially reconstruct and interpret the past. The records are "snapshots" of specific moments in time, of both mundane and significant events that speak to brief episodes in women's lives and their relationships to other individuals. As the book attempts to recover a largely unknown history, its goal has been to piece scraps of evidence together, like the pieces of a puzzle, in order to build a larger picture—no matter how incomplete or partial—from which to detect and draw conclusions about larger social, cultural, and economic patterns. To aid in the process, I have applied Emma Pérez's suggestion, in the *Decolonial Imaginary: Writing Chicanas into History,* that we listen to and interpret mexicana, indígena, and Chicana voices that have been silenced and relegated to the margins, to passivity, and to "interstitial spaces."[10] In many instances, particularly when the silences emerge in the records, I have attempted to give meaning to the inaudible and invisible by suggesting and hypothesizing about the motivations and implications of women's actions and of the measures taken against them. Pérez reminds us that despite the silences, women's words "survive and persist whether acknowledged or not."[11]

The records I have culled from the Spanish and Mexican periods, though sometimes "thin," are richly textured, descriptive, and nuanced. They offer a window onto the lives of Spanish-speaking and Native American women, and men, at all levels of society. The paper trail generated in the American period pales in comparison. The English-language texts, although abundant, are largely legalistic and formulaic documents, and they often fail to tell us much about individuals or about the details surrounding a particular case. Consequently, to some extent, I have relied on quantitative material, such as censuses and baptismal registers, as well as that which is qualitative in nature, such as memoirs and court-room testimonies, to bring into sharper relief women's experiences in the post-conquest period.

In examining the ways in which women shaped and were shaped

by their times, this book—like those of other feminist historians—uses an interpretive framework that incorporates gender, race, class, and sexuality as categories of analysis.[12] By asking gender-specific questions, my findings provide insight into the connections among male-female relations, ethnicity, and class. This approach also enables my work to describe the multiple roles women performed and fulfilled in their families and community. Women inhabited a world where the "public" domain of politics and government and the "private" space of the domestic hearth—commonly identified in nineteenth-century Euro-American women's history—blurred and frequently merged. As recent scholars have found, Mexican women's activities in and outside the home, traditionally viewed as "private" and "public" realms, often overlapped and were interdependent.[13]

This book contributes to the body of knowledge that demonstrates that patriarchy varied across time, space, and locale. By showing that mexicanas contested the limits of male rule and insisted that patriarchal relationships be based on reciprocity, in which husbands and wives, fathers and daughters had mutual obligations, the book expands our knowledge of how patriarchy functioned and evolved. By demonstrating that the shift in sovereignty from Mexican to American rule altered power relationships between men and women, this study also reveals how historical conquests transform social relationships in the family and community.[14]

Building on the work of Castañeda and Bouvier, part 1 focuses on how gender, patriarchy, ethnicity, and culture shaped the military and spiritual conquest of California from the 1770s to the 1820s. Chapter 1 shows that Spanish beliefs and practices about men and women's roles and relations in marriage and the family and native peoples' "place" in Hispanic society were central to the settlement and development of the region. It examines how the encouragement of marriages between Spanish soldiers and women from Mexico's northern provinces—particularly local neófitas—and of the colonization of Spanish-speaking families was used in an attempt to diffuse the soldiers' aggression and, at the same time, to assist Spanish authorities in settling, populating, and developing provincial California.

Chapter 2 explores marital, familial, and community gender relations in Mexican Los Angeles and the greater region, and it probes the interaction of women of different ethnicities with the patriarchal legal system.

It finds that those relations were sometimes characterized by gender conflict and negotiation, in which men and women contested the meanings and boundaries of male and female roles and obligations. A close exploration of the gente de razón's legal and social understanding of marriage, sexuality, and the family shows how Californio, Mexican, and Native American women, across the socioeconomic spectrum, used local institutions to contend with men who exceeded their patriarchal authority. Women's appeals were usually successful, but in those instances where abuse continued, many women resorted to extralegal means to escape their troubled households. Such action invariably alarmed civil and religious authorities as well as men wary of any threat to male-dominated households and the norms of the larger community. Men who abandoned their households faced few repercussions, which reveals the sexual double standard and gender inequalities with which women had to contend in Mexican Los Angeles.

As chapter 3 reveals, the right of many women to hold property in their own name provided them with powerful means to assert their individuality and to achieve a measure of independence within the family and the community. Those women most successful in skirting patriarchal control were gente de razón who owned significant amount of ranching and agricultural land that enabled them to gain economic independence and entry into the highest level of society. The property also served to distinguish them from other, poorer Californio, Mexican, and Native American women in the community. Regardless of whether a woman had been born or had married into the elite or had joined it as a result of her wealth, the independence she gained resulted from her complete legal control over substantial property holdings. Differences in ethnicity, however, influenced the extent to which women held property and hence economic power. Neófitas and especially gentiles had little real property and suffered from impoverishment, which left them socially marginalized.

Part 2 of the book shifts to the first three decades of American sovereignty, to focus on how Spanish-speaking women and men contended with the imposition of a foreign political, legal, economic, and linguistic framework in the initial transition to U.S. governance. It examines how the American conquest altered power relationships in marriage, the family, the law, economy, polity, and society. Following approval of the state constitution in 1850, Californios had to contend with the loss of property rights; the American common law; a foreign language; an increasingly Euro-American and Protestant population and culture; the Americanization of the Catholic Church; the rapid development of a capitalist, farming economy; and the decline of the ranching economy.

Chapter 4 demonstrates that the shift in the legal system altered gender and patriarchal relations. Under common law, women had the opportunity to divorce, a recourse forbidden under Mexican and church cannon law. Despite the persisting influence of those early prohibitions, many women took advantage of this option or threatened to do so. The ability to divorce not only reinforced their ability to challenge wayward husbands but also enabled them to sever intolerable marriages. It also provided the legal opportunity (if not the reality) to recover personal property and their share of community property; gain custody of their children (difficult to do in the Mexican period); and seek support for themselves and their children. Thus, this significantly increased their leverage in contesting patriarchal authority, though the poverty of their former spouses usually meant that the law produced little in the way of actual support. Most women did not opt to disrupt cultural norms by divorcing, but the women who did file for divorce represented a small yet significant sector of the Spanish-speaking community undergoing cultural transformation.

Changes in the political and legal systems gave women the right to divorce, but they also further undermined women's economic status and their ability to support themselves and their families. Chapter 5 examines how land laws, machinations in the courts, exorbitant costs for litigating cases, and steep interest rates on loans combined to dispossess most female (and male) landowners of their property, and thereby of their independence and livelihood. Despite women's attempts to retain their property, by the 1880s they faced increased landlessness and impoverishment, forcing many of them to find alternative sources of survival in the capitalist economy. Ethnic biases in the laws and courts also severely affected Native Californian women, neófitas and gentiles both, curtailing the land rights and most civil rights that they had held prior to the American conquest. In the 1850s and 1860s, the California legislature enacted laws that excluded Native Americans from the legal, cultural, and social worlds inhabited by "whites"—Californios, Mexicans, and Euro-Americans.

The Euro-American conquest not only undermined women's economic status and ability to sustain themselves and their families, but it also brought about larger social, economic, demographic, and cultural changes—"social dislocation"—that impacted in other ways the lives of women of Spanish and Native American ancestry. Chapter 6 discusses why illegitimacy increased dramatically in the post-conquest period. Beginning in the first decade of American sovereignty, the percentage of Californio, Mexican, and Native American children born outside of a state-sanctioned marriage rose dramatically, and those rates did not begin to decline until around the beginning of the 1880s. As the chapter reveals, the dramatic rise in illegitimacy was not a consequence of changing attitudes toward sexuality and marriage but rather to transformations already underway in the late Mexican period, which accelerated following the American conquest. Primary among the destabilizing elements were the impoverishment and marginalization of the Mexican population and the rapid population decline in the Native American community; the migration of Spanish-speaking men to other parts of the state and to Mexico; the resulting abandonment of Mexican women by their husbands; and the decision of those women to take up with men other than their spouses, who would support them and their children.

Scholars agree that recovering and reconstructing the daily lives and experiences of women who left few written or other sources are difficult tasks. For me, it has been a labor of love. By assiduously seeking out and carefully analyzing rarely examined sources, I have sought to produce a book that provides a complex and nuanced understanding of women's challenges, accomplishments, and shortcomings. Above all, my purpose in doing the research and in writing this book is to honor and recognize women of all ethnic backgrounds, social classes, and regions, who established households, nurtured and reared families, and rose above personal adversity in societies that often ignored, overlooked, and rendered them invisible.

Acknowledgments

Many generous people—mentors and colleagues, archivists and administrators, friends and family—provided the intellectual, personal, and financial support that made the completion of this book possible. To them I owe a debt of gratitude, and to them, I also dedicate this book. First and foremost, I would like to thank Norris Hundley Jr., the chair of my doctoral committee and advisor, for consistently working with me in my effort to recover, rewrite, and reinterpret the history of women and men of Spanish, African, and Native American ancestry in nineteenth-century California. The achievement of this study would not have been possible without his guidance, patience, and generosity throughout the years. More recently, he has "come out" of his retirement on numerous occasions to work with me in seeing this project to its completion. He is truly a remarkable person and role model, and I have been blessed to have such a supportive mentor and friend. From the bottom of my heart, I also thank his supportive spouse, Carol Hundley, for her patience and encouragement.

George J. Sánchez, a mentor and advisor, also deserves special mention, for he offered me invaluable support and took a chance on me in the early stages of my graduate career. Without him, the path to academia would have remained beyond my reach. George also provided me, as well as many graduate students at UCLA, insight on the inner workings of life in academia. I would also like to acknowledge the other members of my doctoral dissertation committee, Laura Gómez, James Lockhart, and Michael Salman, who read and discussed ideas with me, provided feedback during the early stages of my work, and offered intellectual assistance.

Other teachers, colleagues, and mentors who deserve special acknowledgment include Ernesto Chávez, a friend who shared with me, as well as countless other students, his wisdom about graduate studies and life. In his own way, Ernie offered all of us vital resources in surviving and thriving in academia. Thanks for being there. To Janet Fireman, curator, archivist, historian, and *amiga*, who allowed me ample time and space to carry out my research at the Los Angeles County Museum of Natural History, I owe *mil gracias*. More recently, Vicki L. Ruiz, a tireless scholar, invaluable mentor, and trustworthy friend on countless occasions has guided me through the publication process and helped me in networking in academic circles. She merits special praise for her mentoring and promoting of junior faculty.

Special friends who pulled me through the early stages of this project include, above all, my confidant, Cathy Ceniza Choy, who continues to be an invaluable resource and is always available to lend a sympathetic ear. Jaime Cardenas, Yun Won Cho, Theresa Delgadillo, Linda Nueva España Maram, Homero del Pino, Josie Rodríguez, and Omar Valerio-Jiménez encouraged me to "stick with it" when all seemed lost. María Raquel Casas, Mike Engh, Michael J. González, Steve Hackel, and Donna Schuele not only shared their friendship with me but also their knowledge and research materials, facilitating many aspects of my work. Without them and their scholarship, my work would not be where it is today. Thank you for your generosity.

Those who have read revised versions of the book and who provided useful insights and feedback include Ned Blackhawk, Monica Brown, Susan Deeds, Susan Ferber, Jack D. Forbes, Deena J. González, Lisbeth Haas, George H. Phillips, Rosaura Sánchez, William Clay Stalls, and three anonymous reviewers. Antonia I. Castañeda, Clark Davis, Camille Guerin-Gonzales, Kevin R. Johnson, Kerwin L. Klein, Cathy Komisaruk, Kevin Terraciano, and Ann Twinam, the Chicana/o Cultural Studies Reading Group at Stanford University, as well as my former colleagues at NAU and my current Chicana/o Studies colleagues at the University of California, Davis, offered support and critical analyses of my work at different stages of my career. I thank all of them for their input.

Long-time friends who have known and encouraged me include my UCLA rowing "buddies," Michelle Brands, Tara (Jones) Eitner, and Margarita Reyes-Williamson, and my UCLA peer counselor-turned *amigo*, Richard Rivera. Several support groups also lent invaluable mental and physiological relief during my time away from my work. Alan Nagamoto, at the UCLA Student Psychological Services, Jmylle Carter, Dan Johnson, Judith Gleba, and the Los Angeles "Leggers," among others, deserve a world of thanks. Special colleagues at the University of California, Davis, who provided much needed encouragement on a daily basis include Kimberly Nettles and Lorena Oropeza.

Archivists who assisted me in numerous ways include John Cahoon, at the Seaver Center for Western History, Los Angeles County Museum of Natural History; Errol Stevens, formerly at the Seaver Center and currently at Loyola Marymount University, who brought several critically important sources to my attention in the early stages of my project; Walsh Washington Jr., formerly the Supervisor at the Records Management Division of the Los Angeles County Recorder's Office, who gave me ample access to Superior Court records—invaluable sources for my study; Hynda Rudd, Jay Jones, and the staff at the Los Angeles City Archives, Records Management Division, who allowed me ample access to the records; Walter Brem, Latin American specialist, at the Bancroft Library, who was always willing to lend a hand with research questions; Bill Frank and the staff at the Huntington Library, San Marino; and the staff at the California State Library, California History Room, all contributed to this project in significant ways. In the course of carrying out this project, I have learned that archivists—with their expertise and familiarity with materials—are oftentimes our best friends. Thank you for your time.

I am the proud recipient of generous financial support from institutions, organizations, and programs aimed at minority and female students. They include the UCLA Graduate Affirmative Affairs Office (with special thanks to Harriet Moss); the UCLA Graduate Division; the American Association of University Women; the National Hispanic Scholarship Fund; the University of California, Office of the President, Postdoctoral Fellowship; and the National Research Council, Ford Foundation Postdoctoral Fellowship Program for Minorities. Thanks also to UCLA, Institute of American Cultures; Northern Arizona University, Office of Research; the Henry E. Huntington Library, San Marino, California; and UC Davis, Office of the Vice Chancellor for Research, and the Division of Humanities, Arts, and Cultural Studies, all of which provided invaluable support, allowing me to read, write, and think, and equally importantly, to publish this book.

I would also like to acknowledge and thank the University of Arizona Press, particularly Patti Hartmann, for taking on my project, Al Schroder, for seeing my project through, and Patricia Rosas, for working wonders with my prose and pushing me to clarify my analysis. Thank you for your hard work.

Special thanks and gratitude go to my wonderful and supportive family. To my *tía* and *tío*, Beatriz and Paco Chávez, who gave me guidance and love when my parents could not be there and provided me with the opportunity to fulfill my life's goals and dreams, I am especially indebted to them for all that I have become. From the bottom of my heart, thank you. My brother, Juan G. Chávez, and my cousins, Alicia Robertson and Gloria Clouss, who endured years of family transition, deserve praise for their support and accomplishments. I only wish we had more time together to share our lives. Ebers García, my spouse, best friend, and biggest supporter, has spent countless hours "counseling" and encouraging me through this process, despite my bouts of doubt and fear. He merits particular mention for his love and attention and for the beautiful map and cover design that adorn this book. *Gracias.* Lastly, I would like to dedicate my work in loving and living memory of my parents, José Chávez Esparza and María Concepción Alvarado, who, though they could not see my brother and me grow and live out our dreams, are constantly with us in our endeavors. *Les dedico este trabajo en su memoria. Que Díos los tenga y los bendiga.*

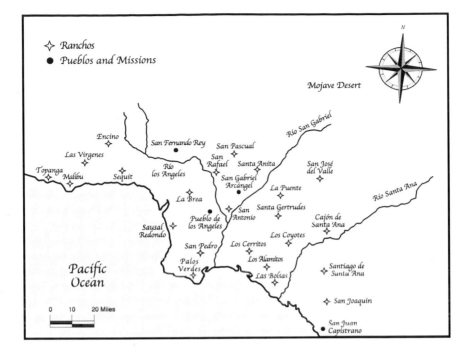

The greater Los Angeles region, ca. 1840

Part I

Women in Spanish and Mexican California

Chapter 1

Gender and the Conquest and Colonization of California

In 1773, a native woman and an eleven-year-old girl from La Soledad, a *ranchería* (Indian settlement), went to see the priests at nearby Misión San Diego. Through a native interpreter who accompanied them, they charged that three Spanish soldiers had raped the girl and a ten-year-old companion, who had died of her injuries. The padres reported this to a sergeant from Sonora, Mariano Carrillo, who promptly had the perpetrators—Francisco Avila, Sebastián Alvitre, and Matheo Ygnacio de Soto—brought before him.[1]

With the soldiers and natives present, Carrillo questioned the young girl. Through the interpreter, she told him that while she and her companion were digging for roots in a canyon, they noticed three soldiers. A few moments later, two came down the canyon in their direction. The girls ran up a hill, but the soldiers overtook them, forcibly grabbed them, and "sinned" with them. When the soldiers finished, she stated, they gave the girls some beads and went on their way. The men, she reported, had raped her companion so violently that she sustained severe injuries to her spine and died two days later.[2]

In 1775, more than two years after the native people reported the assault, officials in Mexico City finally initiated a formal investigation. Distance, poor communication, and, in this case, misplacement of the file had led to the delay.[3] Avila and Alvitre had remained imprisoned in San Diego. Soto, who had been jailed at the mission in Velicata, Baja California, had escaped while laboring on public works.

The governor of Ambas Californias (Baja and Alta), Felipe de Neve (1777–1782), took up the case. He questioned the two soldiers, who denied any wrongdoing, and Avila accused the old woman and the interpreter, whose Spanish was poor, of forcing the youngster to fabricate the story. According to Avila, when Sergeant Carrillo had asked the girl if she recognized Avila and his two companions, she said nothing until the old woman spoke to her in their language. Only then did the girl acknowledge recognizing the men. The reason for the complaint against them, Avila insisted, was that in self-defense, he had previously shot a man from their ranchería.

Following a lengthy investigation, Neve forwarded the case to Viceroy Antonio Bucareli y Ursúa, the highest civil and military representative of the Spanish Crown in New Spain. Because the administration of Alta California (as well as the other provinces on New Spain's northern frontier) had been removed from the viceroy's jurisdiction, however, the matter ended up with Teodoro de Croix, Commandant General of the *Provincias Internas* (Internal Provinces).[4] Two years after it was forwarded to Bucareli, Croix's legal advisor, Pedro Galindo Navarro, concluded that the only evidence was the child's testimony. He believed that testimony had been compromised by the interpreter's incompetence in Spanish. Moreover, since the men had already served a "rigorous and extended" imprisonment of five years, Croix freed Avila and Alvitre and sent them north to the *presidio* (garrison) of Monterey.[5]

This incident reveals the grave difficulties in administering justice in the northern territories, particularly Alta California. The distance between Mexico City and the frontier, the Spanish bureaucracy, and insensitivity to the rights of indígenas usually meant delayed justice and, often, no justice at all. Jurisdictional conflicts between secular and religious authorities, particularly those concerning the California native population, also compromised equity and contributed to instability in Alta California and elsewhere on the northern periphery.

The soldiers' assault was not an isolated incident but, rather, part of a larger pattern of sexual attacks against native women and, sometimes, against the native men who sought to defend them. Missionaries constantly complained to the authorities about the soldiers' sexual abuse of women and girls. The padres understood that this undermined conversion efforts. The behavior also threatened to incite rebellion against the gente de razón by the more numerous native Californians, the cultural and racial "other."[6] As a palliative, Father Junípero Serra, the president of the California missions (1767–1784), called for the settlement of families imported from other regions of New Spain and the marriage of Spanish soldiers to women from those families and to local neófitas (Christian native women). The presence of families and marriageable women, Serra believed, were essential for preventing the soldiers' aggressive behaviors and for establishing a stable Spanish society on the frontier. As suggested by the values reflected in Serra's appeals, gender, patriarchy, ethnicity, and culture shaped the military and spiritual conquest of California from the 1770s to the 1820s. Spanish beliefs and practices about male, female, and native roles in Hispanic society were central to the region's settlement and development.

To understand how the Spanish conquest shaped relations based on gender, patriarchy, ethnicity, and culture requires an understanding of the Spanish Crown's larger aim in conquering and colonizing the region and how the military and Church participated in those efforts. It is important to have an appreciation of the precarious nature of the early expeditions and settlements and how the soldiers' repeated assaults against native women in particular contributed to the instability of the entire venture. Comprehending these factors sets the stage for an analysis of how the colonization in Alta California by casta (racially mixed) women of Spanish, Indian, and African ancestry diffused the soldiers' aggression and made possible a viable Spanish settlement.

In 1768, Viceroy Carlos Francisco de Croix, under orders from the Spanish Bourbon king, Charles III (1759–1788), appointed José de Gálvez as Visitador General. De Gálvez was charged with occupying and fortifying Alta California by creating settlements at San Diego and Monterey. Until then, much of the territory remained terra incognita to Spaniards and other foreigners.[7] According to the *Siete Partidas* and *Recopilación de las leyes de los reynos de las indias* (thirteenth- and seventeenth-century compilations of law for governing at all levels of Spanish society), the king's power to direct the military and spiritual conquest of Alta California derived from his divine authority as God's vicar, or representative, on earth and his position as sovereign ruler of the Spanish kingdom. In Spain, the king, as absolute and natural lord (by virtue of royal dynastic succession), held proprietary rights to all lands in the Spanish realm. As a practical matter, he governed through the Council of the Indies, an agency responsible for all affairs in New Spain.[8]

The *patronato real* (royal patronage), a system of rights and privileges resulting from a series of papal bulls issued in the late 1400s and early

1500s, also authorized the Crown to direct the Catholic Church in the Indies in all matters except doctrine and religious discipline. In effect, the Crown became the secular head of the Church when it came managing patronage and ecclesiastical taxation, or tithes; introducing and maintaining the Church; instructing and converting the native peoples; and founding all churches and disposing of ecclesiastical benefices in the Indies. The Catholic Church became an arm or instrument of the Spanish Crown in conquering and colonizing New Spain's northern frontier.[9]

In colonial Mexico, as in Spain, government was highly centralized, though disputes often erupted among royal officials. The king's authority rested, first and foremost, with the viceroy, the supreme civil and military leader, and the Audencia, the highest court of appeals. The viceroy's jurisdiction, though extensive, was limited, as he had to answer to the king, the Council of the Indies, and Spanish law. The Audencia could voice strong opposition to his decisions, but it could not override them. At the local level, provincial governors, appointed by the Crown, possessed authority over all local civil and military affairs. Archbishops and bishops or, where none existed, as in California and New Mexico, missionaries and secular clergy as well as the president of the missions, also technically selected by the king, handled all religious matters.

In California, the Franciscans' principal duties were converting indígenas and transforming them into the loyal Spanish subjects at the missions. Like presidios and, later, pueblos, missions helped defend the frontier, pacify the natives, and open the country to European settlement. Lines of jurisdiction between religious and civil authorities, such as the governor and the president of the California missions, could blur, especially over matters pertaining to the native peoples. Although the Crown had given the Church the right to save souls and advance the Spanish frontier, increasingly it granted governors the right to enforce edicts that often clashed with and undermined the missionaries' duties and goals. The result was constant conflict and litigation. The Crown, which trusted none of its agents in the Indies for fear they would become too powerful, gave secular and religious leaders overlapping jurisdictions to ensure that no single interest group gained leverage or power over another.[10]

With the king's orders in hand, Visitador General Gálvez traveled to Loreto, Baja California, the seat of authority over Ambas Californias, arriving there in 1768. He ordered Gaspar de Portolá, the civil and military governor of the Californias, and Captain Fernando Rivera y Moncada, the military commander of forty men stationed at Loreto, to lead separate overland contingents to the future site of San Diego. In addition, he commissioned three ships, the *San Carlos*, the *San Antonio*, and the *San José* (which vanished with its crew), to carry personnel to San Diego and then on to Monterey.[11] The troops traveling by land managed to reach their destinations with few casualties and desertions, but those contingents that traveled by sea suffered many losses, which proved nearly disastrous to the success of the entire operation. Of the original 219 who departed on foot or by ship from Baja California, only 126, including six priests, reached San Diego by middle of 1769.[12] Within a few months, the crew on board the *San Carlos* and the overland company led by Portolá finally met at Monterey. By June 1770, the secular and religious wings of the Spanish Crown had formally founded San Carlos Borromeo de Monterey.[13]

Noticeably absent from these early expeditions were women—Spanish, Indian, mestiza, mulata, and other castas.[14] According to Spanish patriarchal norms, military and religious conquest was a male enterprise and responsibility.[15] Military men left their wives, daughters, and mothers behind in Mexico and Spain. When their husbands went off on their adventures, upper-class married females, primarily *españolas* (Spanish women), stayed at home and managed their households and educated their children; single and widowed women engaged in legal affairs and handled transactions involving their personal property; and poor women, usually casta and native, worked outside the home to support themselves and their families.

Invariably, however, there were exceptions to this pattern. Three years after the first incursions into Alta California, two neófito couples reached San Gabriel in 1772. They were to serve as role models for the newly converted native Californians at the missions. The women's duty, in particular, was to assist the missionaries in the instruction of neófitas. As the missionaries anticipated, the arrival of the couples pleased the native Californians, for they had yet to see any women or families among the colonists. One of the women was María Dolores, a neófita from Misión Santa Gertrudis in Baja California, who came with her husband, Sebastián Taraval. María Dolores did not remain long at San Gabriel. For reasons that are unclear, but likely due to harsh living and working conditions, she, Sebastián, and another man ran away from the mission.

She and the other man perished in the Mojave Desert. No other women came to the region in the first five years of the conquest.[16]

As with the missionaries, the lack of Hispanic women concerned the authorities, who feared that the soldiers would sexually abuse the native women. Their worries were grounded in the experience of centuries of imperial conquest. Spanish officials knew that under conditions of colonization or war, native women, as members of the conquered group, were targets for sexual violence. In a patriarchal and ethnically stratified society that devalued females and non-Europeans, native women occupied the lowest rung of society and were treated as spoils of war. Spanish soldiers' rape of these women symbolized the subjugation of native peoples, in general, and the domination of women and castration of men, in particular.[17]

In Alta California, Visitador General Gálvez and, later, Pedro Fages, a Spanish-born military commander and governor of Alta California, worried—with justification—that soldiers would molest native women and, in turn, incite native men and their entire communities to retaliate. To avoid such unrest and perhaps even rebellion, in 1769, Gálvez instructed Captain Portolá to warn soldiers about the "need for treating Indians well." If they disobeyed this command, then Portolá should "punish them," since "any molestations or violence toward the native women . . . besides being offenses against God, . . . could also endanger the success of the expedition."[18]

Despite such orders, soldiers proceeded to harass and rape native females of all ages, sometimes killing the men to get at the women. No sooner had two priests, Angel Somera and Pedro Cambón, and about a dozen soldiers founded Misión San Gabriel in 1771 (fig. 1.1) than two of the latter raped a native woman, the wife of a chief. In response, the chief and some of his followers launched a surprise attack against the culprits, but the Spaniards, with their superior weapons, held off the Indians and killed the chief. Afterwards, as a display of power and dominance, "they cut off his head and brought it in triumph to the mission," reported Serra.[19] The soldiers' sexual assaults at San Gabriel worried Serra, who conveyed his fears to Viceroy Bucareli and Rafael Verger, his superior at the College of San Fernando: "This . . . [action] gives me the greatest cause for anxiety," for "the secular arm was guilty of the most heinous crimes, killing the men to take their wives."[20] Such acts, Serra believed, not only undermined his ability to attract pagan natives and convert

Figure 1.1
Misión San Gabriel, founded in 1771, as it appeared the 1870s or 1880s.
(Courtesy of the Seaver Center for Western History Research, Los Angeles
County Museum of Natural History)

them to the Christian faith but also threatened to disrupt the entire
venture in California. As Serra feared, the coastal and inland peoples,
enemies until that time, united and rebelled in an attempt to rid themselves of the Spanish. They failed to execute their plan because additional
Spanish troops, on their way to establish another mission, arrived and
strengthened the mission guard.[21]

The sexual assaults continued the following year. In 1772, the priests at
San Luis Obispo, San Diego, and San Gabriel reported outrages against
native peoples to Serra. The troops at San Luis Obispo "are the most
notorious molesters of [g]entile women," and many of those at San Diego,
according to Father Luis Jayme, "deserved to be hanged on account of
the continuous outrages which they are committing in seizing and raping the women. There is not a single mission [among the five established in the first three years of settlement] where the gentiles have not
been scandalized and even on the roads, they are committing a thousand
evils, particularly those of a sexual nature."[22] At San Diego, that same

year, four Spanish soldiers repeatedly raped two native women—Yuman-speaking Kumeyaays—at ranchería El Corral. Natives at another populous ranchería near the mission, Jayme reported to Verger, had threatened to attack them. "The gentiles . . . have been on the point of coming here to kill us all, and the reason for this is that some soldiers went there and raped their women," while other soldiers "allowed their animals to graze on [the natives'] crops."[23]

In 1773, Serra complained to Viceroy Bucareli that "the soldiers [at San Gabriel] . . . without any fear of God whatever in their hearts, give such scandal. . . . In the morning, six or more soldiers would set out together on horseback and go to the far distant rancherías," causing "both men and women at sight of [the soldiers to take] to their heels. . . . The soldiers, clever as they are at lassoing cows and mules, would catch an Indian woman with their lassos to become prey for their unbridled lust."[24] When the native men tried to defend these women, they were shot.[25] Married soldiers, too, committed rapes, prompting Serra to ask that "serious measures be taken to stop such awful outbreaks of debauchery."[26] Such heinous acts, he told Viceroy Bucareli, "occur every day; it is as though a plague of immorality had broken out. . . . It is unavoidable that the poor gentiles, until now as gentle as sheep, will turn on us like tigers."[27] Two years later, Serra's predictions' were realized. In late 1775, several hundred Yuman-speaking indígenas, from at least fifteen—perhaps as many as forty—rancherías and Misión San Diego, struck the mission in the cover of night. They killed Father Jayme and two Spanish artisans, and they burned the settlement to the ground.[28] When the authorities asked some of the native peoples about the reasons for the attack, they responded: to "live like before the [Spanish] arrived."[29]

That was among the reasons given by Toypurina, a Gabrieleña medicine woman, who planned a rebellion at Misión San Gabriel in 1775. She gained a powerful cohort in Nicolás José, a renegade neófito and chief, who convinced Christian converts at the mission and gentiles living nearby that Toypurina had the power to "kill the padres with her big magic." On the eve of the intended assault, a soldier of the guard overheard them discussing their plans and alerted his superiors. Toypurina and Nicolás José were promptly arrested along with several fellow conspirators. When interrogated, she boldly explained her motivation: "I hate the padres and all of you for living here on my native soil . . . [and] for trespassing upon the land of my forefathers and despoiling our tribal domains."[30] Her explanation did little to lessen her punishment. Authorities imprisoned her for two years at San Gabriel and then sent her into exile at Misión San Carlos de Borromeo. Her male comrades were publicly flogged as a warning to other would-be rebels.[31]

Although many native peoples responded to the soldiers' attacks by launching assaults against the foreigners, other indígenas distanced themselves, both physically and spiritually, from the Spaniards in order to preserve and protect themselves and their culture. Before his death in 1775, Father Jayme reported to his superior in Mexico City that local natives had deserted their homes and food sources and retreated deeper into the hinterland "so that the soldiers will not rape their women as they have already done so many times in the past."[32] But retreat proved no panacea. "The distance" of the rancherías, observed Serra about a similar situation at San Gabriel, "was not enough to protect them from the soldiers' abuse."[33]

The indígenas also returned to their traditional practices to heal themselves. In an effort to cleanse themselves from the effects of the sexual assaults, native women turned to customary practices and beliefs—all adamantly opposed by the Catholic priests. Women who were raped or in other ways sexually violated were obligated by tribal custom to undergo a long purification, such as sweating and drinking herb teas. If pregnant with a Spanish man's child, a woman sometimes induced an abortion or committed infanticide.[34] In 1772, a partially blind woman, who had been raped and impregnated by Spanish soldiers at San Diego, tried to abort the fetus but, when she failed, she resolved to kill it at birth. The priests tried to change her mind but "to no avail," reported Father Jayme.[35] Jayme, as well as priests at the missions of San Gabriel, Santa Clara, and San José, vigorously condemned these practices, but the soldiers' continuing attacks, complained Jayme, made it difficult, if not impossible, to root out the "evils" of abortion and infanticide among the native peoples.[36]

The soldiers' assaults and rapes not only hindered the missionaries' spiritual work and caused indígenas to flee from the settlements, but it also demoralized the priests and stalled the establishment of additional missions. A priest at Misión San Gabriel "who saw a soldier actually committing deeds of shame with an Indian who had come to the mission . . . [was] sick at heart [and] took to his bed." Eventually, on the advice of others, the priest left his post and "retired to San Diego."[37]

Establishment of several missions was delayed for years as a result of the chief's murder at Misión San Gabriel in 1771. Military officials, fearful of retaliation at San Gabriel, reassigned the troops that had been earmarked for the new missions at San Buenaventura, San Francisco, and Santa Clara. The construction of Misión San Juan Capistrano, though already underway, was delayed for the same reason.[38]

The soldiers' sexual attacks also had pernicious effects on the health of the native population. Women and children, particularly, were the first to contract the deadly sexually transmitted diseases, primarily syphilis.[39] Although it took several decades for the secular and religious officials to recognize the effects of the diseases—first among the neófitos and, later, the gentiles—it resulted in massive population losses. This was greatest at the missions where living conditions—close, cramped, and damp quarters with poor sanitation and little ventilation—enabled the diseases to spread rapidly.[40] Indeed, by the early 1800s, priests, soldiers, and civilians throughout the region testified that *gálico*, or syphilis, was rampant among the neófitos. A decade later, in 1814 and 1815, priests stationed in missions along California's coastline from San Francisco to San Diego reported that syphilis was the most prevalent malady "from which a considerable number die."[41] At Santa Bárbara, the padres noted that "[a]ll are infected with [syphilis] for they see no objection to marrying another infected with it. As a result births are few and deaths many so that the number of deaths exceed births by three to one."[42] Apolinaria Lorenzana, an orphan from Mexico who, as an adult, nursed Christian native women at Misión San Diego, also noted that "*sífilis*" was a common ailment among the *indias* (Indian women) in the infirmary.[43] The end of the mission era, in the 1830s, brought little relief from the ailment, for Spanish settlers, as well as neófito fugitives, had spread it among inland and other non-mission native peoples. In 1831, Mexican Governor Manuel Victoria noted that "venereal diseases [were] devouring the [natives] horribly."[44] By then, syphilis had contributed to approximately 10 percent to 30 percent of the deaths within the missions and an unknown, but likely devastating, number elsewhere.[45]

In Father Serra's view, the military commanders bore the brunt of the responsibility for the soldiers' continued outrages against the native peoples, women and men. Their greatest offense was their failure to restrain their subalterns and set a good example for them. Serra took particular aim at Governor Pedro Fages and, later, though to a lesser extent, at

Governors Rivera and Neve. He told Bucareli that Fages had "unbearable manners" and forced his underlings to endure privations—"long hours of work and a lack of food" made them *violentíssimos* ("extremely violent").[46] Moreover, Fages was incompetent and morally lax, for he allowed his soldiers to live in concubinage.[47] Not until the priests at San Antonio de Padua complained loudly about a corporal living with a woman who was not his wife did Fages dismiss the soldier and send him to San Luis Obispo where his conduct became even more flagrant.[48] Father Jayme, like Serra, complained bitterly about Fages's failure to punish soldiers for their sexual transgressions.[49]

Clerics' complaints about military leadership served only to exacerbate already tense relations between the soldiers and the churchmen in Alta California.[50] At the root of the dispute were conflicting views about the Church's role in the conquest and colonization of California. Father Serra strongly believed that the Church's responsibility for evangelizing and converting "infidels" to Christianity took precedence over all other temporal matters. In contrast, the secular arm of government, including the military, saw the friars and the Church as instruments for furthering the conquest.[51] Governor Neve believed that the mission was a state agency, whose duty was to "remold the [native] population" and to teach them to work and form a stable community.[52] Military officials also complained that the priests exacted hard labor from their wards. At the missions, "[t]he Indians' fate [is] worse than that of slaves," declared Neve.[53] The divergent views led to continuous quarreling between the Church and the military, with priests accusing soldiers of intervening in their affairs.

These strained relations prompted Serra to make an arduous journey to Mexico City in late 1772, where he pleaded for political and economic support in his cause against the military. At the viceroy's request, Serra drafted suggestions for improving the government and administration of Alta California. The resulting thirty-two recommendations called for, among other things, the replacement of Pedro Fages with an officer who, at the request of any missionary, would recall soldiers, especially those who set "bad examples," replacing them with soldiers who were "not immoral or scandalous."[54] To clarify conflicting lines of jurisdiction over Christian natives, the padre urged the viceroy to order military officers to acknowledge and respect the priests' authority over the "training, governance, punishment, and education of [neófitos]," as those activities "belong[ed] exclusively to the friars."[55] Serra's requests had the support of Spanish law, which identified the missionaries as the legal guardians of newly converted native peoples, who, for all intents and purposes, were "wards" of the Church.[56]

To prevent the soldiers' sexual exploitation of native women and encourage family life, Serra urged the viceroy to promote marriages between Spanish-speaking soldiers and neófitas. Marriage, kinship, and women, Serra reasoned, would lessen sexual assaults on native women, ease tensions between the Spanish and native peoples, and create a permanent and increasing population of gente de razón.[57] "Thus, we could [purge the land] of all of the scandalous persons," concluded Serra, "and have such a troop as conquests of this kind require."[58] Livestock and mission lands were allocated to induce soldiers to marry California-born neófitas, and steps were taken to relocate soldiers from the presidios to their wives' missions.[59] For soldiers who brought their families from other regions of New Spain to Alta California, he recommended an increase in pay as well as the supply of animals and other provisions. The presence of wives would help dispel the popular belief among native peoples that the unmarried Spaniards now in California had come only to make war, find riches, and sexually abuse the Indian women. Additionally, the presence of at least some soldiers married to Hispanic women would aid in ridding the natives of the notion that the Spaniards were the offspring of mules, for those animals, reported Serra, "were the only members of the female gender they saw among us."[60]

Viceroy Bucareli accepted Serra's recommendations and had them codified as the *Echeveste Reglamento,* the first regulatory code in California.[61] Bucareli removed Fages, named Captain Rivera y Moncada as California's new ruler, and recognized the missionaries' authority over the neófitos.[62] The Reglamento led the Spanish authorities to promise land and livestock to soldiers who married neófitas and to agree to pay transportation costs and an annual salary and to provide rations to those who moved to Alta California with their families.[63]

Using similar incentives, Serra recruited artisan families from Mexico, which included Hispanic men and the first Spanish-speaking women. Twenty-three colonists arrived in California in 1774 aboard the *Santiago,* an annual supply ship. In the course of three months, the *Santiago* sailed from San Blas to San Diego and then on to Monterey. The group included a surgeon and artisans, as well as their wives and children, and a crew of eighty-eight. The eight Spanish-speaking women aboard the vessel were either married or of marriageable age, and it is likely that they were of diverse ethnic backgrounds.[64] It was hoped that the single women, who were between the ages of eighteen and twenty, would marry soldiers and remain in California permanently with their newly formed families.

The duties of Spanish-speaking women who came to California included teaching neófitas how to cook, clean, sew, and perform other womanly duties in the Spanish manner.[65] The authorities expected them to instruct the native converts in the basics of Spanish Catholic family life, which meant being subservient to men and respecting the sanctity and permanence of marriage, monogamy, and sexual purity or virginity before marriage and chastity in widowhood. The settlers, by example and instruction, would help root out native practices of polygamy, *joyas* (in which persons of one sex, usually males, took on the social roles of the opposite sex, usually females), abortion, and infanticide, thereby advancing the spiritual conquest and growth of the *gente de razón* population.[66] However, these efforts were only somewhat successful. Of all the women in the group of artisans recruited by Serra, only one remained in California. The rest returned to Mexico with their families after the men's six-year contracts expired. This occurred primarily because the families received few of the incentives promised them. The lesson was not lost on other artisans in Mexico, for few went to California with their families in the future.[67]

More successful in encouraging the growth of families in Alta California was the government's colonization of soldiers, civilian settlers, and, later, convicts and their families from other regions of New Spain.[68] In late 1774, the first of two groups of colonists from Sinaloa reached Monterey under the command of Captain Fernando Rivera y Moncada, military leader of California, who effectively replaced Pedro Fages as governor. The viceroy instructed Rivera to recruit "sturdy Spanish families" by offering them rations, clothing, and food and a promise of more goods as well as land grants upon arrival in California. Though Rivera fell short of recruiting the eighty soldiers called for in the *Echeveste Reglamento,* he attracted fifty-one people, including women and children.[69]

Captain Juan Bautista de Anza, military commander of the presidio at Tubac in Sonora, led a second, even larger colonization party. In 1775, the year after Anza opened an overland route from Tubac to Misión San

Gabriel, the viceroy called upon Anza to make a second trip with the purpose of founding a mission at San Francisco as well as at two other locales. Realizing the significance of gender in Spain's plans to conquer and colonize the region, the viceroy directed Anza to enlist married and marriageable soldiers and to instruct the married ones to bring their wives and children.[70] Acting on his instructions, Anza recruited Sonoran and Sinaloan soldiers (and their families), offering them clothes, rations, and an advance on the soldiers' annual salaries.[71] Most of these colonists—and likely those with Rivera as well—were racially mixed and poor, existing on the margins of an economically depressed region. Thus, they had little to risk and everything to gain in joining the venture. After departing in 1775, Anza's company of 240 souls covered 1,600 miles by sea from Culiacán, Sinaloa, to San Miguel de Horcasitas, Sonora, and then overland to Tubac. From there they pushed on to Alta California and established San Francisco in 1776.[72]

Despite the long and harsh journey, the colonists suffered few casualties and only one death, that of Antonia Pañuelas de Féliz, who died in childbirth.[73] Of the other nine or ten pregnant women who started out with Anza, five suffered miscarriages and three had successful births. After the party arrived at San Gabriel in 1775, they remained for about a month and then continued on to Monterey and to the new mission, St. Francis of Assisi, at the site of present-day San Francisco. Despite Serra's desire to have women settle at the missions to serve as role models for the natives, most of the women in Anza's company, being wives or daughters of the soldiers, lived in the presidios.[74]

The government and Father Serra's expectations for marriages between soldiers and California-born neófitas were dashed when, in 1791, the Spanish Crown rescinded the policy of awarding land to such couples.[75] The first wedding between a soldier and a neófita—that is, between Martín Reyes, a retired soldier from the San Diego presidio and a resident of Los Angeles, and María Celia, a Christian native woman originally from the Yabit ranchería, a nearby settlement—was celebrated in 1795 at Misión San Gabriel. It was also the last in the Los Angeles region during the Spanish era.[76] No doubt, the lack of incentives and the few soldiers in San Gabriel and Los Angeles—no more than six in the 1770s, eight in the 1790s, and eleven in the 1800s and 1810s—explain the single marriage.[77] Despite Los Angeles's significant population of retired military men— some fifteen in the 1790s—nearly all were already married.[78] The result was that racially mixed marriages—between Spanish-speaking soldiers and California-born neófitas—in San Gabriel and Los Angeles accounted for less than one percent of the total matrimonies during the colonial period.[79]

In Monterey, where the number of soldiers was higher—twenty-six in the 1770s, eighty in the 1790s, about seventy in the 1800s, and a hundred in the 1810s—mixed marriages were more common, constituting 15 percent—about twenty—of the nuptials during the Spanish era.[80] Even so, the soldiers at Monterey and their neófita wives, like the artisans and their families, were bitterly disappointed with the government's failure to provide the promised land and livestock. In 1775, three Catalan soldiers (Manuel Butrón, Domingo Arús, and Antonio Torba) who had married neófitas (Margarita Domínguez, María Seraphina, and María de Gracia) petitioned the Crown for their missing incentives: land on which to settle, salary for two years, and rations for five years.[81] The soldiers told Serra, who penned the petition for them, that if their commanding officer "had not given them assurances [about their rewards], they would not have married."[82] Butrón's petition was successful, and he received land in 1775. The records are silent on the outcome for other petitioners.[83]

The effort to encourage marriages and settle families continued into the 1780s, especially after viceregal authorities recognized the importance of Alta California as an outpost for defending Spain's northern frontier. In 1776, the viceroy, under royal orders, transferred the capital of Ambas Californias from Loreto to Monterey.[84] That same year, in a further attempt to create an effective government for its northernmost territories in New Spain, the Spanish Crown placed Alta and Baja California, Nuevo México, Nueva Vizcaya, Coahuila, Téjas, Sinaloa, and Sonora into a single political unit, the Internal Provinces. This effectively removed them from the viceroy's jurisdiction and put them directly under the Spanish Crown.[85] Three years later, in 1779, as part of those efforts, Governor Felipe de Neve, Rivera's successor, rewrote the laws governing California and issued the *Reglamento para el gobierno de las provincias de Californias*, which called for strengthening the military and renewing colonization efforts. The means for doing so were familiar: increased material and pecuniary incentives for soldiers and their families who would settle in the region. The reglamento also called for additional presidios as well as the establishment of agrarian communities, or *pueblos*. In the latter, *pobladores* and *pobladoras* (male and female civilian settlers) were expected to produce enough food for themselves as well as a surplus for sale to the presidios. The goal was to diminish reliance on the missions and supply ships, which often failed to make their annual journeys to the provinces.

To entice potential recruits, Neve offered male heads of families or the eldest sons in female-headed households an annual salary, land for a *solar* (home) and a *suerte* (agriculture land), rights to *ejidos* (communal lands), and allotments of livestock, seeds, and tools. In exchange, settlers had to erect public buildings and construct a central plaza, church, dam, and an irrigation ditch. As before, Spanish officials encouraged married men, families, and single, marriageable women to enlist in the venture.[86]

Father Serra vigorously opposed Felipe de Neve's proposal for civilian pueblos, believing that these settlements would expose neófitos to the temptations of the secular world.[87] "[T]hey are our children," Serra complained to Commandant General Teodoro de Croix in 1778, "for none except us has engendered them in Christ. The result is we look upon them as a father looks upon his family. We shower all our love and care upon them."[88] The padres' paternalistic approach to the natives required keeping neófitos at the missions in order to facilitate the instruction and "protection" of "their children."[89] "Missions," Serra declared, "are what this country needs," not pueblos, which lack priests.[90]

Serra's protests notwithstanding, Spanish officials established two pueblos at the sites of present-day San Jose and Los Angeles: San José de Guadalupe, founded in 1777 with fourteen families from the presidios of Monterey and San Francisco, and La Reina de los Angeles, established in 1781 with eleven families (forty-four settlers—twelve men, eleven women, and twenty-three children under the age of eighteen). Rivera had recruited all these settlers from Sinaloa and Sonora. Fourteen years later, in 1795, the Spanish authorities founded Branciforte, the last pueblo established by the Spaniards in California, which they located across the river from Misión Santa Cruz. Three years later, three families and six single men had been recruited to settle the town. Its population grew somewhat, never surpassing one hundred people, and then it began to decline. The site was abandoned in the early 1800s.[91]

The officials' attempts to encourage colonization by importing orphans were only slightly more successful. In 1800, two years after the first convicts went to California, nineteen orphans—nine boys and ten girls—arrived from the *casa de cuna* (foundling home) in Mexico City. Spanish authorities distributed them among families, with the expectation that they would eventually marry, establish themselves, and help increase the gente-de-razón population. That plan, which originally had called for sixty boys and sixty girls, proved only modestly successful.[92] Although it did not lead to subsequent migration of orphans, most of those who arrived in 1800 grew to maturity, eventually married, and remained in California. None of these three colonization efforts had any affect on the pueblos of Los Angeles or San José, for the colonists either ended up in the presidios of Monterey, Santa Bárbara, and San Diego or returned to Mexico.[93] Not until the Mexican government sent a colony of artisans, teachers, merchants, farmers, and other skilled men and women in the 1830s—collectively known as the Híjar-Pádres expedition—did the pueblo of Los Angeles, in particular, receive a significant number of trained and educated individuals to increase its population.[94]

Many settlers at San José and Los Angeles, like those at the presidios, had racially mixed backgrounds and were from the lower strata of Mexican society, having lived most of their lives in the impoverished northern provinces. For example, in Los Angeles, José Antonio Navarro, identified in the 1781 census as a mestizo, had come from a poor neighborhood in Rosario, Baja California. His wife, María Soto y Rodríguez, and his three unnamed children were described as mulattoes. To Navarro and other poor and socially marginalized individuals, the Spanish government's incentives to relocate in California were doubtless attractive, though tempered with uncertainty.[95] With the exception of a handful of high-ranking military officers and the volunteer soldiers from Catalonia in Spain, the retired soldiers who settled with their families in Los Angeles and elsewhere in Alta California were of casta origin and from the lower economic strata. Like the pobladores, they had been recruited in the northern provinces, primarily from presidios in Sonora, Sinaloa, and Baja California, where most of the soldiers were natives and mestizos or other castas, with many being conscripted criminals or vagabonds.[96]

The lower-class origins and mixed racial ancestry of the soldiers and settlers and their descendants did not deter them from distinguishing themselves culturally and, later, ethnically from the indígenas residing in rancherías and at the missions. The gente de razón also forged a cultural and social bond as increasingly over time they downplayed (and forgot) their own mixed heritages and saw themselves as españoles (and eventually Californios). They upheld Spanish (and, in time, Mexican) law and custom, subscribed to Catholicism and the belief in one God, spoke the Spanish language, lived in settled towns, and worked in agriculture or ranching. To ensure the social stability of the community, particularly the family, which was viewed as the basic social unit, they enforced a rigid system of patriarchal beliefs and practices that emphasized the authority of husbands and fathers over women, sexual purity or virginity before marriage, fidelity and monogamy during married life, chastity in widowhood, and shame in all bodily matters.[97]

The impoverished Spanish-speaking mestiza, mulata, and casta women who settled in the pueblos, presidios, and missions in the 1770s, 1780s, and 1790s were essential to the social, cultural, and biological reproduction of Spanish society on the northern frontier.[98] Throughout the region, women bore and reared children, established homes and families, and aided in the development of the gente-de-razón population.[99] Women's capacity to produce offspring was critical because the last sizeable colonization party arrived in the 1790s. Until the 1830s, when an increasing number of Mexican nationals and foreign-born settlers arrived in Alta California, the number of inhabitants rose primarily through natural increase.[100] In the Spanish period, over 90 percent of Spanish-speaking women bore at least one child, with some having as many as twelve or more children. On average, women gave birth to three children. In the 1830s and 1840s, in the Mexican period, that figure rose slightly at the presidio of Santa Bárbara and pueblo of Los Angeles, where women had an average of four children. Although families generally remained small-to-medium in size, infant mortality rates were low, and the birth rate outpaced the general mortality rate by three to one. It is likely that the favorable climate contributed to women's reproductive capacity.[101]

During the early decades of settlement in Alta California, as they struggled to nurture the families they had produced, the wives of soldiers stationed at the presidios and, later, at the pueblos, suffered deprivations and physical hardships. As result of the irregular arrival of supply ships, the colonists lacked provisions and were sometimes near starvation. When ships did arrive, the food was often spoiled or meager. These women and their families had no housing, little privacy, and few household items. Even clothing was hard to come by. Also in short supply was fresh water for drinking, cooking, and cleaning.[102] A few families at the presidios and pueblos had the assistance of native laborers, whom they paid in kind, with beads or blankets. However, most Spanish-speaking women and their families had to rely on their own resourcefulness to shelter, feed, and clothe themselves until permanent dwellings had been built and crops were being harvested on a regular basis. At the pueblos and presidios, women rose in the early hours of the morning and spent their days fetching water, wood, and other necessities and performing time-consuming and tedious household chores, such as cooking, cleaning, washing, and sewing. Women used part of their days to tend small garden plots, on which they grew vegetables for home consumption, and they raised small farm animals, such as chickens. Those who had native servants or manual laborers had to supervise them. In general, these women—most of them accustomed to privation, having been raised in the remote outposts of Sonora, Sinaloa, and Baja California—adapted to their environment and, in the process, with little economic incentive, they recreated the rudimentary contours of Spanish life.[103]

Spanish-speaking women at the missions, like those at the pueblos and presidios, aided in reproducing not only the social and physical environment of Spanish society but also the ideological and institutional bases of Hispanic life. These women assisted missionaries in the instruction and supervision of neófitas, socializing them with European-defined notions of gender, marriage, and sexuality. They taught them the domestic arts: grinding corn, needlework, sewing, weaving, washing, and cooking. As *llaveras* (keepers of the keys) and matrons, Spanish-Mexican women kept watch over the sexual virtue of neófitas by managing the *monjerios* (nunneries at the missions), where neófitas over the age of seven lived until they married.[104] According to Eulalia Pérez, a llavera and widow who worked at Misión San Gabriel in the early 1820s, an older Christian native woman usually locked up the resident females after dinner at night and gave the keys to Pérez (fig. 1.2). Apolinaria Lorenzana, who worked at Misión San Diego, recalled that to guard against sexual indiscretions, the matron "never lost sight of [the girls]."[105] If there was doubt of a woman's virginity, midwives inspected them to make sure they remained *doncellas* (virgins) and, thus, attractive marriage partners.[106]

Women filled many roles in the mission work force: supervising the cooking and distributing food in the *pozolera* (communal cooking and eating area); storing, inspecting, and disbursing supplies; and supervising the neófitos who were cooks, seamstresses, soap makers, and wine makers.

During the Spanish era, only one doctor resided in California, so

EULALIA PERZ, 139 YEARS OF AGE.

Figure 1.2
Originally from Loreto, Baja California, Eulalia Pérez, photographed here in
the 1880s, lived and worked as a midwife at the *presidio* of San Diego. She
later served for many years at Misión San Gabriel as housekeeper, *llavera*,
cook, and teacher. (Courtesy of the Bancroft Library)

women also played an important role as health-care providers. In the
1880s, Pérez recalled having been "the best midwife around."[107] Apolinaria Lorenzana and María Ignacia Amador, who lived at Misión San
Gabriel with her husband, Francisco Javier Alvarado, learned from the
native peoples about folk healing and medicinal herbs.[108] Lorenzana, in
particular, sometimes took ill neófitos and neófitas to the hot springs
of Agua Caliente, a ranchería situated in the mountains twenty-four
leagues (one league is approximately 2.6 miles) from San Diego. There,
she would nurse them for up two months at a time.[109] When a new-

born's health was failing and death seemed imminent, *parteras* (midwives) sometimes could do no more than baptize the child. María Guadalupe Silvas christened twins—María and Romualdo Ruiz—shortly after their birth on February 17, 1821, in "fear of [their] imminent death."[110]

As this chapter has demonstrated, Spanish-speaking women, marriage, and Hispanic families were central to the success of Spain's attempt to conquer, colonize, and defend Alta California. The earliest efforts to populate the territory with neófitos and Spanish subjects met with little success, especially after Spanish soldiers assaulted, violated, and raped native women and killed native men in the process. Those incidents produced violent confrontations between native peoples and the Spanish, which, in turn, put the entire venture in jeopardy and touched off stormy disputes between the military and the Church. The subsequent colonization of Spanish-speaking women and families from other regions of New Spain and the promotion of marriage between Spanish soldiers and California neófitas curbed soldiers' sexual attacks and lessened the discordant relations between the indígenas and the colonists. Although throughout California only a handful of soldiers wed Christian native women, the Hispanic women who came and stayed in Alta California bore and reared children, created homes, and instructed the native peoples in European notions of work, gender, and sexuality. These women were also critical to the reproduction of the population, for few arrivals came to California after active colonization ended in the 1790s. Not until the late 1820s and early 1830s would significant numbers of colonists from Mexico and immigrants from the United States and European countries arrive in California. Along with their families, these women and their descendants helped recreate the social, physical, ideological, and institutional foundations of Spanish and Mexican society and culture on New Spain's northernmost frontier.

As we will see, both Californio and native women were active agents in contesting and negotiating social and cultural norms pertaining to gender relations in marriage, the family, and community. Women sought redress from local institutions when they suffered abuse or neglect from men who were exceeding their patriarchal authority. When assistance from civil and religious authorities was not forthcoming, however, some women took it upon themselves to resolve their marital conflicts by leaving their households or spouses, an action that almost always alarmed judges and priests. Such behavior, the authorities believed, threatened the stability of marriage and the family as well as the larger community. In response, women who violated cultural mores, by consorting with men who were not their spouses or having children out of wedlock, received harsh treatment. On the other hand, men who committed similar transgressions faced few repercussions, which reveals the double sexual standard that permeated California society in the Mexican period.

Chapter 2

Patriarchs, Power, and Sexuality

In 1844, Francisca Pérez went before the Los Angeles *alcalde* (judge) and asked that criminal charges be filed against her husband, Mariano Silvas, for abusing her physically and verbally. Her husband had beaten her, she told the judge, "following a dispute over my will." The fight began "when I was lying down resting from my chores. At that moment, my husband entered the room and, using offensive words, he questioned my decisions in drawing up the will. I responded by pointing out the crude nature of his language and behavior. Then, suddenly, . . . he dealt me three blows, . . . pulled me out of bed and dragged me by my hair, and left me on the floor bathed in blood." This was not the first time he had beaten her, she informed the judge, but she would have no more of it and wanted the full weight of the law brought down on him. The judge took the case under submission, but three weeks later, before he could render a decision, Pérez reappeared in court. "Though I brought criminal charges against my husband . . . he has expressed regret and has promised me a new life," she said. "Because I want to avoid disgracing him, I have forgiven him and now retract my charges." She asked the judge, however, to do what he could to make sure her husband would reunite with her in "good faith." Predisposed to saving marriages whenever possible, the judge dropped the charges against the husband but sternly admonished him, "If you continue your [violent] behavior, you shall be severely punished."[1]

By going to the judge with her complaint, Pérez had boldly shown her unwillingness to tolerate her husband's repeated abuse. However, by recanting, following his promise to reform, she revealed the typical response of most Mexican wives to abusive husbands: demonstration of faith in the sincerity of a husband's promises and submission to social and religious pressures to maintain the marriage and respect a husband's place as master of the home.[2] Spanish and Mexican legal and social norms were permeated with a patriarchal ideology that recognized the man as the head of the household, whom the wife and children pledged to obey and honor. Women, in particular, were expected to maintain their sexual purity before marriage and marital fidelity afterward. Those who dishonored husbands or fathers with sexual indiscretions brought dishonor to the entire family.[3]

These same patriarchal values also placed restrictions and responsibilities on men, who were expected to maintain their authority over the family while providing its members with food, clothing, and shelter. Honorable men, however, did not use excessive force in guiding and instructing their wives, children, and household servants. As in the case of Francisca Pérez, when a man flagrantly abused his authority, it prompted some women to invoke the law to protect themselves and, when necessary, their children and other members of the household. Like Pérez, most women who came before judges did not seek to usurp the husband's position as the head of the household or to overthrow the ideological and practical system of patriarchy. Rather, they sought to challenge patriarchal authority figures who had failed to behave according to the gender and social roles prescribed for them. Through the tribunal, women sought to ensure that the system of patriarchy worked for them, though justice frequently eluded them, especially when the courts interpreted the law in ways that reflected deeply rooted gender biases.

Marital, familial, and community gender relations are revealed in the interactions between the patriarchal legal system and women of different ethnicities. Those relations were sometimes characterized by gender conflict and negotiation in which men and women contested the meanings and boundaries of male and female roles and obligations. Following an examination of how the dominant gente de razón legally and socially interpreted marriage, sexuality, and the family, the chapter shows how Spanish-speaking women and indígenas in all the socioeconomic classes used local institutions to contend with men who exceeded their patriarchal authority.[4] Receiving close attention are the principal reasons women turned to local officials: physical abuse, inadequate support, adultery, and unlawful coercion. Women's appeals were usually successful, but when abuse continued, many women resorted to extralegal means to escape their troubled households, an action that alarmed civil and religious authorities as well as men in the pueblo of Los Angeles and the surrounding region, who were wary of any threat to the norms of male-dominated households and the larger community. Patriarchal fears occasionally led to the punishment or even banishment of troublesome women, especially those who turned for help to men who were not their husbands or fathers. Considered particular pariahs were those women who cohabited with men other than their spouses or who bore children out of wedlock. Men who committed similar transgressions faced few repercussions.

Spanish-speaking settlers and their descendants, Californios, inherited from Spain strong convictions about the centrality of marriage, sexuality, and the family to the survival of civilized Catholic society. These convictions seemed self-evident to the residents of Los Angeles and other communities on the northern frontier. At the most elemental level, stable marriages and families produced children who would secure the future and assure the continuity of the settlers' cultural and moral values. Closely regulated sexual behavior—before, during, and after marriage—was key to maintaining honorable and legitimate families and producing the children that would pass on to future generations the cultural and material inheritance of their families. Socio-sexual codes of behavior required women to maintain their *honor* (sexual virtue) through virginity before marriage, fidelity during marriage, and chastity in widowhood. To violate these cultural norms brought *vergüenza* (shame) to them and dishonor to the men in their homes and to their families in general. Expectations for men's sexual behavior were much lower. Legally, unless they committed rape or adultery, they faced no repercussions for their sexual activity. Their role was to defend female virtue and, if necessary, restore the honor lost to their households as the result of a wife or daughter's sexual improprieties. A man had the right to place a woman in seclusion in order to protect his or the family's reputation and social standing. Men thus enjoyed the benefits of a sexual double standard that reinforced their authority in marriage and the family.[5]

In the eyes of the clergy, sexual relations were confined to a man and woman joined in marriage, a sacrament for the procreation and the education of children as well as for companionship. The padres preached that marriage remained indissoluble except through death, a church-sanctioned annulment, or an ecclesiastical divorce (which allowed couples to separate but not to remarry others).[6] There were some regional differences. In Mexico, for example, ecclesiastical divorces were permissible when one spouse was extremely cruel or had physically abused or threatened to kill the other. Additional grounds were abandonment or inadequate support that forced a spouse to commit a crime, such as prostitution. Absolute proof—eyewitness accounts—was necessary to substantiate the transgression. A spouse's confession was insufficient.[7] In Los Angeles, however, these transgressions, even extreme cruelty, were not sufficient cause for ecclesiastical divorce. The priests' reluctance to grant divorces to unhappy households underscores the weight given to the family as the mechanism for maintaining order, reproducing the population, and developing the region. To keep marriages intact, the clergy frequently sought the help of the local civil authorities, but if their support was not readily given, the clergy sometimes publicly berated them and went over their heads to higher officials.

Legal strictures in Alta California supported the region's religious and cultural norms. The relevant civil codes on marriage and the family were derived from Spanish laws and decrees.[8] Permeating those codes was the widely held tenet of patria potestas (paternal authority), which came from deep in the Iberian past and was embedded in the *Siete Partidas* and *Leyes de Toro*. These thirteenth- and sixteenth-century compilations of laws located familial authority in the male heads of household, under an assumption that this assignment of power would assure orderly families and a stable society.[9]

Thus, a man virtually had complete authority over his dependents— wife, children, and any servants or slaves in the household. They, in turn, owed him their obedience in all matters, including public and personal relations. A man's authority was qualified by his obligation to support, protect, and guide his spouse and legitimate offspring. *Hijos naturales* (those born out of wedlock) or *hijos espurios* (those born as a consequence of adultery), on the other hand, derived few, if any, benefits from patria potestas. Fathers were expected to provide support for illegitimate children, but they did not have to provide them with an inheritance.[10] Laws and social mores also required a husband to respect his wife's person, but he had the right to mete out "mild punishments"—the meaning of which varied with time, locale, and circumstance—to her and his other dependents as a way of guiding or teaching them. His ability to discipline them was symbolic of his authority over and governance of the household.[11]

In Los Angeles, the *casa de honor* (honorable home)—regardless of socioeconomic status or racial and cultural identity—was a place where husband and wife treated each other well, supported their dependents, practiced their religion, remained faithful to one another, and otherwise set a good example for their children.[12] Men who abandoned or neglected the well-being of their households or engaged in excessive punishment of their dependents violated not only the law but also the norms of the community.[13]

As members of the community, women had the right to hold men responsible for fulfilling their obligations or for not exceeding their power and authority as household heads. When a husband failed in his duties, women sometimes felt compelled to turn to the Court of First Instance. Depending on the issue, that tribunal convened a civil or criminal trial, with an alcalde presiding in the *juzgado de primera instancia* (Court of First Instance), or a *juicio de concilio* (conciliation trial), with a *juez de paz* (justice of the peace) presiding in the *juzgado de segunda instancia* (Court of Second Instance). In particularly violent and abusive relationships, the alcalde—with the consent of the individual issuing the complaint, usually the woman—would order a criminal trial. Physical violence in the home was a crime punishable by imprisonment or banishment. In matters that involved so-called "light" *(leve)* crimes of physical abuse or some other relatively "mild" transgressions, such as bodily injuries not resulting in death, justices ordered a civil trial or conciliation hearing, in which plaintiff and defendant each appointed an *hombre bueno* (literally, "good man"). A feature of the Spanish legal tradition, this referee or arbitrator served as an advisor to the court. Like most judges, the hombre bueno had no formal legal training but was someone knowledgeable and generally respected in the community.[14]

In the case of a married couple, the goal was reconciliation to preserve the marriage for the good of the family and social stability. In the case of an unmarried couple, the purpose was to separate them.[15] In many instances, these sessions functioned only as "quick fixes," which failed to restrain a violent husband. Women wanting legal separation or annulment usually received a hearing in the civil branch of the court, even though the clergy preferred to handle such matters through ecclesiastical channels.

In the criminal, civil, and conciliation courts, women voiced a host of complaints against heads of households. Spanish-speaking married women protested about husbands who physically abused them, failed to support them and their children, or set a bad example in the household. Luisa Domínguez's troubles with her spouse are representative. In 1843, she went to the conciliation court, complaining to the justice of the peace about her husband, Ángel Pollorena. "My husband's treatment is insufferable," she told the judge and the hombres buenos. "He constantly beats me, [and] I am asking for a separation." To prove how badly she had been abused, she exposed her body, revealing the scars left from the wounds. Pollorena responded, "My wife is a bad woman. . . . The fight began after I punished one of her children and, as she has [already] had three children outside of our marriage, she wants to return to the same [behavior]." "I've had two children outside of the marriage," Domínguez admitted, "but now that I am with him, he doesn't support me."

The judge and hombres buenos believed that the marriage could be saved, and they ordered the couple to attempt a reconciliation. After some persuasion, Domínguez agreed. "I agree to reunite with my husband," she said, "but with the condition that he treat me well, not punish my children excessively, or set a bad example for them." Pollorena accepted her demands, though he, too, set a condition. "I promise to educate the children, comply with my obligations, and forget the past as long as she [is] prudent." To ensure that Pollorena kept his promise to Domínguez, the judge appointed several men to keep close watch over his behavior.[16]

Complaints like those of Luisa Domínguez were often accompanied by accusations of infidelity from women as well as men. Adultery, which the authorities treated as a criminal act and a flagrant threat to marriage and the family, prompted women to appeal to the conciliation court and, if they felt especially wronged, to file civil or criminal charges against their husbands. Sometimes they even asked for the indictment of his accomplice on the grounds that the other woman had provoked the marital troubles. In 1844, Francisca Pérez accused her husband and his *amasia* (lover) of adultery, telling the judge that the other woman had "caused my husband's infidelity and refusal to support me."[17] Marina García likewise informed a judge in 1845 that she had a *mala vida* (bad life) with her husband Francisco Limón because of Manuela Villa, his lover, "who is living with him."[18] To ensure an end to adulterous relations, wives demanded the banishment of such women. "Having caught my husband in flagrante delicto with Nicolasa Carreaga," Marta Reyes told the justice of the peace in 1843, "I ask that [the court] punish him and banish her from the town." When Reyes's husband admitted that he was at fault and "put himself at the court's disposal," the judge, with the agreement of the hombres buenos, ordered him to "treat his wife well" and sent Carreaga to an undisclosed destination.[19]

A woman's decision to file a formal complaint against her spouse for abuse or adultery did not come quickly or easily. In most instances, women turned to the courts only after a prolonged period of contentious relations. Their testimony is usually filled with numerous examples of earlier abuse. Typical was the case of Ramona Vejar. "My husband, Tomás Urquides," Vejar stated to the alcalde in 1842, "hits me because of Dolores Valenzuela [with whom he] has been living . . . for more than two years. . . . He has hit me so many times with a rope or whatever else he can find that I cannot recall the exact number." Witnesses verified Vejar's account and testified that Urquides had fathered a child with Valenzuela. Urquides admitted knowing Valenzuela but denied having an affair with her. He also acknowledged hitting his wife, though he said he did so in order to correct her insolence. "One day, she came to my mother's house," he informed the court, "looking for someone, and when I asked her what or whom she wanted, she responded, 'I am looking for that *puta* [whore or sexually promiscuous woman], who is your friend, and your mother, who is [a common] *alcahueta* [procuress or pimp]. . . . I only hit her when she gives me cause to do so," he insisted, "not because [Valenzuela] tells me to do so; I do so when she neglects the children or leaves without my permission."

When Valenzuela was called to testify, she admitted to a long affair with Urquides. The judge moved quickly to end the relationship. He ordered that Valenzuela live at least ten leagues (about twenty-six miles) from the town in a casa de honor, where she and her children could be watched. Urquides, on the other hand, received only a reprimand for physically abusing his wife and a fine of ten pesos for his sexual misconduct. Within six months, Vejar was back in court complaining that Urquides had returned to his old habits. "I ran to take shelter [from him] in a nearby home," she told the judge, "but he pulled me out, beat me, and then tied me up with a rope." Before the authorities could apprehend him, Urquides fled town, forcing them to suspend the case until he could be located. Despite her sentence of banishment, Valenzuela remained within the pueblo's limits for at least another eight years. Why local authorities failed to force her to leave is unclear, though perhaps the scant number of officials made enforcement of the law irregular.[20]

Like Ramona Vejar, Luz Figueroa experienced years of abuse. In 1849, having suffered for nearly a decade, she fled from her husband, Juan Riera, and she sought the advice of the local priest. "What should I do?" she asked him. He responded, "Return to your husband." Dutifully, she returned home, only to be beaten again. This time, she turned to the court for help, describing for the judge her husband's years of abuse and his latest attack. He "picked up a leather rope and he struck me once in the face and repeatedly on my back," she stated. "Luckily I was able to escape . . . and found help in a nearby house. But soon my husband found me and pulled me from the house, dragging me through the streets and telling me to follow him or else he would kill me with the knife he had hidden in his pants." She showed the judge the scars that the many beatings had left on her body. "What [punishment] do you request for your husband for having beaten and publicly humiliated you?" asked the judge. "I request his banishment from this city because I fear that he will injure me gravely. He has given me a miserable life, and in the twelve years I have been married to this man, there have been numerous relapses into his indecent behavior."[21] The judge ordered the arrest of Riera, whom he questioned and then imprisoned, pending a full criminal investigation. What that investigation revealed is unknown since the surviving records indicate only that Riera was freed but not the reasons why. What is clear was Luz Figueroa's attempt to have him removed from her life. Yet, despite her efforts, her relations with Riera continued into the 1850s, when she went before the American tribunal complaining about his excessive use of force.[22]

Women challenged not only abusive and unfaithful husbands but also coercive fathers. Though fewer issued complaints against fathers than husbands, those who did so frequently won the support of local authorities.[23] In 1842, Casilda Sepúlveda, who was about seventeen years of age, complained to the civil court that her father, Enrique Sepúlveda, with the support of her stepmother, Matilda Trujillo, and the local priest, Tomás Eleuterio Esténega, had forced her to marry against her wishes.[24] Both Spanish civil law and the Church forbade parents to coerce their children to marry. The Royal Pragmatic on Marriage, issued in 1776 and applied to Mexico's northern provinces in 1779, authorized parents to forbid the union of a child under the age of twenty-five, but it prohibited them from forcing a child to marry.[25] When Casilda Sepúlveda went before the judge, she accused her parents and Esténega of usurping her "liberty" to choose a marriage partner. She asked the judge "for the protection of the law against such an attack on my personal liberty" and for an annulment. The judge examined witnesses, including the girl's grandmother, who testified that Enrique Sepúlveda had beaten his daughter and forced her to marry. With the testimony concluded, the judge ruled that, indeed, Casilda had been married against her will, and he nullified the marriage. That ruling set the stage for a prolonged church-state conflict.

When the judge informed the priest of his decision, Esténega, in turn, notified Francisco García Diego y Moreno, bishop of Alta and Baja California. The bishop was outraged, accusing the judge of exceeding his authority and interfering in a religious matter. From the bishop's residence in Santa Bárbara, he wrote to the head of the *prefectura*, Santiago Argüello, who was the highest civil authority in southern California and directly subordinate to the governor.[26] "Judging the validity or nullity of marriage is absolutely reserved to the ecclesiastical domain," declared Bishop García. He then ordered Esténega to speak privately with Casilda and urge her to reconcile with her spouse. If she refused to do so, then she and her relatives should go to Santa Bárbara and plead her case before the ecclesiastical tribunal. At first, she balked, preferring to "present her reasons in writing to the Bishop," but with Father Esténega's prodding, she consented to go.

Before her departure, Bishop García ordered her confined in *depósito* (seclusion) in a casa de honor, the home of Abel Stearns and Arcadia Bandini, a well-to-do and socially prominent family. Esténega directed Stearns "not to permit . . . communication" between "[Casilda] and her parents or relatives . . . so as to avoid any possibilities of influences or threats to her safety and so that she will be able to go to the bishop to validate and prove . . . the nullity of her marriage."[27] Stearns was also responsible for protecting her sexual virtue and family honor from any "stains" that might be brought about through her interaction with men. In California, as in central and northern Mexico, a "loose" woman—a woman physically and sexually free of the patriarchal control of a husband or father—posed a risk of bringing shame on herself and dishonor to the larger family. Women needed "protection" and regulation of their sexuality and person.[28]

Shortly before going to live with the Stearns, and much to Esténega's dismay, Casilda began communicating with her grandmother and aunt. Esténega chastised Stearns, ordering him to send the girl to Santa Bárbara immediately. Stearns refusal led to more outbursts from Esténega.

When she finally appeared at the Santa Bárbara hearing, the Bishop García decreed that Casilda had been coerced into marrying, and he granted the annulment. Her success in attaining an annulment, a rare occurrence in California and Mexico, was a triumph over paternal authority. Her victory, however, did not come without a price.

A few weeks after returning to Los Angeles, she was again in court, this time complaining that her father had retaliated against her. "I don't want to return to my father's house," she declared, for "he refuses to support me, refuses to recognize me as his daughter[, and] wants to disinherit me. What shall I do?" According to Spanish civil law, a father had the right to disinherit a legitimate daughter, but only when she married against his wishes.[29] Because the court record is incomplete, nothing is known of the outcome of Casilda's appeal or her relationship with her father and family. But even if the alienation from her family was short-lived, this case reveals the risks that women in this frontier community were willing to take to challenge patriarchal authority figures.

Casilda's conflicts with her family did not deter her from starting a family of her own. Within four years, she had married Ramón Duarte, and they had baptized their first daughter.[30] Her father, on the other hand, continued to live in a conflicted household. Less than a year after the Santa Bárbara hearing, his wife, Matilde Trujillo, went to the local authorities, accusing him of beating her. The court ordered the couple to attempt reconciliation. Sepúlveda agreed to carry out his obligations as a married man. However, as he died a year later of smallpox, it is unclear if he complied.[31]

Casilda Sepúlveda identified herself as a member of the gente de razón, as did all the women who used the courts to challenge male heads of household. The extant court records involving native women—a total of eleven cases—provide not a single instance of a neófita or a gentile bringing a complaint against a spouse or father. Perhaps the neófitas took their complaints against family members to the priests or governors who exercised greater direct authority over their lives than the local authorities did.[32] Gentiles dealing with similar problems avoided the courts in favor of tribal customs. At San Gabriel, for instance, when a non-Christian husband mistreated his wife, usually she simply left him and returned to her family. This action amounted to "divorce," for as the priests at San Gabriel noted in 1814, the California natives did not "recognize the permanence . . . that [Christian] matrimony demands."

The local gentiles, reported the priests, cohabited as man and wife "as long as both [partners] were satisfied and living in harmony."[33]

Of the 11 cases brought by indigenous—Christian and non-Christian—women in the Los Angeles and San Gabriel region, only one involved abuse, but by a *non*-family member. Vitalacia, a married Christian Indian at Misión San Gabriel, was the only neófita (the other 10 were gentiles) to bring a complaint to the local court, in this case the criminal court. In 1841, she told the judge that Asención Alipas, a Mexican man who was not her husband, had "maimed and cut [her] with a knife." "Last week," she informed the court, "I was at the mission gathering wheat, when Lorena [a native woman who worked at the mission] told me that Alipas had arrived." With a knife in hand, he "approached me and in a denigrating tone asked, 'Why do you no longer want to be with me?' When I told him [again] that I didn't want to be with him anymore, he took the knife and cut my hand and my braid." When questioned by the judge, Alipas stated that "he had been having relations with Vitalacia for about four or five years and had sacrificed the earnings of his work in supporting her." When "I arrived at the . . . the mission . . . I saw an attitude in Vitalacia that I disliked, [and] I became violent and grabbed her, cutting her hair with a knife." The cut on her hand was of her own doing, he insisted. In "trying to take the knife away from me, she grabbed the blade, and because she refused to let go of it, I pulled on it, and she cut her fingers."[34]

The judge was angered by their extramarital relationship, not the violence. "What do you have to say about using a married woman?" he asked Alipas. "It is true," Alipas responded. "I acknowledge my crime, but an offended man becomes violent." Puzzled, the judge pressed his inquiry. "What offense did she commit against you; she is not your wife." Alipas attributed his anger to Vitalacia's disregard for her obligations to him, particularly the sexual services that she owed him for his economic support. "She never appreciated that," he stated. The judge was unsympathetic. He found Alipas guilty of adultery and injuring Vitalacia, and he sentenced him to labor on public works. He urged Vitalacia, whom he also found guilty of adultery, to stay away from Alipas although he apparently did not sentence her. This case is significant because it shows that a woman occupying a subordinate position in the community vis-à-vis the gente de razón could use the court successfully to extricate herself from an abusive relationship, in which the abuser's gender and ethnic status would normally have given him dominance over her.

Women often had the assistance of their immediate families when they turned to the courts or other civil or religious authorities to deal with men in the larger community. Fathers or brothers often represented daughters or sisters, particularly in instances of sexual assault.[35] The socially and politically prominent gente de razón viewed rape not only as a grave offense against a woman's reputation, or sexual virtue, but also as a stain on the husband or father and on the family's honor and social standing. Hispanic law reflected this attitude, as it allowed male members of a family to kill a perpetrator who was caught in the act of rape.[36]

The threat of family and patriarchal dishonor that rape posed for the elite was clearly apparent in an 1840 criminal complaint filed by María Ygnacia Elizalde, wife of José María Aguilar, a prominent former local official in Los Angeles.[37] She accused Cornelio López of attempting to rape her. "López broke into my house and entered my room," she told the judge, "with the intent of using my person in the [sexual] act when he saw me alone." "With great effort," she added, "I managed to resist the force with which he surprised me. [It was not] until Raimundo Alanis arrived that López let go of me, which allowed me the liberty and opportunity to come [to the court] to report this."

The judge ordered a full investigation, followed by a trial at which Elizalde repeated her complaint. López, she testified, "tried to force me to have a [sexual act] with him, but I absolutely denied him. He told me, 'Why don't you want to have relations with me? Haven't you already been with others?' But I continued to resist and, eventually, he relented, but only momentarily. At that point, he looked out the [bedroom] door to see if anyone else was around, and then returned to my bed to try to force me [to have relations]. He remained an hour, after which time he left, no doubt [because] he saw Alanis . . . I then went immediately to complain to the authorities so that they would restrain him." When López took the stand, he denied trying to force Elizalde, claiming that earlier she had promised to have sex with him. When he had asked her to comply, she refused, which incensed him. He was even angrier, he declared, because of an extramarital affair that she was having with another man, José Avila.

Presenting the case for the prosecution was Elizalde's husband, Aguilar. The court typically either appointed a prosecutor or asked the aggrieved party to select one. Family members could be chosen for the task. Like Aguilar, the selected representatives were usually socially or politically prominent men in the community. "During my absence," Aguilar began, "while I was traveling to Santa Bárbara, Cornelio López took advantage of my wife's solitude, and he boldly profaned the home of an honorable citizen." He continued, "Yes, sir, on the morning of the nineteenth of the past month, my wife was resting in her bed from her domestic work, when suddenly Cornelio López appeared and, as if possessed by the devil and using the most obscene words, attempted to force my wife to have carnal relations. My wife, who was shocked to see him, heroically resisted . . . this treacherous man, who . . . attempted to use her for his pleasure." López's attack, he argued, "disregarded the respect that [was] due to the institution of marriage and [that was among] the duties of a man in society." Upset about the effect of the attack on his authority and position in his family and his social standing in the community, Aguilar declared that "López has made me look like a common alcahueta in public . . . and [has] offended my honor." Furthermore, he told the court, López's "immorality" had not only threatened his marriage, but also that of José Avila. To redeem the "offended honor of [my] wife and family," Aguilar asked the court to banish López for five years to the presidio of Sonoma "where work and reclusion will teach him not to commit such excesses and to respect the society in which he lives; and perhaps then he will be an honorable citizen."

The defense, headed by Juan Cristóbal Vejar, argued that Elizalde's biological sex as a female and López's as a male were to blame for his behavior. "Man is susceptible to the inclinations of the female sex," Vejar argued. "That the defendant approached an honorable woman is not a crime." López's behavior may have been improper, but it was not criminal, and it was initiated by impulses of the flesh beyond his control. On the other hand, acknowledged Vejar, Aguilar had every right to be angry with López, for his anger is "founded on the insult that López caused by approaching his wife and disrespecting her [married] state." But, Vejar emphasized again, an insult is not a crime.

Before rendering a verdict, the Los Angeles judge waited more than two years for the authorities in Monterey to convene the Superior Tribunal, an appellate court composed of three justices. Until that time, appeals had gone to the governor, but legislation enacted in Mexico in 1837 required that a higher court review all verdicts and sentences in criminal cases, including those in California, which led to the creation of the Superior Tribunal in Monterey.[38] Ultimately, the Los Angeles judge found López, who all the while had been incarcerated, guilty of the attempted rape of Elizalde. "For having wanted to use a married woman violently . . . I condemn him for the public satisfaction of José María Aguilar so that the honor of this man's wife is free from damage." Since López had been jailed for nearly three years, the judge believed he had served his sentence and set him free. Presumably, he also thought that Aguilar's honor and Elizalde's sexual virtue and reputation had been restored. Following that decision, the Superior Tribunal automatically reviewed by case, responding with mixed approval to the courtroom proceedings and the sentence: "since the [court] proceedings lack the formal prerequisites that are necessary in overseeing personal injury cases . . . and given the time that Cornelio López has suffered in prison, the judge's decision to free López is approved." López deserved freedom, the Superior Tribunal continued, because the Los Angeles judge had committed a procedural error that mandated López's release and "not because of the [need for] public satisfaction" of José María Aguilar. The tribunal's ruling reflects its view that compliance with legal procedures took precedence over restoration of honor among elite families.[39]

Although sexual assaults by Mexican men on Mexican women were considered an affront to the honor of the women and their families, similar attacks on non-Christian native women brought dishonor only to the Mexican men and their relatives, since indígenas were seen as lesser beings who occupied the lowest level in the socioeconomic, gender, and racial hierarchy, and who thus possessed no honor that could be insulted. As such, they were outsiders to gente-de-razón culture and society. This was the message of an 1844 rape case involving a native woman. A gentile named Anacleto accused two angeleños, Domingo Olivas, an assistant of the court, and Ygnacio Varelas, a friend of Olivas, of raping his wife at their ranchería near Rancho San Bernardino. Anacleto filed his charges with the local ranch owner and judge in San Bernardino, José del Carmen Lugo, who gathered evidence and persuaded a Los Angeles judge to hold a criminal hearing at which the evidence was presented. According to Anacleto and other witnesses, the incident occurred shortly after Olivas and Varelas arrived at the ranchería with the intent of taking Anacleto to the court in Los Angeles (for reasons that do not appear in the public record). They found Anacleto, who was blind, and his wife inside their home. The two then "took the woman," Lugo told the judge, "and used her by force, threatening her with a knife and saying they wanted to kill them both." About this time, "some indios and a Mexican approached," and Varelas "threatened [them] with the knife." When the "men warned Varelas that they were going to inform the local authorities about what had occurred, he fled the scene."[40]

Varelas challenged Lugo's testimony, insisting that he and Olivas had not sexually assaulted the woman but had offered her money for sexual relations, and she had consented. By portraying her as a common prostitute, they hoped to deflect the charges against them. When Olivas testified, however, he contradicted Varelas and admitted to having committed the crime. He attributed it to drunkenness, since he and Varelas had imbibed aguardiente, which "had blurred their senses and led to the lewd acts." He begged that the crime not be made public. "In view of my remorse and frank confession, please consider that I am married and have children, and I live in good harmony with my family. Therefore, I ask and beg you that this situation not be made public." He also pleaded with the judge for "a punishment that is prudent and discreet" in order to spare him and his family any dishonor that would likely result from the publicity of the rape.

The judge was moved by Olivas's appeal, and he understood the social and cultural implications of making the crime public. "The confession and guilt of Olivas and Varelas have been established," the judge ruled. "The former has violated a woman by force, and the latter was his accomplice. I should condemn Olivas to service in public works," he declared, "but in order not to disrupt his marriage [or] . . . harm . . . his minor children . . . I order Olivas to pay a fine of twenty pesos and his accomplice to pay ten." The judge made no effort to compensate the native woman for her (or her family's) loss of honor. Indeed, he made no reference to a dishonored household. He obviously placed greater value on Olivas's reputation and that family's honor and social standing than on the crime committed against a non-Christian native woman or on her or her family's sexual virtue or shame. Clearly, gender, ethnic, and class biases influenced the court's decision. Since this is the only surviving case illustrating those biases, the frequency with which they influenced court cases is unclear. Nevertheless, this case reveals the low status of indigenous peoples, particularly, women, vis-à-vis the gente de razón, and their vulnerability in the larger society.

Amply available, however, is evidence showing that both Mexican women and neófitas devised extralegal means to contend with authority figures when their abuse was not effectively checked by local officials.

Some women simply fled violent households. In 1845, María Presenta-ción Navarro, a single Spanish-speaking woman, left her home in Los Angeles because she feared the wrath of her father. Earlier that year, Antonio Reina, a married man who befriended her father and family, had gotten her pregnant. Frightened of her father's rage, she asked Reina: "[H]elp me escape from my father's side. . . . I fear that he will kill me." Reina took her to Rosarito in Baja California. Her father asked the authorities to apprehend them and punish Reina, who, he believed, "ha[d] forcibly pulled [María Presentación] away from her family."[41]

The couple was captured and returned to Los Angeles where a full investigation and trial soon got underway. During the trial, the judge learned about the tense relationship between Navarro and her father. Recognizing her physical danger as well as the possibility that, in her emotional distress, she or perhaps even her father might kill the child, the judge ordered her "put in reclusion [in a casa de honor] . . . under the care of the owners of the house, [who] will oversee her pregnancy so that an infanticide will not be committed." Keeping her from the public's view would also lessen her shame and her family's dishonor and the damage to their social standing in the larger community. As for Reina, the judge banished him "to the port of San Diego until Navarro reaches *estado* [twenty-five years of age] or she leaves the municipality," whichever came first. The goal was to separate them until she obtained adulthood.

Although it was more common among Californio and Mexican women, neófitas also ran away from abusive households. They, too, had to deal with disapproving male authority figures, particularly husbands. In 1841, because of prolonged mistreatment by her Mexican husband, Estanislao Valenzuela, a retired military man, Manuela, a neófita, left Los Angeles and fled south to her mother's home at Las Flores, a native pueblo. She employed a ruse to escape, asking Estanislao for permission to go to the center of town, where she hid in a house, waiting for an opportunity to leave the pueblo. When two Mexican men passed by on horseback, she asked them to take her to Las Flores. They agreed, but in the meantime, her husband alerted the authorities. She was apprehended at Las Flores and taken back to Los Angeles, where she was brought before the judge. When asked why she had left, Manuela explained that her husband "always hits me and has me locked up." The judge refused to believe her, concluding that the two men had seduced her, convincing her to leave her spouse. He ordered Manuela to return to her husband, found the men guilty of abducting a married woman, and sentenced the two to labor for several months on public works. Despite her willingness to chance an escape, the court thwarted Manuela's effort to flee from her abusive husband.[42]

To get away from an unsafe environment, some women in Los Angeles took the even more drastic measure of cohabiting with someone other than their own husbands. This brought down on their heads the wrath not only of their husbands but also of religious and civil authorities and the entire community. Petra Varela's decision to leave her spouse for another man in 1847 resulted in her husband, Esteban López, bringing charges of illegal cohabitation and adultery against her and Antonio Valencia, a former employee of the household. "I found my wife and Antonio Valencia locked in a bedroom," López reported to the criminal court, "and although I overlooked this incident, they have since then continued with their relations. I finally decided to leave the house," he continued, "and yet Valencia remained there, setting a bad example for the family."

When the judge questioned Varela about her behavior, she denied the charges. López "is my servant," she told the judge. "Since the day he arrived, he has consulted only with me; everything [in the household] belongs to me." Under persistent questioning, she finally admitted to cohabiting with him. Her explanation: "My husband is uninterested [in me] and doesn't work . . . and [he] fails to support me." Witnesses corroborated her complaints, testifying that her husband had not supported her for years. She had been forced to work in order to cover household expenses, including the wages of several laborers, and even so, she had fallen into debt. López's failure to fulfill his marital and household responsibilities, she argued, had absolved her of any sexual obligations to him and freed her to live with Valencia. The judge held otherwise. "Petra Varela must reunite with her husband and carry out her obligations of matrimony," he ordered. López, her husband, "must [meet his obligations] because there are indications that he does not fulfill [them]." To guard against a reoccurrence of the incident, the judge banished Valencia to the port of Loreto in Baja California.[43]

Religious authorities also vigorously condemned sexual improprieties. When Juana Gómez left her husband in 1837 for another man, the clergy denounced the couple and used the occasion to preach about the moral evils of adultery. Gómez had abandoned her unhappy marriage in Sonora and gone north to live with Manuel Arzaga in Los Angeles, taking her two children with her. When Tomás Esténega, the priest at Misión San Gabriel who had made so much trouble for Casilda Sepúlveda, discovered that the couple was living as "husband and wife," he went to Narciso Durán, head of the ecclesiastical tribunal in Santa Bárbara, and obtained permission to ask the civil authorities to end the scandalous relationship. "Arzaga is living with a Sonoran woman named Juana . . . and cohabits with her as if she is his proper wife," Esténega wrote to Gil Ybarra, a local judge, urging him to apprehend the woman and confine her at Misión San Gabriel until her husband could take her home. Ybarra agreed and promptly carried out the request.

With Gómez under Esténega's watch at San Gabriel, Ybarra traveled there to ascertain the reasons for her behavior. "Who is your spouse? Please state his name and where you were married." "I am a married woman," she responded. "They say I married in Sonora and [that] my husband is there, but that is false. I consider Manuel Arzaga to be my husband. Since the first time we were together, he has supported and maintained me, and I have lived with him." Her explanation did nothing to change the civil and religious authorities' view that she and Arzaga had committed adultery. Durán declared them "sacrilegious profaners of holy sacraments," and recommended that she "be restored to the authority of her legitimate husband who will either forgive her or demand that she receive the appropriate punishment, which shall be best, as it will serve as a lesson to all." Judge Ybarra accepted Durán's recommendation, ordering Gómez to return to her husband and banishing Arzaga to San Diego, forbidding him to have contact with her.

Despite that sentence, Gómez remained in Los Angeles, living and having more children with Arzaga until 1845, the year he died. Gómez continued to live in the pueblo for several more decades and never returned to her legal spouse in Sonora. Why the authorities failed to keep them apart is unknown, but perhaps the dearth of local officials or pressing political concerns, especially over the California governorship in the mid-1830s, made it difficult.[44]

Notwithstanding the infrequent lapses in enforcing social and cultural norms, the religious and civil authorities also kept watch over indígenas who in any way threatened the honor of households. One native woman who faced harsh consequences—banishment—for threatening a gente-de-razón marriage and family was María Pegui. In 1840, Durán wrote to the prefect complaining about "the notorious public scandal caused in [the] community by . . . María Pegui."[45] Pegui's crime, Durán informed the prefect, was cohabiting with the Irishman "Santiago Bore" (James Burke), who was separated from his wife, Josefa Boronda, "that worthy but unhappy woman." Bishop García, frustrated by Pegui and Burke's continuing relationship, asked for Prefect Argüellos's assistance. "Pegui has had the extreme and unheard of impudence of following and enticing Don Santiago, [whether] through the streets, into houses, on corners, and [she has] even gone into his home in plain sight of his legal wife," Durán charged. "Were it not for [Pegui's] evil provocation, it is . . . believed that the husband would have desisted from such an immoral life." Rather than lay any blame on Burke for the extramarital relationship, the bishop condemned Pegui for dishonoring Burke and Boronda's family, which is yet another indication of the sexual double standard that existed not only in the Los Angeles community but also throughout Alta California. Her ethnicity as an indigenous woman also reinforced the belief that Pegui had tempted Burke, for members of the community tended to condemn indigenous people of both sexes as initiators of corporal and sexual "excesses."[46]

To end "the persistent scandal," preserve "public morals," and achieve the peaceful reunification of "the honorable [Burke and Boronda] family," Durán persuaded the governor, who had ultimate say in matters involving indigenous peoples, to banish Pegui from the territory. Burke received no punishment other than a warning that he would be "severely punished" if caught "having the slightest personal communication" with Pegui. In this case, Burke's status as married man and member of the gente de razón excused him from his responsibility in the liaison, while Pegui, an indigenous woman with little or no social standing, suffered the full consequences of their relations.[47]

Women who transgressed sociocultural norms not only had to deal with civil and religious authorities but also with male members of the community. Men occasionally took matters into their own hands when they believed the authorities had failed or would fail to enforce law and community standards of propriety and to control women who affronted the "morals" and "security" of decent society. This was a vigilante committee's justification for the public execution of a married woman and her lover in 1836. Two years earlier, María del Rosario Villa had apparently tired of her spouse, Domingo Félix, and she left him to take up with

Gervasio Alipas, a local vaquero and native of Sonora. Villa and Alipas lived together as husband and wife despite Félix's repeated and unsuccessful attempts to persuade her to return to him. Frustrated, Félix asked the *ayuntamiento* (town council) to apprehend her, which was finally done at Misión San Gabriel. As was the custom, the judge, who was also the head or president of the ayuntamiento, held a conciliation meeting between Félix and Villa. When that session appeared to have successfully reunited them, the judge allowed the couple to return to their home at Rancho Los Féliz. All was not well, however. Before they reached their destination, they encountered an angry Alipas, who had vehemently resisted Villa's return to her husband. Alipas attacked Félix with a knife, killing him almost instantly. With the assistance of Villa, who expressed joy at being reunited with her lover, Alipas tied a reata to Félix's body and dragged it off the road and down an embankment. There they covered it with leaves and dirt, expecting that no one would find the dead man.[48]

Days after the murder, however, the authorities unearthed Félix's body and arrested the lovers. On hearing the news of their capture, residents in the community became agitated and demanded justice. At a special meeting of the ayuntamiento, town leaders resolved to handle the trial and prosecution of Alipas and Villa under the utmost security. They called on a group of citizens to aid in maintaining order while the authorities investigated the matter. Few residents came forth, however, for most had already concluded that the two lovers were the murderers and deserved a punishment that fit their crime: death. Because the Superior Tribunal in Monterey had yet to be established, convictions in California for capital crimes and death sentences required the review of jurists in Mexico City. That process could take up to a year or more. Rather than suffer a delay of justice, men in the community concluded that they should take the law into their own hands.

A few days later, an armed group of fifty men met at John Temple's home. There were thirty-seven Californios and thirteen Mexicans. Most were socioeconomically and politically prominent. They organized a vigilante committee, calling themselves the "*junta defensora de la seguridad publica*" (public security defense council). At the meeting, they elected a president, secretary, and commander of armed forces, and drafted a proclamation expressing their indignation at "the horrible crime committed against Domingo Félix" and "the frequency of similar crimes [of passion] in this city." The reference to "similar crimes" is unclear, however, for no surviving record suggests a comparable event. Nevertheless, they continued, "Fearing for this unhappy country a state of anarchy where the right of the strongest shall be the only law, and finally believing that immorality has reached such an extreme that public security is menaced and will be lost . . . [we] demand the execution or the delivery [of Villa and Alipas] to us for immediate execution." They disparaged Villa as a "faithless . . . abominable monster who cruelly immolated her . . . husband in order to give herself up without fear to her frantic passions and to pluck by homicide from the slime of turpitude the filthy laurel of the execrable treason." "Let the infernal couple perish," they declared. Later that day, the committee gave the town council its demands. When the authorities balked, the vigilantes seized the keys to the jail, took Félix and Villa outside, and shot them, leaving their bodies exposed as an example to the public of the fate of those who threatened public safety and the institutions of marriage and the family. The vigilantes' actions seem to have worked, as no other person, woman or man, married or unmarried, committed a similar crime of passion, that is, killing the legal spouse of their lover in an effort to maintain the extramarital relationship.[49]

Women, like Villa, who openly defied patriarchal authority and sociocultural norms of female sexuality, virtue, and shame not only encountered extreme threats—physical violence—but also less severe, yet pernicious, reprimands for their lifestyles. Spanish-speaking women who had children out of wedlock and lived with men who were not their spouses, or who consorted with married men, faced personal and public accusations that tarnished their social standing in the community and damaged the honor of their families. In the Spanish era, authorities sometimes publicly shamed such women by shaving their heads and one eyebrow and forcing them to stand outside the church after mass on Sundays. One widow who experienced such humiliation was Anastacia Zúñiga, an angeleño, who had an extramarital relationship with a carpenter from Misión San Gabriel, José Antonio Ramírez. The liaison resulted in the birth of a daughter in 1818. After appearing in church with her head and eyebrow shaved, the governor ordered the Comandante Militar José de la Guerra y Noriega, Los Angeles's *comisionado* (a military official with authority over local affairs), to remove her to the presidio of Santa Bárbara and place her in seclusion in a *casa de honor* for six months. She was obliged to serve in the household and "lead a religious life as a Christian woman." Ramírez, in contrast, only had to labor for one month on public works. The governor encouraged him to marry Zúñiga and, if he refused, to pay for the child's support.[50]

Though the practice of displaying "fallen" women in church fell out of favor by the end of the Spanish period, in the Mexican era, women like Zúñiga had to face other forms of public humiliation. In the 1836 and 1844 *padrónes* (censuses)—which provided an individual's name, age, profession, place of birth, current residence, and marital status—census takers identified women who transgressed moral and social norms of sexual behavior as individuals who led "malas vidas," indicated by the initials MV following their names.[51] In this case, a mala vida meant leading a sinful life (rather than having an unhappy married life). The 1836 and 1844 censuses identified forty-two Spanish-speaking women (thirteen in 1836 and thirty-five in 1844, six of whom appeared in both records) as leading malas vidas. All but eleven (nearly 75 percent) had had children out of wedlock. Most were single and widowed (only three were married). In age, they ranged from relatively young to "middle-aged," with the average 25.6 years in 1836 and 31 years in 1844. They occupied upper, middle, and lower economic levels of society. The preponderance of unmarried women who were labeled MV reveals that, as socially independent females who often headed their own households, community leaders saw them as potentially immoral and "loose" women who needed to be regulated and kept under surveillance by patriarchal authority figures.

Dolores Varelas, for example, was cited as leading a mala vida in 1844. She was a single mother who had had the first of her seven hijos naturales (children born to unmarried parents who were eligible to wed) in 1830, at the age of fifteen. Of her other illegitimate children, she identified three as the offspring of José López. Whether Varelas and López lived as man and wife in a consensual union is unknown, but it is known that Varelas never married López. Her father, Cayetano Varelas, an elderly widower, with whom she lived with her children, provided most, if not all, of the support for her and her children. (Her mother, Hilaria Avila, had died years earlier, in 1821, at the age of thirty-two.) The authorities not only belittled Varelas by designating her "MV," but they also attempted to hide her "shame" from public view (by recommending that she be placed in depósito or forced to leave town). They also tried to make her to marry in order to legitimize her children. Despite all that, she remained single for her entire life.[52]

Teodacia Saiz's extramarital relationship with José Antonio Sánchez, with whom she had two of her five children, also earned her an MV in the 1844 census and a public reprimand. One night in 1844, Saiz, a widow who used a room in her home as a bar and gaming parlor, hosted a card game at her establishment. Sánchez, a participant, accused Hilario Varela, another player, of stealing from him. After failing to resolve the matter, Sánchez took his complaint to the local judge who, rather than resolving the civil dispute, fined all of them, including Saiz, for gambling and participating in an illegal card game. The judge, who also learned that Saiz and Sánchez lived together out of wedlock, ordered them to separate. They nevertheless continued to have relations for at least two more years.[53]

Illicit sexual behavior, such as that of Teodacia Saiz and Dolores Varelas, did not result in high rates of illegitimacy, however. During the six decades of Spanish and Mexican rule, baptismal records from Misión San Gabriel and the Los Angeles Plaza Church reveal that only 11 percent of the children born to gente-de-razón mothers (293 of 2,592 infants baptized in the Catholic Church) were hijos naturales or hijos espurios, a relatively low rate.[54] For example, in Mexico City between 1830 and 1842, illegitimacy rates were more than double those in California, ranging from 18 to 30 percent.[55] In Cuba in 1846, the illegitimacy rate among "whites" and the "coloured" (persons of African heritage) population was 19 and 75 percent, respectively.[56] The relatively low rate of illegitimate births in the greater Los Angeles region contradicts accounts by travelers and traders in the 1820s, 1830s, and 1840s, which portrayed California women, particularly those in the lower classes, as immoral and sexually promiscuous.[57] Contrary to the traveler's images of women, there was tight social control, few extra-marital relations, and thus, low rates of illegitimacy.[58]

Arguably, the practice of classifying a certain group of women as leading a mala vida may insinuate that they were prostitutes and that the community sought to censure and publicly vilify them as transgressors of law and community standards. The fact that some of these women had multiple partners and that their children had different fathers may also lend credence to the idea that they conducted business in the "oldest of professions."[59] A close examination of the records, however, refutes that. There is little evidence that these women were prostitutes. Rather, the records suggest that by using public denigration, the local authorities attempted to control and, ultimately, end women's perceived sexual misconduct. The "MV" was meant not only to belittle and stigmatize them and the members of their household but also to warn residents, particularly women, of the consequences of immoral excesses. Because the town and the region remained thinly populated throughout the Mexican era, most angeleños doubtless knew the women and were familiar with the accusations against them.

Women who were labeled with an MV, like Saiz and Varelas, belonged to a larger cohort of 115 unwed mothers in the greater Los Angeles region, most of whom were not identified in the censuses as leading malas vidas. A review of the civil and ecclesiastical records corroborates that most of the women labeled as MV were also brought to court for sex-related offenses (not prostitution, but such things as living with someone other than their husbands). Thus, the MV label may have implied violations of social norms that went beyond merely being the mother of an illegitimate child. Why the census takers and civil and religious authorities failed to publicly berate these other single mothers for leading malas vidas is unclear. Perhaps they successfully hid the birth of their child from the civil authorities taking the census, or they gave birth during a time in which personal and public scrutiny of sexual behavior was less intense. (Earlier pueblo censuses, for example, make no reference to "mala vida" or a person's legitimacy.) Between 1780, when the first gente-de-razón child was baptized at Misión San Gabriel, and 1848, the end of Mexican rule, 115 women, not including the ones identified in the censuses, had hijos naturales. These women were also mostly unmarried, from all economic levels, and relatively young. They included Nicolasa Carreaga and Eugenia Valencia, who engaged in sexual relations with men who were not their husbands and eventually faced formal charges for their illicit sexual unions.

In contrast, Mexican men who had children out of wedlock or who consorted with married women or women who were not their spouses faced few legal or social repercussions for their illicit sexual behavior. Those men benefited from a double standard that nearly excused gente-de-razón males (recall José Antonio Ramírez) for sexual misconduct yet vilified women for the same acts. Even when a California Mexican woman openly identified a man as the father of her child, he not only was not publicly shamed but, for the most part, he retained his honor, reputation, and social standing in the community.[60]

One man who fathered several children outside of marriage but who apparently faced little social or cultural pressure or open condemnation of his lifestyle was Bernardo Sepúlveda, a member of a socially and economically prominent family. Sepúlveda essentially led two lives as the head of two households. Sometime in 1832, as a single young man, Sepúlveda fathered a natural child with Josefa Domínguez. Although they did not marry, the couple had one more child in the course of twelve years. In 1844, he finally got married but not to Domínguez. Instead, he wed María Rafaela Antonia Verdugo, the daughter of Julio Verdugo and a member of another well-known family, which owned Rancho San Rafael. In the same year, Domínguez was identified as leading a mala vida as a consequence of her sexual conduct. Apparently, Domínguez's public denigration failed to separate her from Sepúlveda, and they had three more children. With his wife, Sepúlveda reared a family of six, bringing the total number of his offspring, legitimate and illegitimate, to eleven.[61]

Likewise, Teodosio Yorba, a socially and economically prominent, married man faced minimal repercussions for his affair with Ynocencia Reyes, a single woman. His long-term relationship with Reyes began after eight years of marriage to María Antonia Lugo, whom he had wed in 1825 and with whom he had had one child. Between 1834, shortly before Reyes's nineteenth birthday, and 1860, the unmarried couple had at least eight children. Yorba's marriage lasted until sometime before 1860 when his wife died of undisclosed causes. Lugo's passing gave the long-time lovers an opportunity to marry, which they did in 1860. That marriage solemnized their union and legitimized their children, enabling them to escape the stigma of illegitimacy and the dishonor that it brought. Their long-term liaison reveals that couples sometimes maintained illicit relations for years or decades at a time, despite social and cultural taboos against adultery and extramarital relations. Why Yorba did not seek a divorce after 1850, when American common law allowed it, is unclear, but it is clear that he took advantage of the sexual double standard, which allowed him to maintain a wife and an amasia or lover with few legal, cultural, or social repercussions.[62]

Other men who benefited from the double standard included several of the vigilantes who participated in apprehending and executing Félix and Villa. Despite the moral conviction and righteous indignation of the committee, several members, including a leader, later engaged in sexual improprieties of their own. Less than a year after Félix and Villa's execution, Manuel Arzaga, as noted above, cohabited with a married woman, Juana Gómez. And though he never killed her husband, he profaned the sacrament of marriage and the family of another man. In the 1840s, Isaac "Julian" Williams, a widower and father of two, had at least three mistresses with whom he had six children. Two of his lovers were California natives and one a *nuevomexicana* (New Mexican), all of whom worked for him in some capacity on his property, Rancho Chino. With María Antonia Apis, an indígena, he had four children, Victoria, Concepción, Refugia, and Feliciano; with María de Jesús, also an indígena, he had Francisca; and with Villanueva, he had Manuelita. Though he rarely publicly acknowledged his relationships with the women or the illegitimate children as his own, he later made modest provisions for their support and education until they reached adulthood or married.[63]

Neófitas also engaged in extramarital liaisons, bore children outside of marriage, and cohabited with persons who were not their "legal" spouses but none were ever publicly berated for this. From 1802, the year when the first neófito child was baptized at Misión San Gabriel, to 1848, the end of Mexican rule, 110 neófitas—residing in the San Gabriel-Los Angeles region—christened hijos naturales. Like women de razón who had illegitimate children, the neófitas were mostly single, though their ages and socioeconomic status are less clear. They came from the nearby missions of San Gabriel, San Fernando, San Juan Capistrano, and San Diego. Neófitas were enumerated in the 1836 and 1844 censuses, but those who had illegitimate offspring were not publicly identified as leading mala vidas. Given that there are few, if any, records of charges of impropriety filed against neófitas, it seems the authorities did not take much notice of the sexual activities of these women. Doubtless, their status as natives and women who occupied a subordinate position in the social structure vis-à-vis Mexicans meant that their sexual virtue and honor had little, if any, value. In contrast to Mexican families, the stain of illegitimacy in neófito households rarely threatened family honor or inheritance and the transfer of property. Most indigenous women and men had little, if any, property to bequeath to their children and had a lowly social standing in the gente-de-razón community. Baptismal records reveal that illegitimacy rates among neófitos were even lower than among the gente de razón. Approximately 6 percent of neófito children (or 114 of 1,807 persons baptized) in the San Gabriel and Los Angeles region were hijos naturales. This suggests that the neófitos who baptized their offspring adhered to Catholic precepts and did so more closely than the gente de razón, though it is likely that many neófitos and most gentiles never bothered to baptize their children, choosing, instead, to live free of European-imposed religious values.[64]

The evidence adduced in this chapter shows that women—Californio, neófita, and gentile—in varying ways suffered from gender discrimination in the cultural, social, and legal systems of Mexican California. That same evidence, however, reveals that they contested, and sometimes checked, patriarchs and their authority, whether that authority was manifested in the law, government, religion, or family, in order to improve their lives and that of any children. The records indicate that women took legal, and sometimes extralegal, measures to protect themselves from men—husbands and fathers and men in the community—who abused them, neglected to provide for them, or unlawfully coerced them. Although some women turned to the civil, criminal, and ecclesiastical courts for help, others took matters into their own hands and fled from intolerable lives at home, even at the risk of severe punishment by secular and religious officials as well as family and community members.

The records also show that women who transgressed socio-sexual codes of behavior faced serious consequences, including physical harm and public denigration and vilification. Men who committed similar violations of sexual mores encountered little, if any, repercussions. Males benefited from a sexual double standard that allowed them to engage in extra-marital relations without harming their honor and social standing. Despite frequently oppressive cultural norms and laws, there were California Mexican and Native American women who boldly sought a better life for themselves and their families.

Chapter 3

Family, Property, and Economic Independence

In 1840, after living for more than nineteen years on Rancho Rodeo de las
Aguas, the widow María Rita Valdez, a member of the gente de razón,
petitioned Governor Juan Bautista Alvarado for legal title to the property. The rancho was located outside the four sitios constituting the
pueblo of Los Angeles (a sitio equals 1 square league, about 6.78 square
miles, or roughly 4,440 acres), but it was within the town's larger governing jurisdiction or district.[1] Valdez had taken this step because the rancho
had recently been invaded by squatters. Her request included as co-
owners Emidio and Ricardo Vejar, who had acquired an interest in the
property several years after she had first occupied it. What began as a
simple petition soon led to bitter controversy: Luciano Valdez, not a
relative of María Rita, protested to the alcalde, Juan Bautista Leandry.
According to Luciano, he too held an interest: "They are denying my
rights and share of the property. . . . It is true that they have more than
sufficient livestock to stock the land [a prerequisite for claiming the
property]," but, he declared, "I own . . . a share of the [rancho] and have
done so for more than fourteen years. . . . Moreover, because my wife is
the widow of an early settler and my children have served the country
[characteristics that privileged individuals to receive land], I am entitled." The alcalde sent the protest to María Rita Valdez and the Vejares,
asking them to respond.[2]

"What Luciano Valdez states in his petition is absolutely false," they
replied in a joint statement. Fourteen years earlier, they explained, the
presiding alcalde had acknowledged their claims. "We would agree to let
[Luciano Valdez] have an interest in the land, but it is too small to

accommodate all of us" as it consists of only 1.5 sitios and possesses "barely sufficient water to support the [present] inhabitants." Because they knew that the law favored awarding land to "honorable" persons, they described Luciano Valdez as an unsavory fellow, a gambler, "who does not work and . . . barely supports his family. We ask that you refrain from giving him rights to the land."

In response, Luciano Valdez now produced a title of his own to the property. He acknowledged that he occasionally gambled but denied that he failed to support his family. After weighing the evidence, Alcalde Leandry denied Luciano Valdez's claim because he lacked sufficient property—livestock, corrals, and other "improvements—on the rancho, as the law required, and he had confessed to gambling." Leandry sent this judgment as a recommendation to the prefect, who agreed with the decision but for different reasons. "Valdez has falsified the [title]," declared the prefect, "and [has] attempted to fool the prefecture, a crime for which he shall be penalized according to law and justice." The alcalde then slapped Valdez with a fine.

Throughout the Mexican period, women like María Rita Valdez proved as successful in defending their property claims as were men. Despite patriarchal attitudes and laws that restricted female power in marriage and the family, women had the legal right to acquire and use property. However, a woman's marital status determined the extent of her control over that property. Widows and single women over the age of twenty-five could acquire and use property without interference from male family members. A married women or a minor daughter under the age of twenty-five needed, respectively, her husband's or father's permission to conduct business related to her holdings.

Many women who acquired ranchos achieved a measure of economic independence and secured a level of wealth that distinguished them from other women in the community. In contrast to these wealthy landowners, mid-strata gente-de-razón women held only small properties in the pueblo of Los Angeles, and indias, neófitas, and gentiles possessed little or no land, making them the most marginalized members of Los Angeles society. The women with extensive landholdings could join the gente-de-razón elite if they were not already members of it. Although entrance into the elite could come through birth or marriage, economic independence came only with significant property holdings over which a woman had complete legal control. Such holdings, which frequently included homes, orchards, and other property in the pueblo, enabled these women to purchase additional property and make investments, which, in turn, gave them a significant level of comfort in their lifestyles and households.[3]

Rights to land in Spanish and Mexican California derived from decrees and statutes originating in the *Recopilación de las leyes de los reynos de las indias,* a seventeenth-century compilation used to govern New Spain, and the *Siete Partidas* and *Leyes de Toro,* thirteenth- and sixteenth-century summaries that supplemented the *Recopilación.* A later document that became particularly important for the governance of towns was the *Plan de Pitic* (c. 1783).[4] During the Spanish era, the monarch, as owner of all lands and natural resources in New Spain, held ultimate authority in allocating rights to property. However, the Crown frequently delegated that authority to viceroys and other subordinates who, in turn, sometimes vested it in others. Grantees, whether corporate bodies or individuals, had to fulfill stipulations for acquiring and holding land, beginning with an affirmation that no one else had a claim to the property and that their claim did not infringe on another's possession. A grant usually conferred on the recipient a usufructuary right, not title in fee simple as in the English colonies. To obtain the right to hold the property in perpetuity and bequeath it to family members or others, the grantee had to use and develop the land, sometimes in quite specific ways. Failure to meet those requirements could result a denouncement, or claim filed against land.[5]

Women, like men, had the right to acquire property not only through grants but also through endowments, purchases, gifts, and inheritance. A widow would inherit half of the *bienes gananciales* (community property) accumulated during a marriage, while her daughters and sons would share the remaining half. Women could also administer, protect, and invest their property, which they did in a variety of ways: initiating litigation; appearing in court and, if they wished, acting as their own advocate; entering into contracts; forming business partnerships; administering estates; and lending and borrowing money and other goods.[6]

Though unmarried women had the right to transact business, they, as well as their married counterparts, often selected male relatives or men familiar with the local political and legal system of the pueblo to represent them. Although it was assumed that the selected individual would advocate for the woman's best interests, he sometimes betrayed that trust. Women gave men power of attorney, which included the right "to claim, collect, receive, and demand of every person the amounts due" as well as "to file suits in writing, prosecuting same through all courts to final legal decision." For example, in 1847, María Francisca Villalobos, a long-time resident and widow, felt that the current administrator of her orphaned grandchildren's estate, the elderly and ailing Luis Bouchet, was no longer competent. She gave José Antonio Carrillo power of attorney. Carrillo, a lifelong angeleño, was well known and politically savvy. With her consent, Carrillo appointed Leon V. Prudhomme, a prominent member of the community, to replace Bouchet as the children's property manager and as their personal tutor. Knowing that the children's livelihood and interests were in Carrillo's and Prudhomme's capable hands, Villalobos doubtless rested easier.[7]

Married women who appointed an attorney needed their spouses' permission. Failure to obtain it would nullify the appointment and any transactions carried out. The practice of giving men power over women's affairs, however, did not diminish a woman's ability to oversee the management of her assets. Rather, the men who advocated on their behalf did so through the authority their female clients had granted them, and these men were accountable to them. A woman who believed her representative had neglected his duties, either inadvertently or deliberately, could have local officials revoke the power of attorney, and she could ask for them to replace the representative with someone else.[8]

The illiteracy of most of these women did not impede their ability to carry out a wide range of business transactions, either through a representative or on their own behalf. Women and men who could not write used *escribanos* (scribes), like Narciso Botello, a local angeleño leader, or they asked literate family members to pen their contracts, petitions, and letters for them. Women could also handle their business matters in person, going before the proper authorities to articulate their needs or decisions. Nevertheless, the inability to read and write presented grave risks to a woman who had to rely on friends and family members who might potentially take advantage of her inability to oversee and verify written transactions.[9]

In matters related to land rights, angeleños and rancho owners turned to the ayuntamiento and the alcalde. During most of the Mexican era, the ayuntamiento held legislative authority (including control over the distribution of public land in the pueblo). The alcalde, who was also a member of the town council, possessed judicial powers for the pueblo and the district, presiding over trials and sending appeals to the governor. From 1839 to 1844, the Mexican central government imposed the prefecture system on California. It abolished ayuntamientos; established three prefectures (in Los Angeles, Santa Bárbara, and San Francisco); created a Superior Tribunal, an appellate court, in Monterey; established a Court of First Instance (for both civil and criminal proceedings) in major towns, including Los Angeles; and affirmed the alcalde's role as mayor but reduced his judicial authority to that of a justice of the peace.[10] The prefecture, in cooperation with the alcalde, now took over the responsibilities involving land that the ayuntamiento had previously exercised for the pueblo and the district: enforcing land laws; responding to petitions for property; distributing *solares* (building lots) and *suertes* (agricultural fields); overseeing the use of *propíos* (rented municipal property); and approving rights to *dehesas* (grazing land) and *ejidos* (communal lands).[11]

Requests for ranches went to the governor. From the outset of colonization in California, the governor had possessed exclusive authority to allocate land for ranchos. At first, such grants were few and went primarily to retired military leaders and other political officials as rewards for faithful service to the nation. The national Congress, which formed after Mexican Independence in 1821, had concerns about, on one hand, the sparse population in Alta California and, on the other, population pressures on land in central Mexico. In response, it enacted colonization laws in 1824 and 1828 aimed at attracting foreign and citizen settlers to California. The 1828 law vested in governors the right to distribute land on a communal, individual, or empresario basis. Community grants usually went to indigenous peoples, such as the settlement established by former mission Indians at San Juan Capistrano, whereas individual grants were given to one, or sometimes two, people. Empresarios, which were rarely granted in California (being more common in New Mexico), encompassed vast tracts of land and were given to individuals who agreed to settle at least 200 families and establish a Mexican colony with its own militia.[12] The colonization laws resulted in increasing numbers of Californians petitioning for ranchos, leading the government to respond in 1833 with the secularization of the missions, an action that had been proposed earlier. That action made vast tracts of former mission holdings available to neófitos with the remainder going to Mexican citizens, who were not identified as indígenas.[13]

Few women benefited from the pressures to expand landholding in California. Only one woman in the Los Angeles district obtained a rancho during the Spanish era. During Mexican period, of the 148 people who received ranchos in Los Angeles, twenty-five were Mexican women and two were native women.[14] Most men received grants directly from the governor. In contrast, the only women who received direct grants were Asención Avila and Casilda Soto, both gente de razón; all the other women acquired their property based on inheritance and kinship ties.

Avila and Soto were widows, related by marriage and kinship to military and political leaders. Avila obtained Rancho El Nigüel under circumstances that were common among well-to-do grantees in the Los Angeles district. In 1841, she and her brother, Juan, petitioned Governor Juan Baustista Alvarado for land on which to graze their more than 2,000 head of cattle. Because they no longer lived with their father, owner of Rancho Sauzal Redondo and a prominent political leader who had served a year on the town council and thirteen years as a *juez de campo* (a rural judge who settled livestock and other disputes between ranchos), they needed land of their own.[15] After the governor resolved a boundary dispute and quelled rising tensions between the Avilas and the inhabitants of the newly established pueblo at Misión San Juan Capistrano, he awarded joint ownership of three-sitio El Nigüel to Avila and her brother.[16] The ease of the transaction was doubtless due not only to Avila's social and economic status but also to the presence of a man (her brother) as a joint petitioner.

Soto attained her land a more unusual way. In 1844, she appealed to Governor Manuel Micheltorena for title to Rancho La Merced, property that originally belonged to Misión San Gabriel. She had lived there since "some time ago," she explained, "when ex-Governor Juan Bautista Alvarado . . . had given [me his] consent and permission to do so." Moreover, she added, she also deserved the land "in exchange for the payments owed by the presidial military to [her deceased] husband." Micheltorena directed the Los Angeles alcalde to investigate Soto's eligibility for a grant. The alcalde's response was straightforward and positive: "Soto is an honorable widowed woman who behaves respectably . . . [and] she has a house and livestock on the land." The priest at Misión San Gabriel, whom the governor also contacted for confirmation that the mission no longer occupied the land, endorsed Soto's request as well. Father Tomás Esténega stipulated, however, that though the property was vacant, she "must pay fifty head of cattle to the mission in exchange for the concession." Only in rare circumstances, such as when a grant infringed on another's property, were grantees obligated to compensate the owner. In this case, the land, though secularized and made part of the public domain, was used to support remaining neófitos and priests who had chosen to stay at the mission. Soto agreed to the unusual terms, and Micheltorena awarded her title to the property.[17]

Unlike Soto and Avila, the other women inherited their ranchos, but, like them, they were also related by marriage and kinship to military and political leaders. The only woman to obtain property in the Spanish era was Manuela Nieto. In 1804, she inherited the five-sitio Rancho Los Cerritos from her father, Manuel Pérez Nieto, a former military officer who had died that year. Her property had been carved out of her father's Rancho Los Nietos, a thirty-sitio grant, which he had received in 1784 from Spanish Governor Pedro Fages for his role as a "founder of the territory."[18] Manuela's brothers, José Antonio, Juan José, and Antonio María, also came into an equal share of Los Nietos, inheriting Ranchos Las Bolsas, Los Coyotes y Los Alamitos, and Santa Gertrudes, respectively.[19]

In 1825, after living on their lands for more than twenty years, Manuela Nieto and her siblings asked Governor José María de Echeandía for title to their properties. Prompting the request was the appearance of individuals seeking to file a denouncement against some of the land, and the siblings' discovery that their father had failed to leave them proof of ownership of their ranchos or his original concession. The problem remained unresolved for years. Finally, in 1834, Governor José Figueroa's secretary, Agustín Zamorano, found evidence of Nieto's grant, which enabled the governor to confirm the heirs' claims. Manuela's rancho was among the largest acquired by a woman in the Los Angeles area. Besides the rancho, she also obtained 2,000 head of cattle, a house, and a number of corrals. She remained the owner until her death in 1843, at which time her husband, Guillermo Cota, a soldier, and her children inherited the property. They subsequently sold it to a local merchant.[20]

All the other women who inherited ranchos did so in the Mexican era, and, typically, they acquired them at the death of their fathers or husbands. María Ygnacia Verdugo, for instance, inherited Rancho Los Féliz in 1840, following the death of her husband Juan Féliz, a sergeant who had served for twenty-three years in California and had acquired the property in 1813. She and her husband had lived on the 1.5 sitio rancho for more than thirty years, but they had yet to gain legal title when he died.[21] As squatters began settling on the property, María became alarmed and, in 1841, appealed for a title to the alcalde who forwarded her petition to the prefect. The prefect then inspected the property for compliance with the grant's original terms. Satisfied by what he found—more than two hundred head of cattle as well as a number of horses, houses, and corrals—he urged the governor to grant title to Verdugo and her son, which the governor did shortly thereafter.[22]

In contrast to women, most men obtained their ranchos directly from the governor. The eleven men who received grants in the Los Angeles district during Spanish rule were soldiers, many retirees. In the Mexican period, as a result of secularization and population growth, 111 men—predominantly soldiers, former soldiers, and political leaders—received land grants.[23] Eighty-nine of the 111 had been born in California or Mexico, with the remainder coming from the United States, Europe, or Latin America. Typical was Francisco Sepúlveda who had served in the military for twenty-one years and had married a Mexican woman, María Ramona Serrano. In 1841, he received title to Rancho Santa Monica y San Vicente, property that a previous governor had allowed him to use since 1828.[24] The government, in its desire to increase the size of the population, also awarded ranchos to fifteen naturalized Mexican citizens and eighteen emancipated neófitos.[25]

Mexican men (whether citizens by birth or naturalization) almost invariably obtained larger ranchos than did native men or Mexican or native women. Fifty-nine of 103 (57 percent) Mexican men were granted one to three sitios, whereas twenty-three (22 percent) received more than three sitios, and twenty-one (20 percent) got less than a sitio. (No empresarios were granted to anyone.) In contrast, only seven of 25 Mexican women (28 percent) received ranchos or interests in such property measuring one to three sitios, while six (24 percent) received more than three sitios. The twelve remaining women (48 percent) acquired less than one sitio. Women received smaller holdings because they were usually carved out of a preexisting grant. Neófitos and neófitas, with only one exception, received less than one sitio.[26]

The naturalized Mexican citizens obtaining grants included eight traders and merchants, all but one of whom were married to Mexicans. For instance, William "Julian" Workman, married to Nicolasa Uriste, and his business partner, John "Juan" Roland, a trapper from New Mexico, married to a New Mexican, obtained the four-sitio Rancho La Puente in 1842 from Governor Alvarado.[27] John "Juan" Forster, a naturalized English trader who settled permanently in Los Angeles in 1836 and married Isidora Pico a year later, petitioned for two sitios in 1845 from Governor Pío Pico (his brother-in-law) because his "present Rancho El Trabuco y La Misión Vieja produced poisonous weeds that, when consumed by his horses, killed them." When Pico had satisfied himself that the requested property was vacant, he issued the grant for Rancho Sierra de la Agua Caliente. Through his marriage to Isidora and by purchases made with his own funds, Forster quickly acquired substantial property. He established political ties with the highest authorities in California, garnering political clout of his own, and he became a judge and held other local posts well into the American era.[28]

Isaac "Julian" Williams also amassed substantial wealth and status in California as a result of his marriage to María de Jesús Lugo, the daughter of Antonio María Lugo, a retired soldier of political and economic prominence. In 1841, Lugo gave Williams the five-sitio Rancho Santa Ana del Chino, along with 4,000 head of livestock, as a wedding gift. A few years later, in 1843, Williams increased his holdings when he applied for and received an additional grant of three sitios at Rancho Chino from Mexican governor Manuel Micheltorena. Within a few years, the Williamses had accumulated significant holdings, including the ranchos and several thousand cattle, sheep, and other animals, and they employed nearly eighty neófitos and gentiles.[29]

Native peoples fared poorly in obtaining ranchos. In view of their number and the secularization legislation that had mandated that neófitos were to have precedence in receiving former mission lands, their twenty grants—eighteen to men, two to women—in the Los Angeles district seem a pitifully small number. The total land allocated amounted to only 3.5 sitios, a minuscule portion of the vast countryside once controlled by the San Gabriel, San Fernando, and San Juan Capistrano missions. Not surprisingly, men received most of this land. Grants to men averaged about 1000 square *varas* (one fifth of a sitio), but women received on average 400 square varas (less than one tenth of a league). In contrast, Spanish-speaking men averaged 2 sitios, and women, 1.5 sitios. Clearly, ethnic and gender discrimination permeated society in Mexican California.

Manuel Antonio, the former mayordomo at Misión San Gabriel,

Figure 3.1
Native women, likely *neófitas*, at Misión San Luis Rey in the 1860s or 1870s.
Despite their legal rights, neófitas received little land as a result of the
Mexican secularization process, implemented in the 1830s. (Courtesy of the
Seaver Center for Western History Research, Los Angeles County Museum of
Natural History)

received the one-sitio Rancho Potrero Grande, the largest grant awarded
to a neófito. Despite his position and years of service, he had an exas-
peratingly difficult experience in securing title to the property. In 1845,
more than a decade after the government had begun secularizing the
missions, Antonio poured out his plight to Governor Pío Pico. "For
eleven years, I have been living on the lands of the old mission with the
consent of the mission [administrators]. . . . Despite my rights [to the
property] . . . and my repeated requests, they have not given me a piece of
land on which to put my meager possessions or to support my family.
Instead, they have taken the land that I requested in order to give it to
others who do not enjoy the same rights or have sufficient livestock.

Please give me title to the land that I occupy." Moved by the appeal, Pico asked the priest at San Gabriel and the town council of Los Angeles to comment on Antonio's request. Padre Tomás Esténega endorsed the appeal: Antonio "should be conceded the land as an award for his service . . . which he has provided from his infancy to the present." The council agreed, noting that "his land is occupied with livestock and a house . . . as well as some corrals." Pico responded by awarding the property to Antonio. Though the grant came late, Antonio's success in getting a grant at all, especially one so large, doubtless reflected his position as overseer at the mission.[30] The overwhelming majority of native peoples were not so fortunate.

In contrast to Antonio, the grant of 200 square varas that Emilio Joaquín received in 1843 was typical of those obtained by native men. "From childhood to today," Joaquín told the prefect, "at which age I am now well past fifty years, I have worked in [the Misión San Gabriel] community. . . . I am tired of it . . . and wish to work exclusively for my family's benefit." To do so, he asked the prefect to have the governor grant him three hundred square varas, and to keep in mind his "continual residence in the community and the personal services" that he had provided for many years. The prefect, as was customary, asked Padre Esténega to comment on the request. With Esténega's endorsement, the prefect urged Governor Micheltorena to make the concession, as it "will serve as an example to his peers . . . so that they will also dedicate themselves to the industry of agriculture and work." Micheltorena agreed, though he awarded Emilio 200, not 300, square varas, explaining that the government planned to give the remaining 100 varas to another individual who had previously requested it.[31]

In only two instances did grants to native men exceed 1000 square varas, and in both cases, the allocations went to several people rather than to a single individual. In 1843, four former neófitos of Misión San Fernando—Ramón, Tiburcio, Francisco, and Roque—asked for one sitio of land for themselves and "their large families" on the grounds that they had "spent much of . . . [their] lives . . . working in the [mission's] fields." They already had a small parcel at El Encino on which they had "a vineyard, forty horses and some cattle," but it was inadequate to support their families. When Father Blas Ordaz at San Fernando and the alcalde in Los Angeles looked favorably on their requests, the governor agreed to the concession. Possession of El Encino did not last long, however.

Within four years, by 1847, Ramón and his co-owners had sold the rancho to Vicente de la Osa for a mere 100 pesos. What compelled the men to sell is unclear, but what is clear is that they were left landless and without the means to support their families and with nothing to bequeath to their descendants.[32]

The overwhelming extent of former California mission land went to non-natives. Twenty neófitos received modest grants from mission holdings in the Los Angeles district. In contrast, nineteen California- and Mexico-born gente de razón and four naturalized Mexicans received considerably larger holdings.[33] One of the largest allocations, Rancho Santa Ana del Chino, was awarded in 1841 to Antonio María Lugo, who already possessed Rancho San Antonio, which he had received from Spanish Governor Luis Argüello in 1810. Lugo transferred his property to his son-in-law and daughter.[34] Of the remaining twenty-two grants, eleven (50 percent) ranged from one to three sitios, nine (41 percent) were less than one sitio, and two (9 percent) were more than three sitios.

Retaining possession of a rancho proved troublesome for landowners regardless of their ethnicity, their gender, or whether their grant came from the governor or was inherited. In the Spanish period, when population pressure remained low, conflicts over ranchos were few, but tensions increased during the Mexican era, especially after secularization, as allocations rose dramatically. Court officials ruled on some thirty-five property disputes, with several being appealed to the governor's office or, during the prefecture years, to the Superior Tribunal.[35] Most battles involved vaguely defined boundaries, especially those for the few ranchos allocated before secularization, when governors rarely provided written descriptions of property and often gave prospective landholders verbal permission to occupy land. Even owners with written titles did not always escape controversy because boundary descriptions frequently contained references to natural markers, such as rivers, trees, or rocks, that were easily misidentified or moved or that could simply disappear.[36]

Women were not exempt from boundary disputes, but they engaged in them less frequently than men because most women possessed inherited property whose boundaries had been clearly established when the land passed to them.[37] Those property titles, however, were sometimes contested, often long after the bequest was transferred. In 1841, for example, María Cleofas Nieto lodged a complaint in the local court against her mother, Catarina Ruiz, for withholding property from her. Since the division of her father's estate in 1833, she told the alcalde, she had struggled unsuccessfully to obtain her share of Rancho Las Bolsas, which her mother had illegally given to her uncle, Joaquín Ruiz. "I am the only legitimate heir," she complained, and the transfer of the property had been made without her consent. The alcalde summoned Nieto and her mother to court for questioning. Because the court records are incomplete, the precise outcome of the dispute is unknown, but Nieto seems to have prevailed, at least temporarily, for in 1849 she was back in court protesting her mother's attempt to sell her share of the rancho. "I owe my mother respect," she acknowledged, "but when she does not look out for my interests . . . what shall I do other than defend them?" The court ordered the mother to desist from any attempt to sell Nieto's half of the property.[38] This put the matter to an end, for court records reveal that she held it until sometime in the early 1860s, when she finally sold it to pay off a debt.[39]

Another woman who successfully defended her inheritance was Vicenta Sepúlveda, the strong-willed widow of Tomás Antonio Yorba, a man of political and economic importance.[40] Her fight with her brother-in-law, Bernardo Yorba, went all the way to the governor. Her husband had appointed his brother as executor of his estate. In Tomás's will, he left his wife and children Rancho Santa Ana, a property he had inherited from his father. The estate included an eighteen-room adobe house, 2,000 head of cattle and other livestock, two vineyards, and fruit trees. Several months after Tomás's death, Vicenta learned to her horror that Bernardo had asked Governor Pío Pico to award the rancho to him and his brother, José Antonio Yorba. Vicenta implored Pico to intercede on her behalf because the loss of the rancho "would . . . ruin me and my family." Pico ordered the alcalde in Los Angeles to inform Bernardo Yorba of the complaint and ask for his response.

Bernardo expressed surprise, insisting that he and his brother did not want the entire rancho but only what they merited, "so that the heirs may be recognized as legitimate owners. . . . Vicenta alleges harm if [the ranch is divided]. I don't understand the reason why this would harm her property; to the contrary, I see that it will benefit all, as it will allow everyone to know their exclusive holding." Even if "she will be harmed, shall I subject myself to harm in order for her to achieve some gain?" Bernardo and his brother also asked for title to the adjacent Rancho La Sierra in addition to portions of Rancho Santa Ana.

Bernardo's explanation only heightened Vicenta's anxiety. He and his brother might not want all of Santa Ana, but they had claimed most of it for themselves. "Bernardo Yorba," she protested, "has taken advantage of the opportunity of having charge of my deceased husband's interests . . . [and] has asked for the largest portion, which will cause great harm to the minor [children by ignoring] . . . their rights."

Pico instructed the town council to survey the land and determine what belonged to Bernardo, Tomás, and other heirs. The investigators concluded that the entire four leagues of Rancho Santa Ana belonged to Vicenta and her children. "The part that [Bernardo Yorba] asks for is the best [of that property] because of its agricultural land, pastures, . . . watering places, and . . . a corral that the deceased Tomás owned and a shack inhabited by the servants who work for [Vicenta Sepúlveda]." Pico found the reports to be persuasive, and he awarded Vicenta title to the rancho, allocating only Rancho La Sierra to Bernardo and his brother. This supports that her brother-in-law had sought to take advantage of her and her children. How many other women in similar circumstances were successfully defrauded of their property is unknown, but it is clear that unmarried women, such as Vicenta, had to look out for their own interests even when members of the extended family were involved.[41]

Women frequently struggled to not only secure their inheritances but also hold on to the property once they had clear title to it. The legal requirement that owners develop and use their ranchos was easier for men to meet than for women, especially aged widows unable to perform labor-intensive chores themselves and without money to hire workers. When a property holder failed (or was perceived to fail) at meeting those responsibilities, other prospective landholders could file a denouncement against the grant. This was the experience of Eulália Pérez, a widow, who faced losing property because of her financial inability to develop the land. Pérez, the widow of Juan Mariner, a Spanish-born artilleryman, had inherited an interest in the three-sitio Rancho San Pascual in 1838. Two years later, because she lacked the means to stock and cultivate the land, Enrique Sepúlveda and José Pérez, her cousin, asked the governor for the property on the grounds that it was *valdío* (vacant). Without protest, Pérez quietly withdrew her claim, whereupon the governor awarded the rancho to Pérez and Sepúlveda.[42]

Like Eulália Pérez, the widow Josefa Cota faced losing her property because of her failure to utilize the land. In 1833, together with her children, Cota had inherited Rancho Santa Gertrudes from her husband, Antonio María Nieto, a son of Manuel Nieto Pérez. Four years later, Manuel Duarte filed a denouncement against her property on behalf of twenty-five families who had migrated from New Mexico and settled on the rancho, where they were growing crops. They had been giving some of the harvest to Cota as *amonestaciones* (fees), in exchange for her permission to remain. Duarte's petition to the town council requested land for the families and an end to the fees. The council forwarded the petition, with a summary of its investigation, to Governor Juan Alvarado. Josefa Cota, according to the town council, "did not have sufficient means to maintain the rancho," whereas "the residents who are established on the land are many," creating a situation that "has led to frequent complaints and difficulties in the administration of justice to those residents." Though not expressed directly, the council seemed to suggest that because Cota had failed to cultivate her property, the land should be divided among the families to benefit of that larger community. Like town councils throughout the Mexican borderlands, the one in Los Angeles preferred to resolve disputes in ways that resulted in the least harm to the community, regardless of an individual's rights.[43]

Swiftly and angrily, Cota appealed to the governor, condemning the council for its report and accusing the squatters on her land of being trespassers and fabricators of the truth. "For some time now, my interests have been damaged because of various individuals who are [on the land] against my will," she told the governor through her representative. "They are not satisfied with acquiring subsistence; they inflict insults and commit thefts of all kinds. To end . . . these scandalous abuses, I went to the authorities of this city so that they might take the necessary steps to handle such idle people," but they have "not responded to my request for justice, . . . even though I submitted my request several months ago. . . . This has obliged me to come to you [for] . . . justice." Though the governor's precise response is unknown because of gaps in the record, Cota won the battle and held her land until she sold it sometime before 1850 to Samuel Carpenter, a farmer and businessman from the United States. Cota's persistence attests to her general understanding of property rights and to the effort she put into business matters.[44]

Cota's case also underscores some of the daily difficulties women encountered in owning and managing ranchos. As a widowed and elderly woman, Cota had to rely on her grown children, particularly her sons, to help her with the physical upkeep of the property, but, clearly, their assistance had been insufficient. In general, women relied on men to carry out ranching activities and business transactions related to their ranchos. Women without husbands or adult sons were forced to hire men in order to survive and to meet the legal requirements about developing the productivity of their ranches. Although cultural norms and physiological differences forced most women to rely on men to tend livestock, cultivate crops, and other physically challenging work, women routinely cultivated fruit orchards and vegetable gardens and performed life-sustaining household chores. Women like Cota, who succeeded in holding on to their ranchos, achieved economic independence and, if they did not already possess it, recognition as elite members of Los Angeles society.

The California ranchos paled in comparison to the great Mexican *haciendas* (large rural estates) of the eighteen and nineteenth centuries. The haciendas were commercially oriented estates that produced foodstuffs, such as wheat, maize, and beef, to be sold to the growing Spanish and casta population in the urban centers of Mexico City, Guadalajara, and Guanajuato. California ranchos were much simpler, smaller ventures and never obtained the self-sufficiency nor generated the wealth found on the haciendas of central Mexico. However, ranchos granted in the Spanish and Mexican periods were endowed with fertile expanses of land that were strategically located in valleys or near water sources, enabling them to produce abundant grasses, which provided plentiful grazing for a large number of livestock, the primary source of wealth among the rancheros.[45]

Before migrating to California and coming to possess ranchos, most civil and military leaders had been ethnically and racially diverse and as impoverished as the mixed-blood migrants from the lower ranks of Mexican society. However, as a hierarchical, land-based society developed in California, they "whitened" themselves. The acquisition of rancho property provided the grantees with a source of not only subsistence but also the distinction of being large landowners—a status long honored in Spain and then Mexico. This placed them socially above other gente de razón and indios. Rancheros gained distinction as their herds, orchards, and vineyards multiplied. By the 1830s and 1840s, the most prosperous of these landowners had reproduced a society in which property, class, and ethnicity were inextricably linked.

Evidence of the landowners' socioeconomic status is revealed in the nature of labor relations. The 1836 and 1844 Los Angeles censuses reveal that most rancheros hired employees, usually native peoples (gentiles and runaway former neófitos) as well as landless Mexicans. These people worked on a seasonal or annual basis as managers, cowboys, and manual laborers, who tended livestock, milked cows, sowed, harvested, and cut timber.[46] Indigenous women were employed as servants, assisting with the time-consuming round of domestic chores, which were always a female responsibility regardless of ethnicity. (An exception was cooking, which was often done by native men.) The employers provided workers with *jacales* (shacks), rudimentary living quarters that were no better than huts, fed them beef and locally grown corn, and paid them in kind, sometimes with aguardiente and at other times with finished goods, such as blankets, clothing, and other items.

The handful of rancheros with ample means hired and housed skilled workers to produce the goods and supplies lacking on the ranchos. Teodosio Yorba, for instance, employed a cigar maker, a hat maker, and a shoemaker as well as a silversmith at Rancho Santa Ana in 1836.[47] Those who could not afford to hire craftsmen relied on local merchants, foreign traders, or the mission padres (before the secularization in the 1830s) from whom they purchased (or with whom they exchanged) finished goods and supplies. If these or other sources could not supply the needed item, even the wealthiest ranchero went without.[48]

The employees also helped to build and furnish the homes of the rancheros. Most ranchos had modest dwellings, generally made of rough timber, whitewashed and plastered, and roofed with tules. Houses often consisted of two dirt-floor rooms, one for sleeping and the other for entry and living space.[49] Rancheros with sufficient resources furnished their homes with beds made of wood, lined with leather, and covered with cotton sheets, blankets, and pillows. Most could not afford such luxuries, however, and instead slept on the floor, with nothing but a cowhide to protect them from the ground. Kitchen furniture, including wood tables, benches, or stools, and utensils, such as plates, cups, and forks and spoons, were also found only among a handful of families. Poorer families ate with clay bowls and forks and spoons made of animal horn. The destitute used, when they had them, tortillas as makeshift forks and spoons. Food was cooked in pots over what José del Carmen Lugo described in the 1870s as a "small adobe stove-like arrangement" or over an open fire. Lugo also recalled in the 1870s that the wealthy ate hearty breakfasts of hot chocolate, bread, tortillas, and wheat or corn porridge, and later in the day, they ate dried meat with red *chile*, onions, tomatoes, and beans. No doubt, they also enjoyed the fruits and vegetables they cultivated. In contrast, the poor had milk or water with *pinole* (parched corn) for breakfast and *frijoles* (beans) with tortillas for the evening meal.[50] Rancheros and their workers also built corrals for cattle, horses, pigs, and sometimes sheep or chickens. They assisted the women with caring for the vineyards, orchards, and gardens that produced grapes, other fruits, and staples, such as corn, beans, and squash. The ranchos produced this food for household and local consumption, and they also produced goods, such as hides and tallow, that were traded to local merchants or shipped to foreign markets in exchange for luxury goods. Although these properties produced less wealth than the Mexican haciendas, retaining control of a rancho was crucial to the livelihood and prosperity of the families that settled on the northern frontier, as ranching and farming were the primary modes of subsistence.[51]

As throughout colonial Latin America, those who possessed estates in the countryside tended also to have an impressive home in a nearby town or city. Their residences, usually located in the center of town, on or near the plaza, became gathering places where the rancheros entertained and conducted business related to their properties. Despite having to rely on the extremely slow oxen-drawn *carretas* (carts), many families spent part of the year living on their ranchos and the other part in the pueblo.[52]

Like men, rancheras who owned substantial land achieved economic independence that became readily evident in the town. In Los Angeles, during the 1830s and 1840s, ten of the twenty-seven rancheras had a home in the pueblo (fig. 3.2). Typical of these affluent women was Francisca Uribes, part owner of Rancho Los Coyotes and possessor of a substantial house in Los Angeles. She had lived there with her husband, Juan Bautista Leandry, an Italian-born merchant, winemaker, and former alcalde. When he died in 1843, he left his wife not only the rancho and the house in town but also vineyards and a winemaking business that she continued to operate.[53]

Similar to Uribe was the case of Victoria Higuera. In 1846, at the death of her husband, former alcalde Vicente Sánchez, she inherited interests in Ranchos La Cienega and Santa Clara as well as large herds of cattle, horses, and sheep. In town, she had a five-room house, a drinking establishment (rented and operated by a local resident), an orchard, and farming equipment.[54] Another widow, Josefa Alvarado, also had a home on the

Figure 3.2
The Los Angeles Plaza and its surrounding neighborhood in 1865. In the colonial and Mexican eras, the business occupied the buildings closest to the plaza, and the well-to-do lived there as well. In the American period, much of the now-marginalized Spanish-speaking community resided in the heart of the pueblo. (Courtesy of the Seaver Center for Western History Research, Los Angeles County Museum of Natural History)

plaza, which was so large government officials requested the use of it for a meeting following the 1837 transfer of government from Monterey to Los Angeles. The sudden change in governance had left little time to plan for the relocation. In exchange for the use of Alvarado's residence, they offered her 350 pesos. Whether she accepted the proposal is unknown, but it is clear that her property offered size and a level of comfort sufficient to accommodate high-level government officials.[55]

The property holdings of such women gave them the independence to engage in their own business and commercial transactions, buying, selling, trading, and investing their capital as well as borrowing money from men, like Abel Stearns, José Arnaz, Henry Dalton, and John "Juan" Temple, the major movers and shakers in Los Angeles's business community. Casilda Soto, María Figueroa, and María Pollorena, like many other women property owners, used their ranchos as collateral in the

1840s to borrow money—in their cases, 500 to 600 pesos each from Temple. They agreed to repay the loans with placer gold at an interest rate of 2 percent per month. Had they defaulted on their loans, it would have meant the loss of their property, independence, and social status.[56] Other women bought and sold goods on credit. María Antonia Domínguez, for instance, bought goods from Stearns and later repaid him with four hides.[57]

Rather than borrowing money, some women went into the loan business themselves. Josefa Cota, Vicenta Sepúlveda, and Tomasa Pico were among the substantial property holders who made loans to others, which sometimes resulted in an expansion of their own estates. In 1844, Cota, owner of Rancho Santa Gertrudes, loaned 600 pesos to her brother-in-law, Rafael Gallardo. When Gallardo's financial situation prevented him from repaying her or his other creditors, Cota accepted property in lieu of the cash owed to her.[58]

Some women set out purposely to increase their rancho properties, expecting that such an investment would bring them economic rewards. In 1847, Vicenta Sepúlveda, after securing title to Rancho Santa Ana, purchased adjacent land from María Andrea Avila for 160 pesos, a hundred of which she paid in goods and the remainder in silver coin. Similarly, in 1834, Tomasa Pico, sister of Pío Pico, bought horses, mules, and cattle on credit from Abel Stearns. Unable to repay the full amount in one installment, but anticipating that ranching would provide a return that would allow her to cover the costs of the livestock, Pico worked out an arrangement with Stearns to pay off the loan over the course of several months. In this case, the incomplete record does not indicate whether she abided by the agreement, but there is no reason to believe that she did not do so.[59]

Women not only invested their capital but also used it to purchase everyday household and personal items, enabling them not only to carve out a life of modest comfort but also to enhance their often rudimentary material culture. The account books of local merchants and rancheros, such as Abel Stearns and Henry Dalton, show that household items, often delivered by foreign ships, were sold to the women of the local elite, such as Francisca Avila, Ramona Sepúlveda, and Catalina Verdugo. Stearns and Dalton traded in household items like copper saucepans, ceramic tea cups and plates, fine fabrics and thread for making clothes, and finished goods, such as silk scarves and stockings, cotton shawls, and boots. To cover their debts, women paid in cash or in kind, with hides (worth up to 12 pesos) or with aguardiente (a barrel was worth up to 9 pesos). And though the merchandise was not extravagant, because commodities were scarce, other angeleños no doubt coveted such "luxuries" and conveniences.[60]

Women of lesser holdings—those of the middle strata, who possessed only solares, *huertas* (gardens or orchards), and *viñas* (vineyards) in the pueblo—could not afford such luxuries, but they nevertheless had the means with which to support themselves and their families. Unlike the elite rancheras who had inherited property, mid-strata townswomen were likely to have gotten their property from the town council. During the Spanish and Mexican periods, the council allocated plots to residents, preferably household heads, so that families would have a place to live and space for subsistence gardening. Although men were far more likely to receive these land allocations, women, in general, were more likely to own a solar than a rancho.[61]

One reason for the prevalence of solar ownership among women may have been the substantial financial resources required for the upkeep of ranches. Within the pueblo, relatively poor women could tend and maintain the gardens that measured about 15 square varas or even the larger orchards of 100 square varas. In contrast, to manage a large rancho required major investments for livestock, corrals, and laborers. Typical of the mid-strata women who possessed land in the pueblo was the widow Matilda Cota. In her 1836 petition to the council, she described herself as "without the means to support [my] family of six children whom I care for alone." She wanted enough land, she explained, "to cultivate five *almudes* [about two hundred and fifty pounds] of corn . . . for my family." Similarly, Bárbara Machado told the council in 1841 that she needed a suerte "to support my large family." In awarding grants to Machado, Cota, and other deserving women, the ayuntamiento admonished them to improve their lands within the year.[62]

Having an unsavory reputation did not disqualify a woman from holding property in town, though a dishonorable woman (or man, for that matter: recall Luciano Valdez) had difficulty in obtaining rancho land. Unlike prospective rancho owners who had to produce at least three witnesses to testify that they were upstanding and honorable citizens, townswomen were held to no such standard. In the small town of Los Angeles, where local events quickly became common knowledge, there is little doubt that angeleños knew of the ill repute of Nicolasa Carreaga, Manuela Villa, and Eugenia Valencia, among others. All three women had been publicly accused, tried, and found guilty in the local court of engaging in sexual relations outside of marriage, and the 1836 and 1844 Los Angeles censuses had identified them as leading mala vidas.[63] In a community that strove to maintain stable marriages and families, such offenses frequently carried serious consequences, but these did not include rejecting requests for town lots on which such women could build homes, grow crops, and support themselves and their families. In all likelihood, town leaders wanted to insure that all members of the community had the means to sustain themselves, regardless of the morality of their behavior. Land allocations would help diminish the council's burden of responsibility for the town's residents.[64]

Although not as significant as those bequeathed by elite families, the inheritances received by mid-strata women allowed them to come into modest holdings. María Jesús Lorenzana, widow of Desiderio Ibarra, a descendant of an early military family, inherited a vineyard of nearly two thousand vines, an eight-room adobe house with furniture, nearly two hundred horses, seventeen carts and oxen, twenty-five cows, and thirteen heifers, as well as tools and other property.[65] Gregoria Espinosa also inherited substantial property from her husband, Mariano de la Luz Verdugo, a retired sergeant who had received land and livestock from the Spanish government. On her husband's death in 1830, Espinosa found herself in possession of over a thousand fruit trees, a vineyard, farming and brewing equipment, a three-room house situated on one of the main streets in town, and cattle, mules, and sheep, which she grazed on pueblo lands.[66] Regardless of how women attained pueblo property—through inheritances or concessions—their holdings varied from large homes with gardens and orchards to small, humble dwellings on tiny plots.

The mid-strata women, like the elite, frequently received challenges to the legality of their holdings, compelling them to seek help from local authorities. Those challenges often came from male family members or other residents of the community, and the litigation involved titles, boundaries, inheritances, and property damage. In 1822, for instance, five women who feared that their husbands were mismanaging their possessions banded together to appeal for help to Comandante Militar José Antonio de la Guerra y Noriega, a *barbareño* (resident of Santa Bárbara) who had been appointed as Los Angeles's *comisionado*, the official with authority over local affairs. Put a stop to the "crude misdeeds perpetrated by our husbands," they begged him.[67] Since a wife had the legal right to contest a husband's misuse of her separate property, Guerra y Noriega investigated the complaint, beginning with an inventory of their possessions, including houses, agricultural plantings, and vineyards. It is likely that this put an end to their husbands' transgressions, as the available records indicate no additional complaints from these women, who took it upon themselves to hold their spouses accountable to the law and to themselves.[68]

Petra Varela also sought to stop her husband's misuse of her property but unlike the group of five women who protested to Guerra y Noriega, she encountered more difficulty in achieving her goal. In 1843, she accused her husband of selling her land without her permission, and she asked the judge to annul the contract. The buyer, Casimiro Carrión, objected, declaring that he had legally purchased the land from her husband. "I saw the title," he insisted. When her husband confessed to violating his wife's rights and offered to return the money to Carrión, the hombres buenos urged the judge to have Petra provide proof of joint ownership, and if she failed to do so, allow the contract between her husband and Carrión to stand. Because the available records fail to indicate whether Petra produced the documents, the outcome of this case remains unknown. Clearly, even though the husband admitted guilt, the burden of proof was placed on Petra, indicating that the court's interpretation of the law sometimes worked against women. How often this happened to women (or to men) is unknown, as the records are fragmentary.[69]

Women who encountered difficulties with the local authorities sometimes went over their heads. Encarnación Sepúlveda, a member of the politically and economically powerful Sepúlveda family, found herself in a conflict with the town council that jeopardized the water rights on her property. However, she appealed to the governor for redress. The principal culprit, she told Governor Alvarado in 1838, was Vicente de la Osa, a council member who had been illegally using her water ditch to make adobe bricks. She claimed exclusive rights to the ditch through an inheritance from her husband, Francisco Avila. She had filed a complaint with the council, but it had sided with de la Osa, on the grounds that her claims conflicted with rights that belonged to the larger community. In reaching its judgment, the council adopted de la Osa's argument that any right Sepúlveda might have was conditional and could be exercised only so long as it did not harm the wider community. As de la Osa was a member of the community, she could not deny him use of the ditch. When Governor Alvarado reviewed the decision, he found the council's reasoning unpersuasive and overruled its actions, affirming Sepúlveda's exclusive rights to the waterway.[70]

Like elite women, mid-strata women also fought to hold on to property. Some of these struggles involved retaining land they had failed to improve. Landholders in the pueblo who recognized that they would not be able to till or build on their plots within the required year would ask for extensions.[71] Those who neglected to do that might forfeit their land. Only under special circumstances did the town council allow residents to keep land that they had failed to improve. In 1847, for instance, the ayuntamiento gave Carmen Navarro, a poor and elderly single mother who lived alone with her daughter, an extension of time to build on her property "because," it stated, "she [was] one of the founders of this town, which [made] her entitled to a solar on which to live." Under Felipe de Neve's *Regulación para el gobierno de las ambas californias*, pueblo settlers had a right to solares and suertes. And even though another resident had lawfully filed a denouncement against Navarro's property, the council granted her an extra year in order to build on her land, enabling her to retain her humble dwelling and means of subsistence.[72]

In battling to retain their property, mid-strata women, like the elite, had to defer to the rights of the larger community, which, according to the local authorities, took precedence over individual rights. In 1836, Josefa Vejar and neighboring property owners lost a battle with the "public" interest. They had petitioned the town council to close an alleyway, which bordered their fenced orchards, because wagons and animals passing through damaged their property. After investigating, the council concluded that the alleyway "is for the good of the public—the majority of the community will be subject to extensive losses if the alleyway is closed, [for] . . . it is one of the main thoroughfares to the river." When damage to their property continued, Vejar and her neighbors returned to the council, this time suggesting an alternative thoroughfare. The council remained unmoved, denying the second plea and reminding them, again, that closing the alleyway harmed the community interest.[73]

Unlike mid-strata and elite women, native women—neófitas and especially gentiles—acquired little or no pueblo and rancho property, even though Spanish and Mexican laws entitled them and their families to former mission lands. Spain's colonization plans, based on the *Recopila-ción de las leyes de los reynos de las indias*, stipulated that indígenas who converted and adopted Spanish cultural practices had a right to royal or public land.[74] In California, the missions became the vehicle for trans-forming the natives into good Spaniards, and secularization was, sup-posedly, the occasion for allocating former mission lands to the neófitos and converting the missions into pueblos. Among the neófitos, household heads and individuals over the age of twenty-one were entitled to 100 to 400 square varas (the amount depended on their circumstances and ser-vice to the mission), livestock, farming implements, and a solar and house in the new pueblo. Additional land was set aside as commons available for use by all residents. Christianized natives living at rancherías consisting of at least twenty-five families were also eligible to receive land and transform their villages into pueblos.[75]

Missionization had failed to acculturate most natives. Like the those at other missions, indigenous peoples at nearby San Gabriel and San Fer-nando missions largely abandoned the area, especially because only a few obtained land as a result of the missions' secularization. Most neófitos went east, into the interior, and the remainder sought work on ranchos and in the pueblo of Los Angeles. These ranch hands and domestics lived at their places of work or in settlements adjacent to the town.[76] The largest such colony developed near the Los Angeles river in 1836 and remained there until 1847 when the town council, with the governor's permission, moved it across the river. That was done in response to gente de razón who complained about "Indian thefts and . . . weekend . . . orgies," among other transgressions.[77]

Though most natives remained landless, approximately twenty ob-tained property. Two were women, Rufina, who later married Manuel D'Oliveira, a Portuguese immigrant, and Victoria Comcrabit, who would marry the Scotsman, Hugo Reid. Rufina's holding consisted of 15 square varas, far less than the 100 to 400 square varas promised in Governor José Figueroa's secularization decree of 1833. She did not obtain her title until 1845, on the eve of the American conquest, and that was due to the efforts of her husband. D'Oliveira asked Governor Pío Pico for title to agricul-tural land and a house near the former mission at San Gabriel that the priest Tomás Esténega had allowed Rufina and her family to use in 1844. D'Oliveira took the opportunity to request an additional 15 square varas, and he appended a statement by Esténega, which read, "to compensate in a just and equitable manner the considerable and frequent services that Rufina has given to the mission, I concede and give her the house in which she lives. [It] contains three rooms and a corridor which measure about 10 square varas and is situated on a lot that measures about fifteen varas." The house, acknowledged the priest, was at present "considerably ruined." Esténega ended by stating: "This [document] shall serve as a title, . . . confirming the legitimacy and property rights of [Rufina]." Usually, before issuing a title, Pico would ask the alcalde to investigate the property in question, but on this occasion, he was satisfied with the documentation and awarded title and the additional 15 square varas of land to Rufina.[78]

Victoria Comcrabit, the only other native woman to obtain land, inherited it from her husband, Pablo, a neófito from Misión San Gabriel. In her 1838 petition to Governor Alvarado for title to Rancho Huerta de Cuati, she described the property as adjacent to the mission, measuring 850 square varas, and containing a lot, house, orchard, and vineyard. The governor agreed to award her the title if the priest at San Gabriel had no objection to the concession. With the priest's approval, Victoria received the property title. An inventory of her estate several years later shows that she made the place productive shortly thereafter. By 1852, the vineyard consisted of 25,000 vines, an adjacent adobe house, and several fruit orchards, three horses, seven oxen, two carts, equipment for making wine, household furniture, including fine trunks for storing clothing and bedding, mattresses, and kitchen furnishings. She owned it until 1852, when she sold it to a prominent businessman, Benjamin "Benito" Wilson, following the death of her second husband, Hugo Reid.

Reid, a Scotch immigrant, appears to have been the only rancho owner who married a neófita. Reid profited from his marriage to Victoria by obtaining the three-sitio Rancho Santa Anita in 1839, after informing Governor Micheltorena that "[m]y [wife and her relatives] have merit [in their claim to the land], since their forefathers and they as well have personally cooperated in developing the . . . lands once and currently held by ex-Misión San Gabriel." When the governor asked the priest at San Gabriel to comment on Reid's request, he elicited a positive response: Reid deserved the vacant land because he was "married to a neófita who gave very good services to the mission." Before his death, Reid became a politically prominent angeleño who served in the 1849 state constitutional convention.[79]

In contrast to the elite and mid-strata gente de razón, the two neófitas (as well as the eighteen neófitos) who acquired land seldom got into disputes over their properties. Extant records indicate that there were only three such instances, and one of them involved not an individual's rights but the rights of a neófito community at San Juan Capistrano. The controversy erupted in 1841 when Asención Avila and her brother, Juan, asked the governor to grant them Rancho El Nigüel, including the common lands of former Misión San Juan Capistrano, now a newly established pueblo. The natives vigorously protested to the governor, who ordered the prefect to investigate the dispute. That investigation led to the Avilas amending their request to omit the commons.[80] A second dispute also involved a commons, this time in Los Angeles. In 1836, the town council allotted a tract of public property to neófitos for a settlement. Two years later, Juan Domingo, a local businessman, claimed ownership of the property and ordered the Indians to leave. They protested to the council, which found Domingo guilty of illegal trespass and fined him 12 pesos.[81]

Neófito landowners, like the elite and mid-strata gente de razón, achieved a measure of upward social mobility and economic independence that distinguished them from other native peoples. Their property enabled them to avoid laboring on ranchos, in pueblos and private homes, or on former mission lands. In contrast, landless natives of both genders who chose to stay in Los Angeles had to find employment or risk being arrested and fined as vagrants. Most of those unable to pay the fines had to labor on public works, or they were auctioned to the highest bidder for their services. By the 1840s, this system had transformed Los Angeles natives into slaves in all but name.[82]

Regardless of men and women's ethnicity, gender, or social class, the onslaught of the U.S. war with Mexico—which was declared on May 13, 1846, and ended on June 30, 1848, with the signing of the Treaty of Guadalupe Hidalgo—irrevocably altered the social, cultural, political, economic, and legal landscape of Mexican California. It also altered women's (and men's) ability to retain property. As early as the 1800s and, especially, in the 1820s and 1830s, Euro-American politicians in the East and Midwest had expressed interest in acquiring California and other territory belonging to Mexico. Early nineteenth-century travelers and explorers published diaries and journals describing the fertile valleys and abundant natural resources in California, and those accounts fueled interest in—and shaped the popular views of—the region. Euro-American men, who had settled in California and had married upper-class Mexican women, painted especially positive portrayals of the land as well as the people. They reserved special praise for elite women, describing them as "virtuous" and of "industrious habits," though they often disparaged lower-class women as "loose."[83]

Other authors did not paint such an admirable picture of Mexicans, men or women, or of the system of government. Richard Henry Dana in *Two Years Before the Mast* described Mexican men as "jealous" and "vengeful" and Mexican women, regardless of social class, as less than virtuous. "[T]heir morality," he wrote, "is none of the best."[84] Those and other similar characterizations fanned the flames of the ideology of Manifest Destiny. This nationalist doctrine, articulated in the mid-1840s, expressly upheld Euro-American racial or biological and governmental superiority as well as the belief that expansion of democracy and other institutions, from the Atlantic to the Pacific Ocean, was a divine and preordained right. These Euro-Americans, or "Anglo-Saxons," believed that they descended from advanced Germanic tribes; thus, they had "pure" and superior racial origins. The mixed racial origins of Mexicans, on other hand, made them a degraded and mongrel race, unfit to govern themselves or the territory or to make the land productive.[85]

Those beliefs, the invasion of Texas in 1836 and its annexation 1845, and the growing presence of Euro-Americans in California heightened American interest in the region. It also heightened tensions between Mexico and the United States. The battle and loss of Texas in the 1830s had begun a decade earlier, after hundreds, and eventually thousands, of Euro-American immigrant families settled in the eastern portion of the territory and refused to abide by the laws and decrees pertaining to colonization. When the Mexican authorities attempted to enforce the law and regain control of their northern border, the Euro-American colonists rebelled and rose up against the "tyranny" of the Mexican government. Under the leadership of Stephen Austin, American Texans, who vastly outnumbered Texas Mexicans, revolted against the Mexican government and declared themselves independent. War ensued between Euro-American and Mexican forces and lasted for several months, with casualties on both sides. Ultimately, Euro-American forces overwhelmed their Mexican counterparts and forced General Antonio López de Santa Anna, president and commander in chief, to concede defeat and grant

Texas independence. Nine years later, after much debate in Congress over annexation and the expansion of slavery into the new territory, the United States annexed Texas, much to the chagrin of Mexican leaders, particularly the Mexican Congress, which never recognized Texas sovereignty.[86]

That loss did not bode well for Mexicans, especially those in California, who witnessed the numbers of foreign and Euro-American migrants and settlers increase. Among those settlers was a military leader who gave Mexican officials particular trouble: U.S. Army officer John C. Frémont. In 1846, prior to any declaration of war, Frémont "illegally imprisoned Californio officials, seized governmental and private property, occupied Sonoma [north of Monterey] and its surroundings, and declared California the 'Bear Flag Republic.'"[87] Frémont's action, though premature, signaled what many Mexicans and Euro-American had anticipated: War was imminent. Months later, after a skirmish in south Texas at the U.S.– Mexico border, President James Polk—known for his expansionist beliefs and writings—declared war against Mexico. Commodore John Drake Sloat, commander of the Pacific squadron, extended that declaration to California. The conflict lasted for two years, with casualties on both sides. A dearth of military supplies and personnel and little, if any, assistance from Mexican authorities undermined the Californio effort to hold off the Euro-Americans. José María Flores, commander in chief of military forces in California, complained to the Mexican authorities in late 1846 about the lack of ammunition, food, and clothing for his troops. Flores stated that his men had not been able to obtain supplies for the war effort because of the American occupation of Monterey and the blockade of trade routes. These circumstances had forced him to trade with local merchants, most of them foreign-born, whose interest rates had skyrocketed. "What can we do?" he wrote. "Abandon the nation for lack of supplies for the war effort or take them at excessively high prices?" "I must accept the prices offered by the merchants or else allow my troops to starve. . . . Either I take [the high price of gunpowder] or have no way to defend myself from my enemy tommorow."[88]

Despite Flores and Governor Pío Pico's repeated petitions to central Mexico for assistance, California Mexican forces remained ill-equipped and on the brink of starvation. That and the loss of men in several skirmishes ultimately forced the Californians to surrender. The war in California ended with the signing of the Treaty of Cahuenga in 1847.

This document gave every Mexican citizen the same rights as U.S. citizens, and it guaranteed protection of life, property, and right of movement and travel so long as Mexican men did not to take up arms against the United States. Meanwhile, the war continued in northern Mexico, until the Americans gained the upper hand by invading Mexico City, a move that all but sealed the fate of Mexican forces. After securing victory, the Americans negotiated the Treaty of Guadalupe Hidalgo with Mexico and agreed to pay $15 million dollars in exchange for Mexico's northern territory, about one third of Mexico, which included present-day California, Arizona, New Mexico, Texas, and parts of Nevada, Colorado, and Utah. The 1853 Gadsden Purchase increased Mexico's loss to nearly half of its original territory.[89]

In California, the shift in the legal and governmental system was not immediately imposed, as it took at least two years for the implementation of U.S. civil authority. In the meantime, American military leaders and officers, who oversaw the day-to-day legal, political, and economic functions, retained the Spanish and Mexican laws and customs to minimize confusion. As early as 1846, even before the war had ended, Commodore Sloat ordered all "judges, alcaldes, and other civil magistrates to retain their offices, and to execute their function as heretofore, [so] that the public tranquility may not be disturbed; at least until the government of the territory can be more definitely arranged."[90] At the conclusion of war in 1847, interim military governor General Stephen Watts Kearny affirmed that order, declaring "[t]he laws now in existence and not in conflict with the Constitution of the United States will be continued until changed by competent authority; and these persons who hold office will be continued in the same for the present, provided they swear to support that Constitution."[91]

Though Hispanic legal practices continued in California, modifications in the law and legal practices began to take shape as early as 1846, foreshadowing the larger changes that would emerge in a few years. The right to a trial by jury, for instance, a highly regarded American tradition, replaced the use of the alcalde and the hombres buenos in settling civil and criminal disputes and was introduced in Sonoma two months before the U.S. occupation of California. By late 1847 and after the war, the trial-by-jury process had become official policy throughout the region. For all cases involving more than $100, a jury of six men was impaneled, and in criminal trials, one of twelve was used.[92] American authorities also altered the powers of the alcalde, for they seemed too broad to Mid-westerners and Easterners accustomed to the independence of the executive, legislative, and judicial branches of government. U.S. representatives also limited and, in some cases, curtailed the number of land grants to private persons. They did this to protect current property owners—who were going to have to submit to a legal procedure for securing and confirming land titles—from squatters or others who might attempt to usurp those property rights.[93]

The transition from Mexican to American governance proved to be even more drastic and difficult for angeleños, especially for those who suffered property losses or those who suffered deprivations in the months immediately following the war. The American troops, commanded by Stockton and Frémont, had marched into the pueblo, ransacking homes and shops and taking food, supplies, and valuables. They destroyed or stole large quantities of assets and goods that belonged to the men and women who lived in the pueblo and its surrounding region. Gentiles and neófitos also took part in the looting, no doubt in retaliation for their continued marginalization and impoverishment in Mexican society. Henry "Enrique" Dalton, a local merchant and ranchero, informed the authorities that Frémont had incited an "insurrection among the Indian tribes to operate against the inhabitants, and during their . . . operations, they plundered a number of animals off my hacienda."[94] To compensate Dalton and others who suffered losses, Archibald Gillespie, a U.S. military officer in charge of Los Angeles until a civil government was established, allowed people to report any lost or stolen items and to receive just compensation from the U.S. government. Though the money did little to make up for the violence and chaos brought about by the hostilities and defeat of the war, it gave pueblo property owners some peace of mind to know that they would be able to rebuild their lives and that, in the short term, the Americans intended to protect the rights of their newly conquered subjects. The extent to which the Americans would uphold those principles remained to be seen.

In 1847, Gillespie appointed a commission of three men, Abel Stearns, Eulogio de Celis, and Charles Flugge, to identify the men and women with claims and to appraise their losses. In the pueblo of Los Angeles alone, forty-three individuals of various social classes, including fourteen women, claimed property damage estimated at 5,580 pesos. The women reported damages averaging 121 pesos, and the men an average of 134 pesos. No neófito or gentile man or woman reported any losses in town or on their rancherías. Because U.S. law severely discriminated against indigenous people in regard to their property rights, the American authorities no doubt did not include them in the compensation for lost or damaged holdings. Non-Indians, on the other hand, were entitled to reparations, and they claimed a variety of missing or stolen items, including foodstuffs, household goods, and farming equipment.

The widow Juana Rendon, for example, not only cited the loss of kitchen and bedroom furnishings but also a cart full of firewood and another of corn, several bushels of frijoles, fifty pounds of potatoes, onions, and chili peppers, as well as a copper pot and cooking utensils. Rendon did not mince words when she told the authorities that she deserved compensation, as she was "a widowed woman who has a young, strong child whom I have to support until she reaches of age [twenty-five years]." Josefa Cota, another widow, informed the local authorities that "[I am] helpless . . . and lack the means to replace what I have lost." Cota had recently sold her rancho and invested the proceeds in her home in the pueblo, but now even that property had been lost. Despite the attempts of her servants to stop the American troops from damaging her house, she complained, they broke two windows and the shutters and took beans, wheat, various cooking and eating utensils, and other household items.[95]

María Villalobos found her home pilfered but with little physical destruction. With the assistance of Julian Chávez, Villalobos, who could not write, claimed that the Euro-Americans had stolen or damaged farming and carpentry equipment; household furnishings, including two beds; and foodstuffs, including fourteen bushels of wheat, two barrels of aguardiente, seventy-five pounds of onions, fifty pounds of chilies, and several bushels of corn and beans. Whether or not the American government compensated these women as well as the other claimants is unclear, for the outcome of these claims is not documented. Nevertheless, the evidence reinforces the idea that property was crucial to securing status, livelihood, and subsistence among the elite and mid-strata angeleños. Those without it, the impoverished residents, were doubtless aware of the significance of property ownership.[96]

Despite the property losses during the war, most residents managed to escape relatively unharmed. Many fled the town with their families as soon as they learned of the American troop advance. In separate reports, Josefa Alvarado and Juana de Dios Rendon declared that they and their families had escaped on the day the American soldiers arrived. Rendon had done so, she said, before "[I] had a chance to protect my modest interests, since all I could do was to lock the doors of my house. . . . the Americans . . . opened my house . . . and carried off everything I had in it, including title papers [to my land] . . . leaving me today without any safeguard to protect my property rights."[97] Another woman, Juana Ballestreros, happened to be at her family's ranch, Los Cuervos, when Frémont's soldiers marched into town and broke down the front door of her house. Among other things, they carried off bushels of wheat and corn, as well as quantities of tallow.[98]

Although Ballestreros, Rendon, and Alvarado and their families managed to escape harm, others came dangerously close to the violence. Dolores Urquides, a Mexican man, recounted the tense moments he and his family endured during the war. On the day the soldiers arrived, Urquides informed the commissioners, "Commodore's soldiers came to my orchard. . . . they were about twenty men, armed, and . . . [then] they surrounded my house and my entire family . . . without saying a word because [I believed] they wanted to kill us." Urquides and his family were not harmed but, "around seven that evening . . . they took whatever they wanted." The next day he reported the incident to Juan Temple and Alejandro Hope, who were business partners, a local merchant and lawyer, respectively, "to tell them what had occurred and to ask them to witness or give an account of what had transpired," but, Urquides stated, "they didn't want to attend to any of my pleadings." Temple and Hope probably did nothing to help Urquides because of their own concerns over the property and goods they had lost as a result of the American soldiers destroying and looting many of the warehouses at the port of San Pedro including some that they themselves owned.[99]

Outside of the pueblo, twenty men (no women), mostly merchants and traders, suffered property losses valued at 33,000 pesos, with the men losing about 1,580 pesos a piece. This destruction and what had occurred in the town proved to be a distressing setback to many of the Californio and foreign-born proprietors in the region. However, it did not prepare them for the economic losses as well as the social, political, legal, cultural, and demographic transformations that awaited them in the years following the American conquest of California. Despite the guarantees of the Treaty of Cahuenga, and later, the Treaty of Guadalupe Hidalgo and promises to protect their property and rights as citizens, men and women—Californios, mexicanos, and foreign-born—would suffer even more devastating losses and would see their lives irrevocably altered.[100]

The events leading to the closure of Mexican sovereignty in California signaled the beginning of the end of the existing patterns of property holding and socio-racial and cultural hierarchies in Los Angeles and the larger region. Before the Euro-American invasion, land ownership throughout the district reflected class, ethnic, and gender divisions as well as ideas about who had entitlement to property. Under Mexican and earlier Spanish law, those individuals who had aided in the military and religious conquest, colonization, and settlement of California—men and women de razón and neófitos and neófitas—had a right to land. In reality, however, those California- and Mexico-born Mexican men and women, including naturalized citizens, with kinship ties to military and political leaders became virtually the only landowners.

Most landowners were men, but a small, yet significant, number of women also owned property. Although men acquired ranchos primarily through direct grants from the governors, the women secured their holdings through marriage and inheritance. Despite most women's inability to read or write and the common practice of appointing men to represent them, through their involvement in business transactions and court cases, it is evident that these women understood the law and their property rights and that they took advantage of their privileged economic and social position.

Those women without kinship ties to military or political leaders, and hence, without ranchos, obtained property in the pueblos. Most possessed solares for their houses and suertes for vegetable gardens or orchards. In a few cases, these mid-strata women were able to acquire larger tracts, greater social recognition, and a measure of economic independence. Neófitos and neófitas, on the other hand, obtained little or no property despite the mandate of the secularization decrees. A few neófitos and even fewer neófitas acquired former mission land, which elevated their status, but most indigenous peoples fled to the interior or became laborers—sometimes being subjected to forced labor—on ranchos and in the pueblos. The American conquest would only accelerate marginalization for them and would begin it for the Californios and the increasing population of Mexican immigrants.

Part II

Women in American California

Chapter 4

Divorce, Culture, and the Family

In 1870, the widow María Elizalde married Andrés Rubio, a man several years her junior. Though she had five children to support, Elizalde made a good marriage prospect. Her deceased husband, Diego Sepúlveda, had left her substantial property, including an interest in Rancho Palo Verde, livestock, and a vineyard. Within a year of celebrating her nuptials with Rubio, however, marital and family relations soured. Her life became so unbearable that she did something that was unusual in nineteenth-century Mexican culture but that was becoming increasingly common in contemporary Euro-American culture: She filed for a divorce.

Before the local District Court judge, the official responsible for divorce matters in the American era, Elizalde recounted the numerous difficulties she and her children had experienced with Rubio during their brief stint as a family. At the time of their marriage, he had no property, she explained, but now he had appropriated her holdings and "was wasting [them] away." Shortly before the hearing, "he had taken some wagons from the rancho and left for his father's house, and he has not returned." His mismanagement of the family finances had left her without funds to run the household and cover the costs of the children's schooling. "Rubio," she argued, "is unsuited to have control of the property or be responsible for the care and custody of the children." "Ever since marrying him," she continued, "he has been brutal and cruel. . . . [H]is language is vulgar, and he throws [objects] . . . as well as strikes, beats, pinches, and curses [me]." He did this, she declared, in front of her children and friends. He had even threatened to kill her. Because of these abuses, she now sought a divorce, custody of the children, the return of her property, and temporary support—alimony—during the suit.

Rubio denied the charges and accused Elizalde of undermining the marriage. It was she who was the aggressor, and she had even encouraged the children to assault him, he countered. Those attacks, he charged, had forced him to flee to his father's home, where he had remained until compelled to appear in court.

Rubio's accusations provoked Elizalde into expanding on her list of complaints. He had not only admitted to taking "all [her] money," but he had also told her to "go live with another man." He acknowledged giving some of her property to his brothers and using physical force to get her to consent to having one of her daughters marry one of Rubio's brothers. Elizalde's testimony was corroborated by two of her sons, who had fled the home, fearing for their lives. After weighing the evidence, the judge ruled in Elizalde's favor, granting her request for a divorce, which would enable her to remarry if she so wished in the future.[1]

María Elizalde's case provides a window onto the cultural as well as economic, political, legal, and social transformations brought about by the American conquest. In post-conquest Los Angeles, the right to divorce introduced ambiguity into gender relations and created dilemmas for Spanish-speaking women, as individuals, as well as for families and the community. Most Californio-Mexican women in the community were successful in suing for divorce—as were Euro-American women who filed divorce suits. However, although a divorce offered possibilities for personal and economic independence, women had difficulty asserting their claims to community property, alimony, or child support because their husbands were often impoverished or had deserted them and could not be found. Regardless of their ethnicity, many divorced women ended up having to fend for themselves and their children.

Some women were unsuccessful in court, and they were either found "at fault" for the marital failure or were denied a divorce altogether. Perhaps fearing those outcomes, some women dropped divorce petitions once their husbands agreed to mend their bad ways, and others opted for a legal separation. Still other Californio-Mexican women took a familiar route in dealing with abusive spouses: They brought criminal charges against their husbands.

The Spanish-speaking women who sought divorces in the American era were challenging fundamental cultural understandings of marriage, the family, and sexuality. In Spanish and Mexican culture, stable marriages were the bedrock of a well-ordered society. To maintain stable families, sexuality before, during, and after marriage was carefully regulated by household heads—patriarchs—who had authority over their dependents.[2] This was still true for the California-Mexicans in Los Angeles after the American conquest. Francisco Ramírez, editor of the nineteenth-century Los Angeles Spanish-language newspaper, *El Clamor Público,* used his publication to reprimand married women who complained to the local priests about unhappy households and spousal abuse. He advised such women to "suffer patiently the adversities . . . of your lot [*suerte*] in life" and to "obey God's will and that of your spouse." Though he expressed no views on divorce, it is highly likely he considered it an assault on the institutions of the family and the Church.[3] In Mexico itself, these beliefs continued well into the twentieth century, as absolute divorce (which allowed couples to remarry) was not permitted until 1917.[4]

In contrast to the Mexican era, when options for escaping an unhappy marriage were limited, in the American era, women's right to bring their spouses before a tribunal and charge them with marital indiscretions or other inappropriate behavior expanded. However, this signified a disruption of the traditional balance of male-female (read dominant-subordinate) roles and family relations, particularly in the California-Mexican community. Hence, the decision to divorce did not come easily or quickly. Women recognized that by filing a divorce suit, they were confronting long-held beliefs and cultural proscriptions. A divorce could stain a woman's honor, making her appear to be sexually "loose." A divorce could harm a family's social standing and reputation, and it could alienate relatives and friends, as well as the larger community, whose members disapproved of such action. A divorce could leave a woman and her children without a means of support and might even leave her open to retaliation by a violent spouse. The Los Angeles community felt "under siege" as it coped with the economic, political, legal, demographic, and cultural changes taking place in the wake of the American conquest in 1848. In that "pressure cooker" environment, a woman petitioning for divorce risked tapping into collective wrath.

Euro-American women who sought divorces also encountered social and cultural resistance, although to a lesser degree. Divorce had been hotly debated at different times and places in the United States. As early as the colonial period, "bed-and-board" divorce *(a mensa et thoro),* or legal separation, allowed a couple to part ways but not marry anyone else, whereas an absolute divorce *(a vinculo a matrimonii)* allowed remarriage.

The Puritans introduced absolute divorce in the seventeenth-century in Massachusetts, but English still law forbade remarriage. Cotton Mather and John Robinson, who disputed the English law and fought for liberalization of divorce decrees in the 1690s, argued that discordant families disrupted social harmony in the larger community. Disgruntled marriage partners, they believed, should be allowed to separate so that they could form other, more harmonious, unions that would set a positive example. Among the Puritans, grounds for divorce included female adultery, male cruelty, bigamy, desertion, failure to provide for the family, and impotence. Those statutes were liberalized in 1773, when women obtained the right to seek divorce on the grounds of male adultery. As a result, an increasing number of women sought divorces in Puritan communities.[5]

Most contemporary Americans disagreed with those principles. Antidivorce advocates argued that marriage was the basis for social harmony and that divorce undermined and disrupted that stability. Colonists in the middle colonies hesitantly agreed, allowing absolute divorce only in cases of desertion and adultery. The South followed the Church of England's cannon law, which prohibited absolute divorce. Ecclesiastical authorities alone had the power to grant bed-and-board divorce, and even then, only on grounds of adultery, desertion, and extreme cruelty. The Revolutionary era encouraged a change in popular attitudes toward marriage and divorce in most regions (with the notable exception of South Carolina, where strict divorce laws persisted until the end of the nineteenth century). Like the revolutionaries who sought to break England's tyrannical colonial ties with America, supporters of divorce reasoned that a couple should be able to sever the bonds of a union that had become unbearable. They also embraced the idea of companionate marriage (with its emphasis on romantic love, reciprocity, and respect) and accompanying challenges to patriarchy, in general, and to men's authoritarian marital position, in particular.

By the nineteenth century, the development of the market economy and technology, which dislocated the household as the primary locus of production, and railroad expansion, which increased social mobility and westward migration, encouraged a highly mobile and individualistic culture that exalted personal freedom over the common good.[6] Especially in the western states and territories, new divorce laws contributed to a popular association of migration with divorce. Under the Constitution, states had jurisdiction over legislation involving divorce, resulting in great variability and increasing flexibility. Indiana, for example, allowed divorce on the "flimsiest of pretexts."[7] Not surprisingly, divorce seekers who found their own states' laws overly prohibitive migrated to divorce-friendly jurisdictions, most of them in the West, in the latter half of the nineteenth century.[8]

Like other western states, California had "liberal" divorce statutes, which had been enacted at the granting of statehood in 1850 and with the adoption of the common law in 1851. During the process to pass the bill to institute the common law (which would automatically establish divorce laws), debates raged over the "divorce" and "woman" questions, championed on one side by nineteenth-century moralists and on the other by advocates for women's rights. Nevertheless, the California Assembly and Senate approved the bill, and women and men were granted the opportunity to sue to sever the bond of matrimony, which had been declared a civil contract in 1850.[9]

Because Native Americans were subjected to severe racial and social discrimination, California law denied indigenous peoples—both neófitos and gentiles—most of the civil rights granted to the conquered Mexican population living in the United States. For instance, the testimony of a Native American could not be used to convict a "white man."[10] Native Americans were also barred from divorcing in U.S. district courts. However, they did divorce through traditional means, which for most groups meant separating based on mutual consent or dissatisfaction.[11] In the 1880s, U.S. government officials accepted the validity of such separations, so long as witnesses corroborated the strained marital relations. In the eyes of the law, those divorces were binding, and the U.S. Indian Service (the Bureau of Indian Affairs) recognized marriages and divorces performed through traditional or "Indian custom."[12]

In contrast, California law allowed California-Mexicans and Euro-Americans to sue for bed-and-board divorce (or legal separation) or an absolute divorce, on the grounds of adultery, cruelty, desertion, natural impotency, extreme cruelty (subject to wide interpretation), conviction of a felony, intemperance, desertion, and neglect over a period of at least three years.[13] An 1870 act reduced the period for intemperance, neglect, and desertion to two years.[14] The Civil Code of 1872 shortened that period to one year.[15] To what extent spouses who claimed "cruelty" or "neglect" or similar grounds in court really suffered such circumstances is open to speculation. Doubtless, with the assistance of a skilled lawyer, many chose their particular grounds for divorce based upon what best characterized their marital situation or suited their purpose.[16]

In 1850, the California legislature established nine district courts in the new state, with the First (later renamed the Seventeenth) District Court having jurisdiction in Los Angeles. A year later, state legislators vested the district courts with authority over divorce, civil, and probate cases as well as cases appealed from county and municipal courts.[17] Under California law, an individual seeking a divorce had to go before the district court accompanied by a lawyer, who assisted them in filing the complaint. The defendant had two to three weeks to respond. If the defendant lived out of the state, the court would publish a summons, which ran for three months in the English-language local newspaper, the *Los Angeles Star,* and its Spanish-language counterpart, *La Estrella.* Failure to respond was technically insufficient grounds for granting a divorce, but with evidence or the testimony of others, including that of the plaintiff, the courts frequently found non-respondents to be in "default" and ordered the marriage dissolved.[18] Divorce was generally available regardless of social class, as costs were usually minimal, $20 to $30, though they could sometimes range as high as several hundred dollars if the case were complicated and the lawyer's fees were high. For impoverished spouses, however, even modest court costs could be an impediment to escaping an unbearable marriage.

Another barrier existed because Californios, Mexicans, and European immigrants were unfamiliar with American common law. During the years immediately following statehood, the Los Angeles District Court relied heavily on common law, and for Californio-Mexican community, in general, and women, in particular, awareness of new statutes and court decisions came only gradually. Judges and lawyers tended to be newcomers to California and were unacquainted with local conditions and community norms. During the Mexican era, the local judges, alcaldes, and other officials, including the hombres buenos, frequently lacked expertise in Spanish and Mexican civil law, but they were usually long-time residents, who were familiar with community values. In American Los Angeles during the three decades immediately following the conquest, only two judges presiding over the Los Angeles District Court—Agustín Olvera (1851–1852) and Pablo de la Guerra (1863–1867)—were Mexican and Californio, respectively. Neither possessed formal legal training in the common law, but they understood the customs and legal practices of the Mexican era as well as the Spanish language. Olvera served only a brief stint on the court, both on and in front of the bench, as judge and lawyer, before becoming a county supervisor. De la Guerra remained in office longer and not only quickly mastered California jurisprudence but also participated in the state's constitutional convention and held the offices of lieutenant governor and United States marshal.[19] Both men served as legal counsel for Mexican and American clients. All other district court judges and lawyers were recent arrivals from other regions of the United States, and only a few, such as Benjamin Hayes, an Irish-American Catholic, understood the Spanish language.

Indeed, language was another tremendous barrier for the Californio-Mexican community because English had become the official language of the courts. Not only the judges but also the court officials spoke little or no Spanish. Though the legislature in 1853 authorized the presence of court interpreters and the printing of laws in both English and Spanish, interpreters and translators were in short supply throughout the government. For example, in several divorce and other civil proceedings, there were complaints that the sheriffs who were responsible for serving court summonses spoke English only, which prevented them from explaining the court orders to Spanish-speaking recipients.[20]

Despite the barriers, a small group of California-Mexican women availed themselves of the new legal system. By challenging cultural and social norms in seeking a divorce, this group was significant in that it symbolized cultural change. Most Mexican women in the larger region undoubtedly remained loyal to traditional legal and religious strictures and refrained from divorce. In all likelihood, cultural and social taboos as well as material realities contributed to minimizing the number of women who sought to sever their marital bonds in the three decades that followed the American takeover. Others certainly chose alternative methods to deal with an unsatisfying or abusive marriage: They and their spouses agreed mutually to separate, or they simply left their households with or without their spouse's consent. Yet, the action of women who chose to carry out a formal divorce represented a break with the past and an engagement of the future. Their decision demonstrates one way in which Californio-Mexicans adapted to and engaged the new dominant society, with its foreign legal, social, political, and economic systems. Despite the linguistic and cultural barriers, these women not only learned to maneuver within a foreign socio-political and legal framework, but they also used it to their own advantage.

Between 1851 and 1879, sixty-nine women, less than 1 percent of the

Californio-Mexican population in Los Angeles, challenged fundamental notions of marriage and the family by seeking a divorce.[21] The records are silent as to the ethnicity of the applicants, but ethnic background can be surmised from the woman's first and last names, language use, place of birth or residence, and other cultural indicators. It is also possible to partially reconstruct a woman's social class and regional origin. Within this group of women, most of those who gave an indication of the value of their assets were from middle level of the socioeconomic spectrum (women who, with their spouse, held $1,000 to $5,000 in real property) or from the elite (those couples with over $5,000). Most who filed for divorce had been born in California, which suggests that impoverished women (those with less than $1,000) and those who had recently immigrated from Mexico were the least likely to file for divorce. Lack of financial resources and of familiarity with the American legal system undoubtedly deterred poor women and Mexican women from seeking a divorce, and it is likely that those who were in unhappy unions resorted to informal separations—that is, they simply left their spouses.[22]

The Euro-American women who sought divorce, like their Spanish-speaking counterparts, represented a small portion of the larger population. The records for Euro-American women, however, provide less information on the value of their real property: fewer than half of the 213 who sought divorces gave an indication of their real wealth. Though incomplete, the extant records demonstrate that those with mid-strata and elite backgrounds took advantage of the opportunity to divorce more often than did the poor. And, unlike Spanish-speaking angeleños, they were recent migrants primarily from the Midwest and East Coast and from European countries. That fact served to reinforce the idea that many women had come to California to divorce or ended up divorced because of their migration to the state.[23]

Though the number of women who sought divorces was small, far more women filed suits than did men. In Los Angeles between 1851, when the first petition for divorce was tried in district court, and 1879, when that court was abolished and the Superior Court was given jurisdiction over divorces, 72 percent of divorce suits were filed by Californio-Mexican and Euro-American women, whereas only 28 percent were filed by men (ten Spanish speakers and 104 Euro-Americans).[24] Some 282 women (25 percent Mexican and 75 percent Euro-American) of different ethnicities, social classes, and regional backgrounds petitioned for divorce. Most did so in the 1870s, when Los Angeles was experiencing the greatest population growth since the American takeover. The significant number of suits filed in the 1870s also reflects Californio-Mexican women's increased familiarity with divorce laws and practices, prompting more of them to turn to divorce as a recourse in dealing with conflictive households, rather than turning to the criminal court, as they had in the Mexican period.

In the same thirty-year period, no native women (or men) filed for divorce in the Los Angles District Court. Their absence is explained, in part, by the legal, racial, and ethnic discrimination they faced. Though no native women sought court-ordered divorces in Los Angeles, many parted ways with their spouses, as tribal customs allowed for couples to "divorce" or to separate, particularly in instances of adultery.[25] According to Hugo Reid, a "Mexicanized" Euro-American who married a Christianized gabrieleño woman, Victoria Comcrabit, a husband's abuse and cruelty were grounds for divorce. If a woman's spouse beat her repeatedly, she would tell her relatives, who, in turn, "collected together all the money which had been paid in at the marriage" and returned it to him. A woman could then remarry if she wished.[26] How many native women in California divorced is unclear.

The experiences of most Los Angeles women seeking to end their marriages mirrored the experiences of women elsewhere. In Contra Costa, Santa Clara, and Sacramento counties, women initiated 65 to 75 percent of the divorce actions between 1850 and 1890.[27] Women throughout the American West also filed more than two-thirds of all divorce suits. In nineteenth-century Mexico City as well as in eighteenth-century Brazil, women also initiated most divorces.[28] Nevertheless, the tendency for Californio-Mexican women in Los Angeles, in particular, to outnumber men in court reflected a pattern stretching back into the Mexican era: Women were more likely than men to bear the brunt of abuse and neglect in troubled marriages and thus to have a motivation to end the relationship. In general, women in Los Angeles, like those in other parts of the state, country, and hemisphere, cited cruelty, neglect, desertion, intemperance, and adultery as reasons for ending their marriages. Most men cited the wife's adultery, desertion, and, less often, mental cruelty.

Apparently, ethnicity played a minor role in women's ability to divorce. Although twenty-three of the 282 cases are incomplete and forty-four women dropped their suits, the files reveal that Californio-Mexican women won thirty-seven of forty-one cases (90 percent) for which the court rendered a judgment. Euro-American women were slightly more successful, prevailing in 167 of 175 suits (95 percent).

Women's racial identity, on the other hand, played a significant role, as no native or African-American women appeared in the court. As noted earlier, under California law, neófitos and gentiles faced social, racial, and legal discrimination. African-American women faced similar barriers. The legal status and socio-racial position of African-American women is uncertain, as few resided in southern California before the end of slavery. In the southern United States, however, African-American women's marriages (and thus divorces) were not legally recognized until after emancipation.

Despite Californio-Mexican and Euro-American women's ability to use the courts successfully to rid themselves of cruel, neglectful, or adulterous husbands, with a few exceptions, they failed to win financial support. Under an 1851 California statute, women were entitled to alimony (a temporary allowance given to women during a pending divorce suit) and future support for themselves as well as for the "maintenance and education" of children.[29] The judge would determine the "just" amount at the time of the divorce, though the court was also authorized "at any time, . . . [to] annul, vary, or modify such order as the interest and welfare of the children may require." In other words, this provision allowed women to return to court for modifications of support arrangements. When this statute was challenged in 1855, 1861, and 1873, the California Supreme Court upheld it. In 1861, it affirmed that a judge possessed "large discretion" in determining alimony and other forms of support for a wife and her children as well as the authority to make such determinations at "different times" and for "different sums."[30] In 1867, the Supreme Court specifically acknowledged that the district court could take into consideration a husband's "earnings or ability to earn money."[31] These rulings meant that former wives and children, rather than having a fixed amount of support, would receive what the ex-husband's circumstances and the district court's appraisal of the situation determined.

The 1872 Civil Code measurably broadened a wife's right to support by authorizing district courts to order husbands "to make suitable allowances to the wife for her support *during her life* [emphasis added], or for a shorter period, as the court . . . deem[ed] just." This gave women a new possibility for gaining support throughout their lives and for children until they became adults. If a man had little cash or most of his wealth was tied up in real property, the court could compel him to provide support from his share of community property or from his personal assets. If he refused to do so, the judge could require him to provide the court with "security" in the form of cash or property. The court would then appoint a receiver to manage those assets and oversee their distribution to the wife.[32] As for temporary alimony during divorce proceedings, the Civil Code granted the court the authority, "in its discretion, to require the husband to pay as alimony any money necessary to enable the wife to support herself or children or to prosecute or defend the action."[33] However, women would forfeit these rights if they abandoned their husbands. Support would resume only when they returned to their spouses or offered convincing evidence justifying their flight. A wife found guilty of extreme cruelty also risked the loss of any support, as shown by an 1877 California Supreme Court ruling. Laws in the Civil Code dealing with alimony, ruled the Supreme Court, did not "require the husband to pay . . . out of his separate property any sum toward the maintenance of the former wife when the divorce was for her offense."[34]

Nevertheless, regardless of their ethnicity, few women obtained support during or after a divorce trial. Of the Californio-Mexican women who won their divorce suits, only three of thirty-seven (8 percent) received temporary or permanent alimony, while Euro-American women who divorced did slightly better, with seventeen of 167 (10 percent) acquiring support during a trial. Women fared slightly better than men in avoiding payment of court costs, with fifty-six—seven Californio-Mexican and forty-nine Euro-Americans—of 204 (28 percent) succeeding in getting their spouses to pay for court costs and attorney fees, expenses that ranged from $20 to $250.

Californio-Mexican and Euro-American women were more successful in obtaining child custody than winning alimony, but few got the support they needed to house, educate, and care for them. Until the enactment of the 1872 Civil Code, the terms of custody were unclarified, thus leaving the matter in the purview of the district courts. The Civil Code somewhat clarified the district court's authority by ruling that it had the power to act "as necessary" for the care, custody, and education of children. In twenty-seven child-custody cases, seventeen Californio-Mexican women prevailed (63 percent) compared to ten men (37 percent). Still, only two of the women (12 percent of the total cases) received child support or alimony. Euro-American women had an equally difficult time in acquiring support. Of eighty-nine child-custody cases, support was ordered in seventy-two (81 percent), yet in only sixteen (22 percent) did the woman actually collect the mandated support. Regardless of ethnicity, women had difficulty in obtaining support.

This finding—that few divorced women, especially Spanish speakers, actually received court-ordered alimony or support—was not unique to Los Angeles. In Sacramento, for example, less than 1 percent of the women who were granted divorces received alimony or support between 1850 and 1872. The primary reason was that husbands deserted their wives and could not be found, or the men simply lacked the means to provide for their dependents.[35] In Los Angeles, Rafaela Carrillo was among those women who got nothing because of her husband's poverty, which forced her to rely on her own means of support. In 1855, she filed for divorce on the grounds of abandonment after her spouse of ten years had been gone for two years. Legally, she needed to prove that she had been abandoned for three years, but she had decided to bring her suit, presumably in the hope of getting relief from the court. He had deserted her in Sonora, Mexico, but she followed him to Los Angeles. "Nine months [after he moved to Los Angeles]," she told the judge, "he wrote me, telling me that he had abandoned me and the children, and he would have nothing to do with [us]." Since her arrival in California, she, her children, and parents had "been living together and supporting each other . . . but he has not supported us in any way and now wants custody of the children. . . . He is a worthless man without means and wholly incapable of caring for and maintaining them."

The judge agreed that her husband was "an unsuitable person to have custody of the two children and is without sufficient means to do so." The mother, he believed (though the record does not indicate the reason for this belief), "is well provided to maintain and educate the children." In this instance, Carrillo obtained custody of the children but no support from the father. Since the law gave judges "large discretion" in determining alimony and child support, the court seems to have concluded that it would be a fruitless exercise to require an impecunious husband to pay funds that he did not possess. This action anticipated the 1867 California Supreme Court ruling that explicitly allowed judges to take into consideration a husband's "earnings" or "ability to earn money" in determining the amount of support.[36]

Like Carrillo, Fannie Gift, a Euro-American woman, failed to obtain support from her husband. The reason, however, was not his lack of means, but his disappearance. In 1862, she had filed for divorce, complaining of her spouse's long-time neglect, extreme cruelty, and adultery. He had been "harsh and tyrannical . . . towards her, which continued with very slight [let up]" for the last seven years, prompting her "finally [to] separate from him." A year earlier, he had rebuffed her requests for support for herself and their two children and then "he left the state, leaving me to the charity of my friends . . . [and with] no intention of returning . . . [or] making any provisions for maintenance or support." She filed for divorce, asking for custody of the children and support for their education and payment of court costs. When the husband failed to appear following a summons, the judge, based on a court-appointed referee's report, granted her a divorce and custody of the child and decreed that the husband pay $45 for her litigation expenses. The judge doubtless made the husband liable for the court costs to free Fannie from that burden, but the husband's disappearance made the issue moot.[37]

The financial hardships for women who did not win support were exacerbated by a failure to distribute community property. In 1850, the California legislature addressed the distribution of marital (or community) property. As a measure of the new community-property law's importance, it was passed even before 1851 enactment of statutes that would define the grounds and procedures for divorce. Drawing upon Mexican and Spanish legal principles, the law stipulated that divorced couples had a right to an equal share of "community property"—"all property acquired after the marriage by either husband or wife, except . . . by gift, bequest, . . . or descent [inheritance]."[38] While Hispanic law held that couples had a mutual interest in that property, the husband actually controlled and disposed of it as he saw fit. California law was similar, "with [the husband having] . . . absolute power . . . as of his own separate estate." The law held that any profits generated from a husband's or wife's personal belongings were community property, and the husband's authority extended to those earnings as well.[39] Indicative of a man's power was an 1863 statute stipulating that any married woman who subverted her husband's rights by disposing of property held in common faced stiff penalties: She could be charged with a felony and receive up to ten years in state prison.[40] A husband's authority over the property, which essentially gave him title to it, allowed his creditors to have access to it, while a wife's debts could only be paid out of her personal holdings. The California Supreme Court reinforced the husband's privileged position in an 1872 ruling that allowed him to give common property to third parties, since he had "absolute power of disposition of . . . [it] as of his own separate property."[41] The 1872 Civil Code left that decision and the statutes intact, as it codified them virtually unaltered.[42]

Notwithstanding a husband's prerogative, the law imposed some restrictions on him. In 1855, the Supreme Court ruled in two separate cases that a husband could dispose of property only during his and his wife's "joint lives," and it forbade him from bequeathing his wife's interest in the property to someone other than her. Moreover, another ruling stipulated that his right to manage ended when the marriage was dissolved.[43] An 1859 decision prohibited a husband from selling, without the wife's permission, property "for the mere purpose of divesting her [the wife] of her claims to it" or during divorce proceedings.[44] The court followed that decision with an 1872 decree prohibiting a husband from giving common property to others in any manner that jeopardized the wife's interests. The Civil Code supported those restrictions by stating that a husband could not give or in other ways dispose of the property without his wife's written consent.[45] Nor could he convey property that consisted of his wife and children's personal clothing or household furnishings, unless his spouse consented. During divorce proceedings, a woman who believed her spouse had illegally conveyed or transferred her property could protest that and request the appointment of a third party, or receiver, to manage the property until the court rendered a decision.[46] When granted a divorce, women had the right to an equal share of the community property. The court would then either divide the property or sell it and distribute the proceeds equally.[47] The state's Supreme Court and Civil Code affirmed those procedures in 1869 and 1872 by vesting the judicial system with the authority to "divide [the community property] between [the spouses]."[48] If the asset was not apportioned at the time of the divorce, each spouse retained an interest in it and could request its division at a later time.[49]

Despite these laws, the property shares obtained by divorcing spouses could vary depending upon personal behavior. In 1857, the legislature gave judges presiding over divorce cases the authority to determine the portion of community property "deem[ed] just" for spouses found guilty of adultery or extreme cruelty.[50] Spanish and Mexican law called for similar consideration in divorces and legal separations involving infidelity. A guilty spouse risked losing his or her share of marital property as well as child custody.[51] In American California, the legislators who authored the act apparently sought to punish spouses who were guilty of "immoral" conduct. The California Supreme Court on several occasions upheld the 1857 statute allowing divorce in the cases of adultery and extreme cruelty. For example, in 1873, the court ruled that "the injured party is to receive, as a general rule, more than one half of the property, and as much as the Court shall deem just."[52]

Though entitled to their share of community property, only twenty-five of 204 women (12 percent)—four Spanish speakers and twenty-one Euro-Americans—who were successful in their divorce suits obtained it. In many instances, there was simply no property to share. In at least twenty-nine of the 204 suits, women claimed entitlement to property held in common, yet the court failed to divide it. The husband may have hidden or have squandered the assets before or during the divorce proceedings, or he may have denied that that the couple had accumulated any property during the marriage, though wives invariably testified to the contrary. Doubtless, in some of the 150 cases where no community property was mentioned, the wife may have lied to the judge, or she may simply have been unaware of the family's situation because she had deferred to her husband in financial matters during the marriage. Whatever the reality, the court did nothing to investigate if community property might have existed in any of the cases brought by women to the tribunal. The reality was that many newly divorced women were left dependent on themselves and others for support, while men remained relatively free of responsibility for their children and former spouses.

Though most women failed to win their share of community property, six of the 204 cases, one Californio-Mexican and five Euro-American women, chose to forego their share in exchange for other forms of support. Some chose to receive a lump sum, while others opted for monthly payments. One Euro-American woman, who successfully proved in 1877 that her husband had been guilty of cruelty, declined a share of community property, valued at about $20,000. Instead, she settled for a $60 monthly allowance for the support of herself throughout her lifetime and for their child until the age of fifteen.[53] Another woman who declined community property was María Antonia R. de Easton, the only Spanish speaker to do so. An 1878 divorce decree awarded her $40 per month in support for her during her lifetime and for her five children to adulthood.[54] Though women rarely emerged with such settlements, the few who did so had wealthy spouses. Generally, most women, especially those from impoverished families (increasingly the condition for Spanish-speaking families in Los Angeles), failed to get their share of the community property or other forms of support.[55]

In at least ten of the twenty-five Los Angeles cases in which women obtained community property, injunctions were brought against the spouses, restraining them from managing or disposing of community property until the court rendered its decision. Among the angeleños making use of the injunction was María Antonia Coronel, a member of a once politically and economically prominent family (fig. 4.1). In 1869, Coronel complained to the district court that her former husband, Alexis Godey, had tricked her into a divorce and was attempting to sell the community property and deny her a share. No doubt, Coronel's situation would have provided opponents of divorce with ample evidence of women's victimization as a result of the legal right to end marriages. Earlier that year, she informed the court, the couple had moved from their Los Angeles home to Kern County. There, without informing her, Godey filed for divorce in the Sixteenth District Court, charging his wife with adultery. When the court served a summons requesting a response to the charges, Coronel asked her husband for a translation since she could not read English. He told her that it was nothing to worry about and to sign, acknowledging that she had received it. After she did, the sheriff gave her a copy, but Godey took it and destroyed it without her knowledge. When Coronel failed to respond to the charges, the judge found her in default and granted the divorce. Godey had not informed the court of the existence of community property, so no provisions were made to deliver any assets to the wife. When he began selling off the property, purchasers informed Coronel of what was taking place. The news led her to ask questions. When she learned of the divorce in Kern County, she returned to Los Angeles where, with the assistance of a lawyer, she filed for an injunction against her husband.

Coronel accused her husband of deception in obtaining the divorce and seeking to deny her a share of the community property. She also claimed that he had physically assaulted her and committed adultery with two Indian servant girls. Because of the severity of his transgressions, she demanded all the community property, which consisted of more than

Figure 4.1
María Antonia Coronel de Godey (left) and Guadalupe Zamorano de Dalton in the 1860s or 1870s. In 1869 in the Los Angeles District Court, Coronel successfully challenged her ex-husband's attempt to sell her property without her consent. Zamorano, apparently a close friend, was married to Henry Dalton, a British trader and ranchero. (Courtesy of the Seaver Center for Western History Research, Los Angeles County Museum of Natural History)

three thousand head of cattle, a couple of hundred horses, thousands of dollars in gold coins, promissory notes, and real estate. She also requested an injunction voiding the sales he had already made and prohibiting any others. Godey denied the charges, insisting that the assets were his personal property. A court-appointed referee found otherwise. Nevertheless, the decision was partially favorable to each spouse. The court granted Coronel an injunction but split the property between her and Godey.[56]

The husband then appealed to the California Supreme Court, on the grounds that the Los Angeles court had no jurisdiction because the divorce had been granted elsewhere. The Supreme Court issued a mixed verdict. It held that the Kern County court had issued a valid divorce decree, while the Los Angeles court had dealt with the issue of community property, granting her "any property to which she might be entitled"—half of the holdings. "The parties stand upon equal grounds in [the division of the property]," the court ruled, "and neither could wholly exclude the other from participation in the property." In the end, Coronel's persistence in pursuing her rightful share of the assets enabled her to regain her property, despite her former spouse's fraudulent actions.[57]

In addition to the right to claim community property, women could claim personal property—that is, the land and any other goods owned before marriage or later acquired "by gift, bequest, . . . or descent [inheritance]."[58] However, very few actually claimed such property in divorce suits. The 1850 California statute that dealt with community property held that personal possessions remained the exclusive property of each spouse during and following a divorce, though a husband had qualified control over his wife's personal property. However, a husband could not dispose of his wife's personal property without her written or oral permission. The latter was granted in a private meeting with a judge or notary, which occurred whenever a wife entered into a contract, thereby ensuring she did so without coercion from her husband.[59] Furthermore, to protect a woman's personal property and to keep it separate from that held in common (and controlled by the husband), the wife could draw up an inventory and register that list with the county recorder.[60] If a woman believed her husband had mismanaged or squandered her property, she had a right to ask the district court to appoint a receiver to oversee her assets. In contrast to California common law, Spanish and Mexican law had granted a woman the right to control the *bienes parafernales* (personal property she brought to her marriage), with the exception of the dowry, which the husband managed. A wife controlled her assets without interference from her husband unless she ceded her rights to him in writing, an action that absolved her of any debts he might incur.[61]

The California Supreme Court upheld the 1850 statute protecting a woman's separate property on at least three different occasions. In 1859, the justices decided that when the "estate [and title] is confessedly in the wife . . . joining of the husband [in the contract or agreement] is not for the purposes of passing . . . [her] title. It is . . . evidence [of] his renunciation of the right to manage and control it."[62] The court made similar decisions in 1873 and 1874, in which it reminded two male appellants that they needed a wife's "assent"—her signature—to sell her separate property.[63]

Despite these legal protections, wives did not gain significant ground in controlling and managing their estates until the 1870s. In 1879, the legislature decreed that any funds generated by a wife's separate estate remained hers alone.[64] (This statute amended the earlier 1850 law, which, as already noted, held that assets generated by property belonging to either spouse became community property.)[65] In 1872, the Civil Code brought an even more dramatic transformation to a married woman's property rights. She could now convey, sell, or transfer her personal assets "without the consent of the husband."[66] Moreover, a wife could receive gifts or purchase movable goods or land and retain (and manage) these items as her separate property. Once divorced, a woman took full control of her personal holdings as well as any community property she might receive.

In Los Angeles and the greater Los Angeles region, only eighteen of 204 women (8 percent)—five Californio-Mexicans and thirteen Euro-Americans—were awarded personal property following divorce. The other 186 women simply had no property to claim or did not declare their holdings to the court, under the assumption that that personal property had no bearing on the marital dispute. Among the minority who claimed separate property was María Antonia Domínguez, who had inherited substantial assets from her first husband. Her troubles began almost immediately after she married her second husband, John Chapman, in 1863. Before the year was out, she had filed for divorce, accusing Chapman of deception, intemperance, and cruelty. This story had an unusual twist. Ten years before their marriage, sometime in 1853, Domínguez had established a friendly relationship with a "Chapman," who, after several years, left Los Angeles. In 1861, after having had no subsequent contact with him, she learned he was in San Francisco and wrote to him, revealing personal matters about her family and business life. At the time, she was unaware that the man receiving the letters was not the Chapman she had befriended but an impostor, who had assumed Chapman's identity in order to take advantage of her. Eventually, the false "Chapman" came to Los Angeles, but, rather than being angry at learning he was an imposter, Domínguez took a liking to him. After a short courtship, they married. Then the trouble began. "Without my consent," she told the court, "he has taken my separate property [including land, livestock, a house, and jewelry] for the purpose of pawning them, . . . and he threatens to take my children." She asked for a divorce, custody of the children, her property, and an injunction prohibiting him from selling her property or mistreating her children. "If I cannot get my property returned to me," she declared, "I want to be compensated in gold or silver."

Chapman denied the charges, arguing that Domínguez and her parents had conspired against him. "Her family forced the marriage to take place," he stated. "She forced me to take control of her personal property, minor children, and servants." At the time of the marriage, "she only held $500, which was used to pay family debts." Since then, he had had to borrow money and pawn her jewelry to pay debts, but he did it, he explained, "for the good of the family." Chapman asked the court to dismiss the case.

The judge ruled against Chapman, awarding Domínguez a divorce as well as the return of those items of her property that had yet to be sold. The property already purchased by others could not be recovered, the judge ruled: "The court has no right to order them [the purchasers] to return it." Presumably, she filed a separate suit to recover that property, as the law forbade a husband from selling a wife's separate property without her written permission, but the records are silent on any such litigation. Alternatively, perhaps she never regained those assets, as the legal framework in California was, by and large, still an imperfect system.[67]

Like María Antonia Domínguez and the four other Spanish-speaking women who claimed separate property, Angelica Baltz and twelve additional Euro-American women fought in court to retain their holdings. In 1866, Baltz filed a complaint, accusing her husband of desertion and neglect. A widow at the time she had married him, she owned a house and three city lots. She asked for a divorce, her property, and $500 in alimony.

Unlike Chapman, Baltz's spouse did not appear before the court to contest the charges, and following an investigation by a court-appointed referee, the judge granted her requests. How, or if, she managed to collect the alimony, given that her husband had deserted her, cannot be determined from the records. Her success, however, seems to have been facilitated by his failure to appear.[68]

Another group of women dropped their divorce petitions. Californio-Mexican women suspended eighteen of sixty-nine divorce petitions (26 percent), while Euro-American women did so less frequently, in only twenty-five of 213 instances (12 percent). The available evidence suggests that women withdrew their suits because they either reconciled with their spouses or decided to pursue a legal separation instead of divorce. Californio-Mexican women exhibited a higher tendency to dismiss suits than did Euro-American women: seven of eighteen (39 percent) reconciled, six separated, and five gave no reason for the dismissal. Euro-American women reconciled in seven of twenty-five instances (28 percent) and separated in four (16 percent). In the remaining fourteen cases, no reason for the dismissal appears in the record. Those who dropped their suits in favor of reconciliation appear to have used divorce as a threat, just as some California-Mexican women used criminal complaints in the pre-conquest era as a way to apply legal and social pressure to force their husbands to end bad behavior. This suggests why Spanish-speaking women were more likely to use the threat of divorce to gain leverage in the household than Euro-American women, who more often went through with the divorce. No doubt, cultural differences and social pressure concerning marriage and divorce played a key role in women's decisions to divorce.

Sometimes reconciliation failed. This was the case with Rosario Dias, who went to court four times in a ten-year span, once filing criminal charges against her spouse and, on three occasions, seeking a divorce. She first appeared before the justice of the peace in 1850, complaining about her husband's abuse and threats to kill her. "He has also used various vulgar and indecent epithets towards [me]," she stated, "such as calling [me] a whore and a street walker and has threatened to break [my] head with a bottles and sticks. . . . [I] do not feel safe." After weighing the evidence, the justice convicted Felipe Rheim of an assault and fined him $10.

This did little to curtail his abusive behavior, as it continued for seven years, culminating in her decision to take more drastic measures. In 1857, she appeared again in the tribunal, this time in the district court, where she requested a divorce. However, she withdrew her petition almost immediately. Two months later, her husband's drunkenness and physical violence had resumed, and she was back in court. "His treatment [of me] has been so bad," she complained, "that it caused me to produce an abortion, endangering my life." She requested an equal share of the community property as well as alimony, custody of the three children, support for them, and an injunction preventing her husband from selling any property during the course of the trial. The judge awarded her child custody and ordered her husband to pay court costs and support for her and her children during the trial. Apparently lacking adequate information about the community property, the judge postponed the decision on that as well as on long-term support for her. Those decisions were never made because she dismissed the case a second time. No doubt, her husband or relatives had persuaded her to reconcile for the sake of the family and in keeping with cultural and moral dictates. Or, perhaps, her own internal conflicts with divorce eventually led her to withdraw her request. Three years later, in 1860, Dias again returned to court with similar complaints of abuse and drinking, but this time she carried through. When her husband failed to appear in court to answer the charges, the judge ruled in her favor, awarding her court costs, custody, and her share of the community property, though she received no long-term support.[69]

Unlike Californio-Mexican women, of the seven Euro-American women who reconciled with their husbands, six seem to have remained married. Among them was Ester Caroline Shugg, who had gone to court in 1856, complaining of a cold, neglectful, and "beastly intoxicated" husband, who had refused to care for her while she was ill. When her family arrived to look after her, the husband told them to leave and threatened to shoot her sister. Shugg asked for a divorce, alimony, her share of community property, custody of the children and child support, payment of litigation costs by her husband, and an injunction restraining him from disposing of their joint property during the trial. She did not request any long-term support. Following an investigation, the judge, with little explanation, awarded her a divorce but, before he finalized it, she and her spouse asked the judge to dismiss the case, explaining that they had agreed to remain together. Presumably, they had settled their differences and, unlike Rosario Dias, there is no evidence that a further divorce suit was ever filed in the Los Angeles court, though, of course, they might have turned to a court in another district or state.[70]

Unlike Shugg and the thirteen other Californio-Mexican and Euro-American women, some women dropped their suits because they believed a separation was the best, and perhaps most practical, solution to their problems. Among the eighteen Californio-Mexicans who dismissed their suits, six (33 percent) separated from their husbands, whereas among the Euro-American women, four of twenty-five (16 percent) did so. This suggests and supports the view that Spanish-speaking women were less inclined to follow through with divorce than their Euro-American counterparts. Though we have no first hand accounts (such as diaries or memoirs) that might provide explanations, it is likely that religious and cultural teachings as well as family and social pressures against severing the bonds of matrimony played a role in couples' decisions to reunite.

Though several women chose to separate legally, others decided simply to live apart from their spouses. Regardless of which approach they adopted, they forfeited their right to remarry, and their spouses continued to control the community property. One woman who brought charges and then dropped them in favor of separation was María Merced Williams (fig. 4.2). After she dropped her suit, she went to live with her grown children.

In 1877, after thirteen years of a stormy marriage to her second husband, José Clemente Carrillo, Williams filed for divorce. She charged him with adultery (with prostitutes at a local brothel who had a contagious disease, which made it "dangerous and unsafe for her to cohabit with him"), mismanaging her property, and mental cruelty. In her complaint, Williams also alleged that he had tried to force himself on her daughter from her first marriage, Cornelia Rains, "in [our] own household." She continued with her complaints, saying that one night, while they attended the theatre, Carrillo acted in such a "rude . . . and outrageous manner so as to stop the acting on the stage and to cause the police to . . . remove him from the theatre." That incident, as well as his compulsive gambling and theft of personal items—given to her by her father, Isaac Williams—which he sold for cash, had driven her to leave her home, taking the children with her. She informed the court of Carrillo's repeated threats: "After I have spent your last dollar," he allegedly told her, "then you can go." Three years ago, "[I] was worth more than $20,000," she stated, but now little remained, as he had squandered the money as a result of his many vices."[71]

Williams's complaints also detailed allegations of Carrillo's mismanagement of property. Soon after they married in 1863, Carrillo took

Figure 4.2
Merced Williams (right), Margarita Bandini (center), and Francisca Williams (left), the daughters of Isaac Williams and Juan Bandini, ca. 1860s–1870s. Merced endured stormy marriages with two husbands, John Rains and José C. Carrillo. She attempted to divorce Carrillo but apparently settled for a permanent separation. (Courtesy of the Seaver Center for Western History Research, Los Angeles County Museum of Natural History)

control of Rancho Cucamonga, which Williams owned, having inherited a part of it from her father and another part from her first husband. Carrillo mortgaged a vineyard and winery to secure a $5,000 loan. When he failed to repay the loan, he was forced to sell those assets. Several years later, he borrowed money again. This time he took out a note for $1,244 against property his wife held in San Diego County—Warner's Rancho, or Valle de San José, which Williams had inherited from her first husband, who had used her financial resources to purchase it in the first place. In due time, the couple failed to make payments, and they lost this rancho as well.[72] At the same time, creditors compelled Williams to pay off a $16,000 mortgage on Rancho Cucamonga, which had been negotiated several years earlier. The couple managed to retain that land for a few years, but by the end of the decade, Carrillo's mismanagement of the couples' financial assets caught up with them. In 1870, the creditors foreclosed, forcing the sale of the rancho to pay not only the mortgage but also back taxes and court costs totaling nearly $50,000. Williams and Carrillo had no option but to move to Los Angeles where, they hoped, the advantages of an urban settlement would allow them to make ends meets.[73]

Joseph Bridger, a friend of the family, witnessed Carrillo's financial disaster. He testified at the divorce proceedings that Williams was, indeed, "in poor circumstances."[74] María Merced concluded the suit by asking the court for a divorce and for custody of the children. The court's decision in the matter was never rendered, however. One week after filing for divorce, María Merced returned and without explanation, she dismissed the suit against Carrillo. Though it is unknown why she retracted her charges—cultural or social pressure or threats from Carrillo or something else—it is known that they lived apart until his death sometime in the 1880s. Apparently, as the gap in the record suggests, María Merced preferred to handle matters in her own way.[75]

Of the two options, formal or informal separations, the former proved to be more favorable to women, as it provided them the opportunity to ask for and receive support, custody of any children, and property. For instance, María de los Angeles Soberanos, who dropped a divorce suit in favor of a legal separation in 1857, obtained $15 in monthly support, $200 for court costs, the sale at public auction of 150 acres of community property, and the equal division of those proceeds with her husband, Gregorio Fraijo. She did not, however, get all the community property. In 1856, Fraijo transferred titles of some properties to his mistress, María Francisca Méndez, whom he had falsely identified as his "wife" for at least three years before the divorce suit.[76] A year earlier, in 1855, Fraijo's assets had been diminished, as he had declared bankruptcy to clear himself of a number of loans he owed to merchants in town. Whether Soberanos asked the court for a share of the property Fraijo had given to Méndez remains unknown.[77]

In dealing with unbearable husbands and miserable marriages, another group of women took an alternative route, one that was familiar to Spanish-speaking women. Rather than seek a divorce or separation, they opted to bring criminal charges against their husbands, as some women had done in the Mexican era. The records indicate that in the three decades after the American conquest, at least thirteen women (or a family member or friend) filed a criminal complaint with the justice of the peace or county court judge against an abusive head of household. (Most of those complaints were issued in the 1850s.) The small number of women who charged spouses with crimes reflects the social and cultural practices that instructed women with abusive spouses to "suffer patiently" and remain in the household for the good of the family and the larger community. No doubt, other women experienced similar circumstances in their households, but they chose to avoid the courts. Changes in the legal system—the shift from Spanish civil to American common law, the increasing and overwhelming presence of non-Spanish speaking Euro-American lawyers and judges, and a move away from community values—likely also influenced women in their decision not to seek redress before the criminal courts. Despite the obstacles of operating within a new legal and cultural environment, women who went to court with complaints of physical and sexual abuse—at least five—were numerous enough to reveal that patterns of domestic conflict had continued into the American era, and that some women challenged their spouses in order to carve out a better future for themselves and any children.

Typical was the experience of María J. Olivera who in the 1850s filed a complaint against her husband, Martín Duarte, accusing him of beating her "for no cause." On the day of the abuse, she told the judge, he had arrived home visibly drunk, tied her to an oak tree, and "whipped her with a . . . reata." She warned her husband that she would complain to the justice of the peace about his behavior. "[Y]ou can do nothing if you go to him," he told her, "as I have all of the authority in my favor . . . [and] you are a woman and the justice will not believe you." Despite his threats, she fled the household and went to the justice, explaining that the beating was not an isolated incident. On several occasions, he had threatened to "kill her" and once, she said, he "hunted for me with [a] pistol [in order] to shoot me and instructed his friends to kill me wherever they find me. . . . I now am afraid that he will kill me and do not wish to stay with him."

The authorities arrested her spouse and initiated proceedings for a trial by jury. María Olivera was the first to testify, recounting the events told earlier to the justice. Duarte contested her charges, insisting that she had fled the household with no provocation. "I came [to Los Angeles] and found her hidden away. I did not beat her then, why should I now[?]"

he asked. She is cohabiting with another man, he declared, "a better man than I, according to her." When he found and confronted her, she reportedly "begged him to kill her." "I told her 'no,'" he stated. The jury found Duarte guilty, and the judge fined him $10 and set him free. The records do not indicate whether María subsequently sought a divorce and freedom from her spouse's abusive behavior, but this court case reveals her resolute determination to end her spouse's abuse.[78]

For those women declared "at fault" in a divorce case, the future was particularly bleak since they seldom received alimony, support, or property. Under Spanish and Mexican civil law, a wife found guilty of infidelity could lose custody of children over the age of three, forfeit alimony, and lose her share of community property. A guilty husband could also be severely penalized, financially and personally: Loss of custody of the children, forfeiture of his share of the community property, and liability for supporting his family and court costs. An innocent wife, forced to separate from her husband because of his adulterous relations, ordinarily received alimony, child custody and support, her dowry, and her share of community property. American common law made similar distinctions between innocent and guilty spouses in awarding support. An innocent wife, for instance, was eligible for alimony, but an adulterous one forfeited her right to the dower (a woman's life interest in a third of her husband's real estate if she survived him).[79] Although American common law prescribed various actions for "innocent" and "guilty" spouses, the broad discretionary authority given to judges meant that they had the final word in determining the economic and personal future of a husband or wife found at fault in the divorce case.

In the three decades following the conquest, Californio-Mexican and Euro-American women were found guilty in almost all of the divorce suits initiated by men. Ten Californio-Mexican and 104 Euro-American men were the plaintiffs in 114 of the 396 divorce cases filed in Los Angeles. All Californio-Mexican men successfully charged their wives with adultery, desertion, or mental cruelty, while eighty (about 77 percent) of the Euro-American men also prevailed.[80] The most frequent charge, adultery, required substantial proof: Name of the person with whom the spouse had committed adultery as well as the location and time of the affair.[81] Further, plaintiffs had to prove that they had not cohabited with their spouses after learning of the extramarital affair. In the eighty four instances in which women were found guilty of adultery, desertion, or mental suffering, all were denied alimony, seven had to pay court costs, twenty-five were denied child custody, and thirteen lost their share of community property.[82]

Gumecinda Cruz was among the women penalized for adultery. In 1870, her husband, Andrés Elias, filed for divorce, charging her with more than five years of adultery with Ignacio Reyes, a boarder who lived with them. Because of her behavior, Elias had left the home in 1865. His wife and Reyes continued to live there and had two children of their own. Why Elias waited five years before seeking a divorce is unknown, but, in doing so, he asked for custody of his son and all of the marital property, including the house in which she and Reyes resided. Cruz denied Elias's charges and rejected his requests. "Elias has abandoned me for five years," she told the judge, and "is habitually drunk. . . . I am in indigent circumstances and . . . am wholly dependent upon my own labor to support myself and my son." She requested that the court grant her the divorce, custody of the child, and her share of the community property.

The judge appointed a referee to identify witnesses who could testify in the case. Most of those testifying cast doubts on Cruz's story and supported Elias's charges. Even her stepfather, a local barber, admitted the shame and sense of family dishonor he felt on hearing rumors about his step-daughter's reputation, and he said he had reprimanded her for cohabiting with Reyes. In contrast, he did not express disdain towards Elias, who had failed to support Cruz and the children during his five-year absence. The double sexual standard for men and women no doubt influenced his perception of Cruz as a disgraced and shameful woman, regardless of his kinship to her. Testifying on behalf of Cruz was Ignacio Reyes who claimed that she had supported herself "from her honest labor. . . . [For] a number of years, I have paid her to wash, iron, and cook for me while I lived in her house . . . and while I have been gone to Sonora, she has taken care of my two daughters." Reyes's testimony did little to convince the judge that Cruz had been living a moral life. The judge ruled that "adultery is determined to be a 'fact'" and awarded Elias the house in which Cruz was living, custody of their son, and all of the community property.[83]

The court made little distinction along ethnic lines when it found women guilty of adultery in divorce actions. Euro-American women fared just as poorly as their Spanish-speaking counterparts did. If a woman failed to appear and respond to charges, she was invariably declared in default. One such woman was Swena Swigart, who was sued for divorce by her spouse, Thomas Swigart, in 1870. He accused her of adultery and intemperance. "I have provided for her all the comforts of life . . . yet she is a habitually intemperate woman, so frequently intoxicated [that] she is wholly unfit and unreliable in all of the duties of a wife toward a husband." Her worst offense, however, occurred "after several occasions of casual separations, [when] she left me to live with [another man]." His demands: a divorce, return of his separate property, and all of the community property. When Swena Swigart failed to respond within a month, the court found her in default and granted the husband's requests.[84]

The loss of a divorce suit could mean not only the loss of alimony, community property, and child custody, but also possibly being forced to reunite with an intolerable or abusive spouse. Four Californio-Mexican and eight Euro-American women failed to prove they had legal grounds for divorce, and they were forced to return to their spouses. A wife's failure to return to a spouse could result in charges of desertion, as the law obligated women to live at the husband's choice of residence, unless the place he chose was unfit.[85] Such was the experience of María Antonia Gastelum de Domínguez who, in 1868, brought charges of desertion and neglect against her spouse, Noah Felch. She also accused him of mismanaging her personal estate—a rancho, which she had inherited from her first husband. Felch had sold it without her consent for $5,000 to Prudent Beaudry, who still owed $2,000 on the property. She asked the judge to place the note under the court's control so that Beaudry's final payments would go to her after the divorce was finalized. She also informed the court that she and Felch owned about eighteen acres of community property, and she asked for an injunction preventing its sale, and the appointment of a trustee to manage the property.

Felch denied her charges of abandonment, neglect, and mismanagement, and he asked the judge to dismiss the petition. The court took the case under advisement, appointing a referee to look into the matter. The referee affirmed that the property had been sold to Beaudry, although it "rightfully belonged to [Gastelum de Domínguez] and not [Felch] and should be restored to her." The referee also reported that three years before the sale, Felch had left the state and failed to support his wife during his absence. Gastelum affirmed the report, while, at the same time, softening its effect: "he hasn't supported me, rather, . . . I have had ample means for support. While he was gone to the East, . . . [I] asked no support from him. On his return," she continued," he told me he could not support me because he was impoverished. . . . For eight months, I supported him." Several witnesses, including an adult son from a previous marriage, confirmed that she was the main source of support for the family. Prudent Beaudry also came forward, admitting he had carried out the transaction with Felch, even though he knew that Felch was dishonest.

Despite the testimony supporting Gastelum's contention, the judge ruled against her, denying a divorce and ordering her to pay her husband's court costs in addition to her own. "I see no proof to justify divorce," declared the judge, nor any "reasons to justify the appointment of a trustee of her separate property." Felch's sale of her property, according to the court, might be questionable, but it was legal. Though California law, as noted earlier, held that a husband had to have his wife's written permission to sell her personal property, the judge, in this instance, interpreted the law as giving the husband absolute control over his spouse's property, with no interference from the wife. The judge acknowledged the existence of lingering questions about the legitimacy of the sale of her property, but he ruled that the case at hand dealt with the divorce and not the note. No evidence exists that Gastelum made a second attempt to divorce, so it seems that despite the disappointing outcome, she arrived at some kind of an accord or reconciliation with her husband.[86]

A European woman seeking a divorce in 1863 suffered a similar disappointment. Charlotte Grabs, an immigrant from Germany who had settled in San Francisco in 1850 and then moved to Los Angeles in 1860, charged her spouse of thirteen years with intemperance, neglect, and failure to provide for her and their eleven-year-old daughter. "I have maintained the child by my own labor," she stated. She requested a divorce and nothing more. The judge issued a summons to her husband, who failed to respond. Rather then awarding Charlotte the customary divorce by default, the judge found against her for two reasons. First, he held that her husband's drinking had not been proven to be a habit, as was required in the law. Secondly, he ruled that "neglect as grounds for divorce" required the "willful neglect on the part of the husband to provide for his wife the common necessities of life, having the ability to do so, for the period of three years." Presumably, in the court's view, there was lack of sufficient evidence proving he was habitually drunk and neglectful. The judge also revealed his skepticism about her actions when he asked: "Why [did you not seek] a divorce in San Francisco three years ago when he was drinking then?" Her request for a divorce was denied.[87]

Despite the possibilities that divorce offered for personal and economic independence, the reality was more often disappointment for the woman, which underscores the personal risks involved in pursuing such a goal. As noted earlier, most women, regardless of ethnicity, age, or regional origins, received little in the way of personal or community property or alimony following a divorce. Many found themselves forced to find a means to support themselves and their children. Women might turn to family and community networks for support. However, this was difficult for those in the Californio-Mexican community, which marked divorced people as disgraced individuals, whose pursuit of "individualistic" goals threatened the traditional family and undermined Catholic precepts. Other women relied on extended family networks—parents, aunts and uncles, brothers and sisters, and sometimes their own grown children—for assistance in making ends meet. Still other women sought the assistance of private and public institutions or took jobs as domestics, which enabled them and their children to survive, if not prosper, in a rapidly changing environment. Though the records are incomplete, the evidence indicates that some women opted to remarry in the hope that their new partners would provide the home environment they had lacked with their previous husbands.

A Spanish-speaking woman who turned to her parents and friends for help, and who later remarried, was Francisca Sepúlveda. Because of his incessant drinking, her husband José Antonio Carrillo, thirty years her senior, had neglected to provide for her during their seven years of marriage. She informed the court that even before the divorce, she had relied on the financial assistance of her parents, José Andrés Sepúlveda and María Francisca Avila. Finally, in 1854, shortly before the divorce, she left Carrillo and went to live with her parents. They apparently respected her decision to leave Carrillo, as they provided her with a secure home environment for more than fifteen years. During that time, she also received emotional support from family friends to whom she wrote, complaining about Carrillo's continued intrusions into her life and his prolonged illness, likely brought about by alcoholism (in the court proceedings, he testified he had been drinking since the age of eighteen). In

1858, her *comadre* (a fictive-kin relationship forged through sacramental sponsorship) and friend, Guadalupe Villareal, wrote a letter to Francisca, imploring her to be patient: "God will reward those who suffer."[88] Carrillo died in 1862, and Francisca remained with her parents until she married James Thompson in 1869.[89]

Like Sepúlveda, María Merced Williams sought psychological comfort and financial support from close friends and family members, particularly from a grown daughter, Cornelia Rains, and her husband, D.J. Foley. This couple not only provided housing, meals, and other basic necessities for María but also for seven of Cornelia's unmarried siblings—three from Williams's first marriage to John Rains and four from her second to José Clemente Carrillo. Williams lived with the Foleys for about thirty years, from 1877, the year she filed for divorce from Carrillo, until her death in 1908.[90]

Williams and Sepúlveda were fortunate to have had family members who supported her decision to divorce. Other women, including women who had migrated from the Midwest, eastern United States, or northern Mexico, had no close relatives in Los Angeles, and so, having divorced, they were forced to turn to community members. As abandoned and neglected women, they survived on the "charity of friends." Charlotte Parker, for example, informed the judge in 1873 that she was "poor, nearly blind, and too ill to earn a livelihood," a condition that compelled her to depend on friends during and after her marriage.[91] Such women also supported themselves by becoming seamstresses, washerwomen, or housekeepers.[92] Those who had some formal education might pursue professional work, though that avenue was rarely open to Spanish-speaking women. Ella Finley, a schoolteacher from the Midwest who divorced in 1877, supported her household on her teacher's salary.[93] Those who lacked professional skills could rely on traditional forms of subsistence, such as cultivating small agricultural plots. Cesaría Valenzuela, for example, who divorced in 1872, supported herself "with the little property left . . . by [her] parents," which included a three-acre vineyard that had been in the family for more than thirty years.[94]

Other women sought the assistance of private and public institutions. Sarah Barter, for instance, divorced in 1872, and she was awarded a small sum for the support of her two children. She turned to the Sisters of Charity, a Roman Catholic order that had founded the Institución Caritativa, a private school and orphanage, in 1856.[95] Julia Benavides, who divorced in 1871 and won child custody but no support, had to put her three children into the Protestant Orphan Asylum because her wages, earned as a dressmaker, were insufficient to support them. The orphanage requested that she pay only as much as she could afford, enabling her to assure her children adequate, if not the best, living conditions.[96]

When they divorced, women not only risked facing shrinking economic resources but also the possibility of retaliation by former spouses. This was especially true in the case of couples that parted ways under strained circumstances. Sometimes reprisal came in the form of verbal threats or physical harm; other times, it involved destruction of property at the hands of a vengeful former spouse. María G. Ferris was one divorcée who felt the wrath of an ex-husband. Her marital troubles began only one month after her marriage to Alfred Ferris in 1876. Following several failed attempts at a reconciliation, she filed for divorce, requesting the division of the community property, which included a home she and her spouse had built. When summoned to court, Alfred Ferris failed to appear, and the judge declared him in "default." María Ferris won the suit and gained control of the house, located on Macy and Center streets, as well as two empty lots in Los Angeles. The house, which she had paid $250 to build, burned down the day the court finalized the divorce. María Ferris knew this was no twist of fate, and she promptly filed a criminal complaint against her ex-husband, charging him with arson.

During the court trial, María Ferris testified that Alfred had "made some threats . . . that if the [district] court should decide against him, . . . he would burn [the house] down." Her ex-spouse denied the charges: "I saw the fire on my way home [from a local bar]" and tried vainly to help before leaving the scene and retiring for the night. He also challenged her ownership claim, declaring that the house had belonged to him long before the divorce. His ex-wife got title only after he "defaulted" and lost the divorce suit, he stated. Alfred damaged his case by attempting to leave town early the next morning. Apprehended, he explained that he had gotten a job with a railroad company in Arizona and was on his way there. Though several witnesses corroborated his claim to have been at a bar when the fire broke out, the jury found his testimony implausible, and it returned a verdict of guilty. The judge sentenced Alfred to three years in state prison, thereby giving María peace of mind and security—at least for the time being.[97]

As most divorced women learned, the opportunities for financial and personal freedom promised by divorce gave way to grim reality: Little or no alimony, property, or child support; the necessity of having to work at menial jobs or turning to others for charity; and suffering risks to their personal safety. Regardless of ethnicity, few couples had community property worth dividing. When property existed, many husbands had already squandered or hidden it. Other husbands fled the community, removing themselves from the jurisdiction of the local district court. Not until the twentieth century would divorced women benefit significantly as a result of better-crafted laws and more sensitive judges, which gave them greater access to alimony, community property, and child custody and support.[98] Despite the contrast between the promise and reality of divorce, divorcées adapted to their circumstances, which enabled them and their children to survive, if not prosper, in a rapidly changing world.

In their pursuit of divorce—an uncommon solution to marital problems—the courage of this small yet significant group of Californio-Mexican women reveals that they not only engaged a foreign legal, political, and social system, using it strategically, but they also challenged long-held beliefs and practices in a way that would fundamentally alter cultural mores. Though atypical, the women who sought divorces were agents of cultural change. They shaped norms pertaining to the family, marriage, and sexuality, and challenged the precepts of the Catholic Church. In divorcing their spouses and in remarrying or remaining single, they introduced ideas and set in motion practices relating to women's equal role in marriage and the family and their entitlement to marital happiness and fulfillment—notions that would lay the groundwork for and influence future *mexicanas* as they forged a better life for themselves and their families.

Chapter 5

Loss of Property and Economic Independence

The right to divorce set in motion gender and cultural transformations that increased women's power in the family. However, divorce often left women financially destitute and forced to work at menial jobs to support themselves and their children. Their prospects were even grimmer because of the land policies that ultimately dispossessed most Californio-Mexican and native landowners—women and men, the elite, the middle strata, and the poor. Articles 8 and 9 of the Treaty of Guadalupe Hidalgo (1848) guaranteed the property rights of Mexicans who remained in the newly conquered territories would be "inviolably respected." "The present owners, the heirs of these, and all Mexicans who may hereafter acquire . . . property by contract, shall enjoy . . . guarantees equally ample as . . . citizens of the United States . . . and . . . shall be protected in the free enjoyment of their liberty and property, and secured in the free exercise of their religion without restriction."[1] However, by the 1880s, the most of the original residents of the region were landless.

For the owners of ranchos, the principal culprit was federal legislation that violated the spirit of the treaty by creating an extraordinarily time-consuming, and hence costly, process for confirming land titles. By the 1880s, nearly half of the rancho owners had sold or lost significant portions or all of their holdings. Apart from the insurmountable debts incurred as a result of the court delays, floods and droughts in the late 1850s and early 1860s (which decimated crops and cattle herds), a generally weaker cattle market (created by the introduction of stronger and better grades of stock from the Midwest), and high-interest loans taken to cover these loses and to pay for taxes (an onerous innovation in the American era) led many to bankruptcy.[2]

For owners of property within the limits of pueblo of Los Angeles, the problem was not federal legislation but rather increased land values and the new property taxes. Within the first decade, Spanish-speaking angeleños found themselves overrun by Euro-Americans who acquired much of the most valuable city real estate. During the 1860s and 1870s, most of the original residents of Los Angeles sold, transferred, or in other ways lost their property. They were reduced to living in an ethnically segregated and economically marginalized barrio, where they were joined by recently arriving and equally impoverished immigrants from Mexico. The Native Americans who had been residing in rancherías on the outskirts of town had been forced off their lands and had fled to other parts of the region and state.

On March 3, 1851, the U.S. Congress approved a bill, introduced by Senator William M. Gwin, subsequently signed by the president, "to ascertain and settle private land claims." Gwin's Act to Ascertain Land Claims in California designated distinct processes for rancho and town property. For ranchos, it called for the appointment of three commissioners, who, with the help of a secretary fluent in Spanish and English, were responsible for determining the validity of land titles dating to the Spanish and Mexican eras. The act required claimants to "present . . . to the . . . commissioners . . . documentary evidence and testimony of witnesses . . . in support of [their] claims."[3] In practice, this meant that rancho holders—Californios and natives, individuals and corporations—had to hire lawyers (all of whom, with one exception, were Euro-Americans) to prove the legality of their land titles under Spanish and Mexican law and, more specifically, under the *Recopilación de las leyes de las indias* as well as the 1824 and 1828 Mexican colonization laws.

Because those bodies of law had had differing requirements for acquiring and holding property, various complications arose around the grants that had been made in the Spanish and Mexican periods. All claimants had to produce documents or oral testimony concerning the authority under which they had received their land grant, the kind of grant received, and when they received it. Evidence of continuous residence and property improvements had to be supplied, along with proof that the owner had been a Mexican citizen. Moreover, the law required property holders to show that they had received the grant prior to July 7, 1846, the day Commodore John D. Sloat took formal possession of California and the U.S. government declared the end of Mexican sovereignty.[4]

The 1851 Land Act also held that all titles, whether rejected or confirmed by the commission, could be appealed within sixty days to the U.S. District Court by either the claimant or the U.S. District Attorney, each of whom would then have the option of appealing that court's ruling to the U.S. Supreme Court. Once a claim was settled, the U.S. Surveyor General's office in California would survey the land. The claimant would then submit the survey to the General Land Office in Washington, D.C., which, in turn, would issue a patent to the owner. Only with the receipt of the patent did an owner have legal title to the property.

The process was burdensome, but, in 1852, when Congress ordered that all the commission's rulings be appealed automatically to the district court, the process became punitive. That requirement would create immense delays and hardships for the Californios. Finally, in 1860, Congress eased the situation somewhat and allowed a claimant to order the survey while title confirmation was being sought in the courts, reducing the number of years it took to obtain a patent. However, because the change came so late and the appeal was still required, it took an average of seventeen years for claimants to obtain a patent to their rancho property.[5]

Ironically, although most claims on ranchos were upheld (604 of the more than 800 presented), nearly half (46 percent) of the original owners in the Los Angeles area went bankrupt in the process of defending those claims. That most titles were confirmed reflects not only the leniency of the land commission but also the diligence with which claimants sought out *expedientes* (files of grant papers). These usually contained the petitions that had been made to local officials and governors in the Spanish and Mexican periods and the documents verifying the resolution of those petitions, as well as documentation of any subsequent sales, transfers, or disputes involving the property. When only a few or no documents were available, witnesses, including former Mexican governors, prefects, alcaldes, and private citizens—men and women both—testified on behalf of claimants.[6] Unsuccessful claimants lost their property.

Native Californians living on rancherías, land that had never been formally granted by the Spanish or Mexican governors, also lost their property. Those lands reverted to the public domain and were opened to settlement and acquisition under preemption or homestead legislation. Preemption laws, enacted by Congress in 1841 and extended to California in 1853, recognized the claims of heads of families, widows, or single individuals to 160 acres of public land, and it allowed them to buy the property at a minimum price of $1.25 an acre. These settlers or squatters had thirty days from the time they occupied a tract to file a claim with the federal land office. The enactment of the 1862 Homestead Act by the U.S. Congress attracted more settlers by allowing squatters on the public domain to acquire a patent to 160 acres so long as they could prove five years of residence on the property. Unfortunately, homestead and pre-emption legislation encouraged squatters to trespass on rancho lands and to take possession of lands on which Native Californians as well as Mexican Californios were residing. Anticipating that the titles acquired in the Spanish and Mexican periods would eventually be denied and that they could then file a preemption or homestead claim to the property, newcomers illegally moved onto ranchos, which provoked conflicts with the owners. Those tensions, in turn, exacerbated racial conflict and further complicated (and, hence, made even more costly) the Mexicans' efforts to confirm their titles.[7]

Confirmation of titles to ranches came slowly for both Spanish-speaking and native peoples, but women, especially married women, encountered additional burdens created by the limitations placed on their rights to manage and control their property. An 1850 California statute gave married women an equal interest in marital or common property, but a husband had the authority to manage his wife's property as if it were his own.[8] Only when the wife had the juridical status of "sole trader," which she acquired by registering an official declaration of her "intent to conduct business in her own name" with the county recorder, could she carry out transactions alone.[9]

The 1850 law also enabled a wife to retain separate property, though her husband (or other legal agent) managed those assets and needed the woman's written and oral permission to sell or transfer her property. Moreover, when it came to separate or community property, a wife could challenge her husband if he grossly mismanaged her share or attempted to dispossess her of it. In such situations, she could ask the First District Court to appoint a trustee, or receiver, to take control of the property.[10] Widowed, divorced, and single adult women, in contrast to their married counterparts, faced fewer difficulties: They could engage in legal transactions on their own, though they (like most other claimants, including Californio men and Native American men and women) often had Euro-American lawyers representing them in the municipal, state, and federal courts.[11]

During the three decades following the American takeover, women and men of different ethnicities brought ninety-four cases before the board of land commissioners to establish title to ranchos in the former Mexican district of Los Angeles. Eighteen (19 percent) involved Californio women, three (3 percent) Native American women, forty-three (46 percent) Californio men, six (6 percent) Native American men, and twenty-four (26 percent) Euro-American men, seventeen of whom had purchased their holdings from original Californio or native grantees in the 1840s and early 1850s. Of the cases petitioned by Californio women, sixteen (89 percent) resulted in title confirmation and two (11 percent) in rejections, but of these, nine (50 percent) sold their ranchos or portions of them during and after the hearings. As for those cases involving Native American women, two of the three claims were successful, and in one of the two successful cases, the owner sold an interest in her rancho while the proceedings were underway. Among the men, twenty-two (92 percent) of the Euro-Americans who filed petitions obtained titles, whereas two (8 percent) did not. During the hearings, eight (33 percent) sold their ranchos. Most of the claims brought by Californios and Native Americans were also successful, though a greater number of cases involving Californio men ended in sales before the termination of the legal process. (Although these landowners did not have clear title to their property, they would transfer it to buyers who were confident that the title would be confirmed and the patent received.) Of the forty-three petitions initiated by Californios, thirty-seven (86 percent) led to title confirmation and six (14 percent) to rejections. At least eighteen of the Californios (49 percent) sold their property during the hearings. Most claims made by neófitos—five of six cases (83 percent)—received titles, and only one (17 percent) was rejected. Only one rancho, claimed by a group of native men, was sold during the proceedings.[12]

The high success rate of all ethnic groups and both genders stemmed largely from the land commission and U.S. District Court's commitment to rule leniently in reaching decisions. The courts ruled favorably even when boundaries remained unclear, title papers had been lost, and grants had been made only days prior to the July 7, 1846, deadline. In an 1852 land case, the board warned all claimants that rancho concessions made after that date were "without authority and cannot be the foundation of a valid claim."[13]

The land commissioners accorded both women and men equitable treatment. Vicenta Sepúlveda's 1852 petition for title to the four-sitio Rancho Sierra, for instance, aroused suspicion but was nonetheless approved. (One sitio is equivalent to a square league or about 4,440 acres.) The grant was dated June 15, 1846, less than a month before the July 7 deadline, and she had not taken possession until July 9, 1846. To resolve any doubts held by the commissioners, she called upon others to testify on her behalf, including a close friend and prominent citizen, Antonio Francisco Coronel. He stated that Sepúlveda, along with her now deceased husband, Tomás Yorba, had lived on the land for more than fifteen years and had erected "some small houses . . . and corrals and [introduced] a large stock of cattle." The commissioners, though noting that "juridical measurement and possession were . . . [completed] after the Americans had [taken] possession of the country," nonetheless concluded that she and her family had lived on the rancho for nearly twenty years before she took legal possession on July 9, 1846. That was enough for them to affirm her title in 1855 and then to appeal the case, as now required, to the district court, which upheld their decision the following year. It took more than ten additional years for the surveyor general to complete the survey and the land office to issue a patent.[14]

Like Sepúlveda, María Rita Valdez won the commission's approval to retain her one-sitio Rancho Rodeo de las Aguas, even though she had failed to produce papers demonstrating that she had received a grant from the Mexican governor. In 1852, she testified that during hostilities with U.S. troops in 1846, she had lost the papers: "After I received the [title in 1838, I] always kept it stored in a . . . trunk. . . . At the time of the political disturbances . . . with the Americans coming to this city . . . my family and I fled our home . . . [and,] on our return, we realized our house had been pillaged and the trunk rifled by unknown persons, [perhaps] Californians, Indians, or Americans. . . . [S]ince then I have not been able to find [the papers]." Abel Stearns, a former Mexican alcalde, testified that Valdez's documents and the original copies in the ayuntamiento's archives had been lost during the war. When "Commodore [Robert F.] Stockton came to this place, with his forces, about the 10th of June in 1844," Stearns recounted, "many families left town . . . and went to various places to be out of the way." "Several houses," he continued, "which had been left by their previous occupants, were broken open." Stearns also told the commissioners that some of the council's records were later recovered, but a substantial portion of those dating to 1838—

the year in which Valdez claimed to have received her grant—were still missing, making it impossible for her to cite public records in support of her claim. The commissioners requested the surveyor general—the keeper of the Mexican archives in the early American period—to search for the records, but he also failed to find them.

Despite the lack of written proof, the board was sufficiently swayed by the testimony of Valdez and Stearns to invite Valdez to bring in others who could support her claim. Among them was José Antonio Ezequiel Carrillo, another former alcalde, who testified that Valdez had occupied the land since 1828. In his capacity as local magistrate, he had gone personally to the property and "established the boundaries by order of the governor." The board then questioned former Mexican Governor Juan B. Alvarado, asking him if he recalled granting her the property. His answer—"I have no recollection"—did not help her claim, but José Castro, the former prefect (the highest-ranking local official directly responsible to the governor), undid the harm by testifying that he had helped her get the grant. "I went and saw the governor," Castro told the commissioners, "and asked his favorable attention . . . and the governor [Alvarado] issued the title . . . and gave it to me in my own hand."[15]

The witnesses convinced the commission, which ruled in 1854, that, "From that evidence [oral testimony], we think the grant was for the rancho claimed and that it was genuine. . . . The boundaries are well defined, and we think this a valid . . . claim." Though the commission took only two years to rule, the district court did not render its decision until 1857. Bureaucratic and other delays resulted in it taking another fourteen years to survey the land and issue a patent, which was finally done in 1871.[16]

Like Valdez, María Ygnacia Verdugo, the widow of Juan Féliz, also succeeded despite lacking proof that California's *diputación*, or assembly, had approved the governor's grant (as required by the Mexican colonization laws of 1824 and 1828). Verdugo's case was further complicated because the boundaries for the claimed land were overly vague. Boundary problems plagued many claimants, both men and women. Perhaps because there was no official surveyor's office in Alta California, the authorities in both the Spanish and Mexican periods did not define boundaries with the precision used in the United States. In 1852, when Verdugo filed for confirmation of her title to Rancho Los Féliz, she supplied evidence that, in 1843, Mexican Governor Manuel Micheltorena had granted 1.5

sitios to her and her son (as heirs of Juan Féliz). However, she could not demonstrate that the diputación had approved that action. She did produce a copy of proceedings of an 1841 civil court case, in which her son, José Antonio Féliz, accused Ramón Orduño of coming to the rancho and causing him "bodily harm." That evidence, though indirect, was enough to convince the commissioners, though they noted the insufficiencies of the claim. "There is no proof that any approval was ever made by the Departmental Assembly." Moreover, "the party endangers [her] case by neglecting to file a traced copy of the [e]spediente [sic], which generally contains a map, and is of essential aid in ascertaining the boundaries of the land claimed." Nevertheless, they ruled, "the proof in this case shows substantial and ample [evidence] . . . of the grant and the record of judicial measurement sufficiently describes the tract granted so that its location may be ascertained [by the surveyor]." Three years later, in 1857, the district court upheld that decision, and in 1863, when the surveyor general completed the survey, the land office issued a patent for 6,647 acres, roughly 1.5 sitios.[17] Altogether, eleven years had passed since she filed her claim. Though shorter than the average time for most claimants, her wait was nonetheless long.[18]

The land commission and federal courts also treated men, regardless of ethnicity, in a fair and flexible fashion. However, like the women claimants, men endured delays. In 1852, when Andrés Duarte, claimant for Rancho Azusa, presented his evidence, he could demonstrate only that he had submitted a petition for 1.5 sitios to the alcalde in 1841, who in turn had forwarded it to the prefect. That official was responsible for forwarding it to Monterey, for action by the governor, and returning a copy of it—signed by the prefect and the alcalde—to Duarte. Apparently, the petition did not reach the governor since Duarte never received confirmation of the grant. Nonetheless, with the tacit approval of the alcalde, Duarte had occupied and developed the land, and he now sought to establish his ownership.

To bolster his claim, Duarte had Abel Stearns testify that the signatures of the alcalde and the prefect on the copy of the original petition, which Duarte produced as evidence of his grant, were genuine. Stearns also attested that Duarte had built a house and corrals and stocked the rancho with cattle. Such evidence was enough for the commissioners. Though acknowledging that Duarte had an "espediente [sic] showing [only] his application for the grant to the prefect," they concluded that "the proof [provided by Stearns] of occupancy and residence . . . shows a substantial compliance with the conditions of the grant." Their decision then went on appeal to the district court, which ruled that the "grant . . . has all the requirements . . . required by the Mexican law and the customs of the country . . . [and] seems perfect in all respects except" one: "the description of the land is uncertain" and must be clarified by the surveyor general before the land office can issue a patent. That problem was resolved when Francisco O'Campo, also a ranchero, provided a general, but satisfactory, description of the boundaries. After affirming the grant in 1855, the district court sent the case for review to the U.S. Supreme Court, which upheld the lower court's decision and authorized a survey. With the survey complete, Duarte filed for a patent and received title to 6,596 acres, nearly 1.5 sitios. He did not receive that title, however, until 1878, twenty-six years after he had first filed his claim.[19]

Neófitos, men and women, petitioned for grants that were much smaller than those of Californios, men and women, but they were just as successful, even when their claims lacked some of the proof required to establish their claims. In 1852, José Domingo, for instance, initially had difficulty because he lacked evidence that he had inherited the property from his father, Felipe, a former mission native at San Gabriel. Domingo explained that Pío Pico granted the property to his father in 1845, after the family had already been living there for years. Domingo produced his father's badly tattered expediente, containing proof of legal possession, and his 1848 will, signed by Felipe, two witnesses, and an Indian alcalde, whom the padres had appointed to oversee the natives. The will indicated that Felipe possessed a "parcel of sowing land for the benefit of my son," but it neither identified the son nor established José's relationship to Felipe. The commissioners expressed skepticism about the claim until Michael White, a former mayordomo at the mission (who was frequently called to testify before the commission) verified that José was Felipe's son and verified the family's long residence on the property. Before the commissioners approved title to the grant, however, they learned that Domingo was not the only heir. They ruled that under Mexican law, Felipe's widow, Pascuala, "was entitled to one-half of all the [marital] property." Though she had not filed a claim, the commissioners awarded titles to both Domingo and Pascuala in 1853. That decision then went to the district court, which upheld the commission's ruling. Eighteen years later, the surveyor general completed the survey, and the land office approved the patent in 1871.[20]

The commission also closely scrutinized and questioned claims made

Figure 5.1
Only a handful of native women, such as Felicita Josefa's unidentified
daughter, pictured here in an undated photograph taken at Misión San
Fernando, managed to acquire property in the Mexican era and retain it in
the American era. Most native men and women were landless and
impoverished. (Courtesy of the Seaver Center for Western History Research,
Los Angeles County Museum of Natural History)

by Euro-Americans. Though lenient, the commission investigated everyone, regardless of gender or ethnicity. For example, the commission denied the joint claim made by businessmen David W. Alexander and Francis Mellus on the grounds that they had failed to prove that the original owner of Rancho Tujunga, Pedro López, had received a grant and had occupied and developed the land. But when the case went on appeal before the district court, Alexander and Mellus this time asked López to provide written and oral testimony that he had indeed received the grant in 1841 and had improved the land within the required period. López's testimony was enough to convince the district court, which overruled the commission's decision. In 1874, twenty-two years after filing their claim, Alexander and Mellus obtained a patent to about 1.5 sitios, 6,661 acres.[21]

The federal courts, though flexible and fair in their decisions, nonetheless rejected claims that rested on grossly insufficient or false evidence. Of the twenty-one petitions filed by women (eighteen Californio women and three neófitas), the board initially rejected six (submitted by four Californio women and two neófitas), three of which (from two Californio women and one neófita) were approved on appeal and the other three rejected.[22]

María Merced Lugo's claim for Rancho San Pascual failed because she had not fulfilled the requirement to cultivate the land. Invariably, the commissioners ruled against claimants, women or men, who had not made the required land improvements or lived continuously on the property. Such lapses were held to be "fatal to the claim" unless petitioners could offer compelling reasons for why they had been unable to make the required property improvements.[23] In her 1852 petition, Lugo produced expedientes verifying that her deceased husband, José Pérez, had held the original land grant. However, she had no proof for her assertion that, with the exception of a brief period following her husband's death in 1842, she had lived continuously at the rancho. The commission denied her petition, citing evidence showing that she had abandoned the property and had gone to live in Los Angeles. That evidence was provided by Manuel Garfías, who had applied for title to the same land. When Lugo's claim was denied, Garfías filed a petition with the commissioners, who awarded him the property. Lugo then filed an appeal with the district court, but before it could render a decision, she dropped her suit, perhaps because of litigation expenses and because Garfías had already received confirmation of his title. In 1863, he finally obtained the patent for the land.[24]

The commission also rejected the petition of an Indian woman who failed to produce sufficient evidence.[25] In 1852, Victoria Comcrabit, the widow of Hugo Reid, who had died that year, failed to establish her title to a parcel of land near Misión San Gabriel. The property, she claimed, had been originally granted to her relative, Serafín de Jesús, a single native woman, who had died intestate. At Serafín's death, Victoria Reid had taken over the property and, acting as the landlord, had rented it to a family. When she appeared before the commission, she produced Serafín's expediente and had Michael White, the former manager at the mission, testify on her behalf. He supported Reid's claim to be Serafín's closest living relative, but he acknowledged that he had never seen a will or other document naming her as heir. In rejecting Reid's petition, the commissioners asserted, "Loose testimony like that before us, merely stating the belief of the witness [White] that the claimant is the nearest relative and next of kin . . . is not the proof which the law contemplates to establish the right of an heir." Further damaging her claim, they declared, was the expediente she produced, for it did not identify Serafín as the original grantee. Rather, they concluded, the original grantee was a man with a similar name. "The terms of . . . the grant show unequivocally that [it was] . . . made to a male and not to a female grantee," the commissioners ruled. They conceded the possibility that Mexican officials might have erred in issuing the grant papers, but "[i]f any mistake had occurred in writing the documents [expedientes] on which the title depends, the claimant [Reid] was bound to give proof of the person . . . whom she claims [is] . . . the grantee named in the title. But no such explanation is given." Reid did not appeal the case, in all likelihood because the evidence against her was too strong and the costs too burdensome.[26]

Unlike Reid and other unsuccessful claimants, most rancho owners secured titles to their land. Sadly, establishing title did not guarantee continued ownership, for more than 46 percent (twenty-eight of sixty Californio-Mexicans and Native American claimants whose titles were found proven) had lost their property by the 1880s. They were dispossessed by financial burdens brought on by the years of delay in getting their titles, high-interest loans, new taxes—which had been unknown in the Mexican era, depressed cattle prices, and droughts and floods that killed livestock and ruined crops in the late 1850s and 1860s. Assessment

Table 5.1

Los Angeles County Property Values, 1851–1880

Year	Values ($)
1851	2,282,949
1856	2,490,750
1860	3,650,330
1867	2,556,083
1873	9,845,593
1880	18,503,773

Source: J.M. Guinn, *A History of California*, 253–54.

records used to tax county property illustrate the losses in that period (table 5.1).[27] County property values, though steady in the 1850s, decreased significantly in the 1860s, with the onset of the cattle and crop devastation of that decade. Not until the 1870s, when the region emerged from the natural disasters, did that trend reverse.

Most ranchers, nearing bankruptcy, were forced to sell part or all of their property before they had the titles in hand. Those sales occurred because of indebtedness resulting from the newly instituted land taxes; from crop and cattle losses, especially in the mid-1860s; and from the heavy costs of proving land titles, which required paying attorneys and court fees as well as the costs for the land survey. Appeals and bureaucratic delays in Washington meant that these costs continued for years, sometimes for decades (fig 5.2). Some married women lost their lands because of desperate husbands who, when faced with personal financial reverses of their own, overstepped their legal authority and disposed of the wife's property. The available evidence indicates that at least eighteen ranchos claimed by Californio-Mexican men, nine by Californio-Mexican women, and one by a Native American woman were lost during and after confirmation hearings. As early as the mid-1850s, this melancholic reality permeated the pages of Los Angeles's Spanish-language newspaper, *El Clamor Público*. "These titles have remained without being decided upon for . . . years," wrote the editor, Francisco Ramírez, "during which time the rightful owners of these *terrenos* (lands) have exhausted most of their assets in obtaining a definitive patent. This . . . is destroying the confidence and love of the [Mexican] people towards the laws and government of this country."[28]

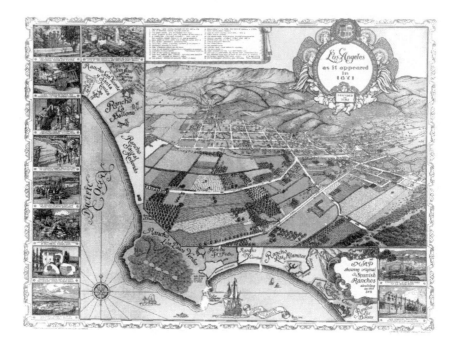

Figure 5.2

Los Angeles and surrounding ranchos as they appeared in 1871. In the 1860s, dozens of Mexicans were forced to sell their ranchos to meet exorbitant debts created by delays in legally confirming the title to their land. The sale and subdivision of those properties resulted in the proliferation of American owned and controlled businesses and property. (Courtesy of the Seaver Center for Western History Research, Los Angeles County Museum of Natural History)

María Merced Tapia and her husband, Victor Prudhomme, prominent members of California Mexican society, had to sell their three-sitio Rancho Malibu Simi Sequit because of debts accumulated in appealing their claim to the district court and in maintaining the property (fig. 5.3). The land commission rejected their petition in 1854 because of their failure to prove that the original landholder, José Bartolomé Tapia, had lawfully obtained the rancho from Spanish governor José Joaquín de Arrillaga in 1804. Though Tapia and Prudhomme could not produce documentary evidence of the Spanish grant, they could demonstrate that the commandant at Santa Bárbara, Felipe Goycoechea, had given Tapia

Figure 5.3

María Merced Tapia de Prudhomme in the 1870s or 1880s. Tapia was
orphaned at a young age and was raised by María Francisca Villalobos, her
grandmother. Sometime in the late 1840s, she married Victor Prudhomme, a
Frenchman. Like others, Tapia and Prudhomme struggled to hold on to their
property, Rancho Malibu Simi Sequit, which they had acquired through
Tapia's family networks. (Courtesy of the Seaver Center for Western History
Research, Los Angeles County Museum of Natural History)

legal possession of the rancho in 1804. That document, however, did not indicate that the governor had authorized the commandant to take such action. "The [U.S.] act of 1851 limits the power of this commission to claims founded on some right or title derived from the Spanish or Mexican government," but "[t]he documents in this case do not show any such concession . . . from either of these governments." The commissioners also faulted Tapia and Prudhomme for failing to provide "sufficient boundaries or other description" of the rancho.

In their appeal, Tapia and Prudhomme produced three witnesses who testified to the couple's long-time residence on the land, but none could substantiate their contention that Goycoechea had the governor's authority to issue the grant. Nor could their lawyer, Jonathan Scott, turn up such evidence, though he searched the archives of the surveyor general and asked family members if they possessed or knew of any documentation demonstrating the legality of Goycochea's action. Without such proof, the district court rejected their claim in 1860. It remains unknown why the court was so strict in its interpretation of the law in Tapia and Prudhomme's case but not in the case of the claims brought by Andrés Duarte, María Ygnacia Verdugo, and others who did not produce all the required evidence.[29] Clearly, the procedural delays ruined Tapia and Prudhomme.

The mounting litigation expenses and several outstanding loans forced Tapia and Prudhomme to sell their rancho for $1,400 to Matthew Keller, a lawyer and real estate investor.[30] Once Keller received notice of the district court's rejection, he petitioned the tribunal for a second hearing, which he received within the year. Keller, unlike Tapia and Prudhomme, found the missing documentation showing that Governor Arrillaga had indeed authorized the commandant to award Tapia formal possession of the land. How that proof was found is unclear: Perhaps Keller fabricated the document or perhaps Attorney Scott had failed to search hard enough for it. Keller persuaded the district court to reverse the commission's denial of title, and that decision was appealed to the U.S. Supreme Court, which ruled in favor of Keller. From the time that Keller took possession of the ranch until the land office issued a patent for 13,316 acres (about three sitios), twelve years had passed.[31]

While Tapia and Prudhomme were accumulating heavy legal expenses, other rancho holders were incurring crushing debts because of droughts and floods that came in 1857 and again in the early- to mid-1860s. Andrés

Duarte, owner of Rancho Azusa, was among those forced to sell properties because of debts acquired as a result of the bad climatic conditions. In 1864, fourteen years before a patent was issued for the rancho, Duarte lost the property because of a debt owed to William Wolfskill, a Euro-American citrus grower and lender. The sheriff foreclosed on the property, selling it at auction for $4,000 to Wolfskill. Other men meeting a similar fate during the 1860s and 1870s included Ygnacio Palomares, a once politically prominent California Mexican and owner of Rancho San José, and Henry "Enrique" Dalton, a U.S.-born former Mexican citizen and owner of Rancho Santa Anita.[32]

Some ranch owners held onto their properties—at least for a while—by subdividing and selling portions of them. For instance, Victoria Reid sold a portion of Rancho Huerta de Cuati in 1858, one year before she received final confirmation of the title, because she needed cash to maintain the property. The sale meant the loss of two-thirds of the original grant, leaving her with only 128 acres.[33]

Catalina Verdugo and her brother, Julio, also lost a substantial portion of Rancho San Rafael because of an outstanding mortgage. In 1852, they had petitioned for confirmation of their title to the eight-sitio ranch. The commission and federal courts affirmed their claim, but the surveyor general had yet to complete a survey. Five years later, and still without a survey, Julio took out a loan for $3,445 at 3 percent interest per month to pay for needed improvements and county and state taxes. By 1869, the debt had climbed to a staggering $58,750, and the sheriff auctioned off all but 2,500 acres of the original 34,000 acres. Catalina died in 1871, at the age of 79, and Julio died five years later, at age 87. These Californios, whose lives had begun in the previous century, witnessed—indeed, they experienced first-hand—the devastating social and economic changes wrought by the American conquest.[34]

In contrast to the struggles of the rancheros, who were coping with the legal system, the economy, and even the climate, landholders inside Los Angeles had fewer difficulties. The process for confirming title to pueblo lands was relatively simple and quick. The 1851 land act vested officials with the authority to affirm private titles to land within the new American towns that had emerged from the former Spanish and Mexican pueblos. Property types included *solares* (building lots) and *suertes* (agricultural lots) granted from *propios* and *ejidos* (municipal and common lands). Acting on behalf of the town were the mayor and members of the

Common Council, positions that had replaced Mexican alcaldes and ayuntamientos. They represented all property holders in the municipality (which, under Spanish and Mexican law, embraced four sitios).[35] Since the land act did not stipulate a process for determining the legality of titles in the towns, the state legislature delegated that responsibility to municipal leaders.[36]

In the case of Los Angeles, it did so implicitly in 1850, when it approved the pueblo's incorporation as a city, giving its leaders "all the rights, claims, and powers of the Pueblo de los Angeles."[37] After Congress passed the 1851 Gwin Act, the state legislature explicitly vested in Los Angeles's mayor and members of the common council the authority "to lease, sell, or otherwise dispose of . . . lands." It also recognized the city's right to commons or other property "not included within its present incorporated limits." An 1849 survey had determined that portions of ejidos lay outside the municipal jurisdiction that covered the four sitios, making it necessary to extend the city's authority to land beyond those limits.[38] Los Angeles's authority over 17,172 acres of pueblo property was made official in 1866.[39]

Town leaders did not wait for such legal niceties to deal with the fundamentally important property issues. In 1849, officials hired Lieutenant E.O.C. Ord to complete the first survey of Los Angeles (fig. 5.4). Ord's map established the boundaries of preexisting properties held by long-time residents, and it subdivided the remaining vacant land into lots of 2,200 square yards (close in size to a Mexican solar). In early 1850, the town council passed the first of several ordinances allowing for the sale of the newly created city lots.[40] The purpose was threefold: to stimulate the growth of agriculture, the town's major business; to attract new settlers; and to stabilize and increase the city's land values and, hence, the revenue that the city could generate from those properties with the land taxes that the council was soon to enact. With the taxes, the council funded public works projects, such as the paving of streets and the building of sewer and potable-water systems.[41]

To speed the distribution of town property and bring more land under cultivation, the council employed Henry Hancock to complete a second survey in 1852. This partitioned additional vacant ejidos that were south and west of the town's center into larger lots of ten and thirty-five acres. Economic growth would be encouraged through a so-called donation system—which began in August 1852 and ended in May 1854—in

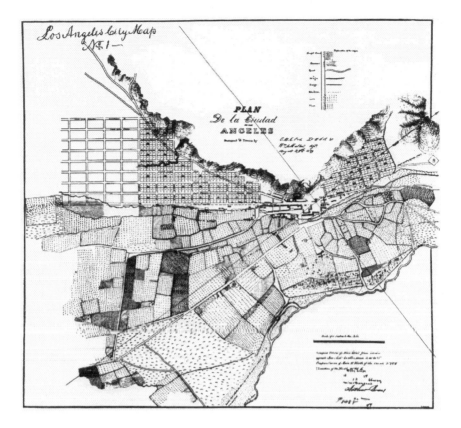

Figure 5.4
The first official survey of the city of Los Angeles. City leaders ordered this 1849 survey as a precursor to the subdivision, sale, and development of land in the city. This foreshadowed some of the larger changes that would take place in the wake of the American conquest. ("E.O.C. Ord 1849 Survey," L. Seebold copy, c. 1875, courtesy of the Seaver Center for Western History Research, Los Angeles County Museum of Natural History)

which the surveyed lots were opened to settlement. To obtain title to a lot, residents had to pay a processing fee of only $10 and make improvements within a year that would increase the property's value by $200. The building of a small home or the planting of fruit trees or gardens was usually enough to comply with that. The donation lands attracted an influx of Euro-American migrants, which led to a general rise in Los Angeles property values. Those best positioned to acquire land under these conditions were the newcomers from the United States, who possessed cash or credit and a willingness to engage in real-estate speculation.[42]

The town council also took steps to facilitate confirmation of Mexican land titles. In 1854, it passed an ordinance that approved the titles of those "persons who themselves or whose ancestors have occupied them without interruption, peaceably, and in good faith for a term of twelve years."[43] Unlike the system for determining rancho titles, this broad declaration led to swift approval and, hence, was a less costly process, even for those who lacked the original title issued by Spanish and Mexican officials or the Mexican ayuntamientos. Petitions for titles or deeds went to the city's "committee on lands," which investigated the claims, usually through an examination of Mexican titles, if extant, or through the testimony of neighbors or former pueblo leaders. The committee then made its recommendations to the mayor, who either confirmed or denied the petitions.[44] The city also used the process to bring the properties into conformity with the boundaries established in the 1849 survey. Though the council had broad powers over town property, it had no authority to settle civil disputes between landowners. That responsibility rested with the First (later, the Seventeenth) Judicial District Court.[45]

When the town council passed its first ordinance, in 1850, Californio-Mexicans made up 75 percent (1,215 residents) of the city's population of 1,610, whereas Euro-American and other foreign-born residents numbered only 395 or 25 percent (table 5.2).[46] During the next decade, the city's ethnic ratio reversed in response to a stream of migrants from northern California and from the eastern United States, especially New York, Missouri, Illinois, Ohio, Indiana, and Pennsylvania.[47] By 1860, Euro-Americans constituted 53 percent (2,316) of the town's 4,385 residents, whereas Californio-Mexicans were now in the minority with 47 percent (2,069). The end of the Civil War brought a significant number of white migrants from the southern states to the region, so that Euro-Americans, by 1870, accounted for 62 percent (3,568 of 5,728) and Californio-Mexicans, despite a slight increase in their real numbers, had dwindled to 38 percent (2,160) of the populace. In another harbinger of the future, immigrants from Mexico had come close to outnumbering the original Californio residents. By 1880, the number of city residents had doubled, swelling from 5,728 to 11,183, with Euro-Americans making up 81 percent (9,017) and Californio-Mexicans, whose real numbers had

Table 5.2

Los Angeles City Population, 1850–1880

Ethnicity	1850	1860	1870	1880
Spanish-speaking	1,215	2,069	2,160	2,166
Euro-American	395	2,316	3,568	9,017
Total Population	1,610	4,385	5,728	11,183

Sources: Griswold del Castillo, *Los Angeles Barrio,* 35; and Newmark and Newmark, *The Census of Los Angeles.*

remained nearly unchanged in the ten years, were only 19 percent (2,166) of the city's residents.

The city's changing ethnic composition paralleled shifting patterns of property holding. In the 1850s, most landowners were Californio-Mexicans, but by the decade's end, they held less land than Euro-Americans. Soon after Ord completed his survey, Euro-American men, who had cash and credit, began to purchase municipal lots that the city sold at public auction. Between 1850 and 1851, the council distributed a total of forty-five acres in city lots. Each measured approximately 2,200 square yards (.45 of an acre), and the sales generated $7,125 in municipal revenue. Euro-American men bought thirty-nine of the forty-five acres (87 percent) for $6,162, whereas Californio-Mexican men acquired fewer than seven acres (13 percent), at a total price of $963. No women bid for city lots. Euro-Americans who made significant purchases included John "Juan" Temple, who paid $1,414 for 9.45 acres (or twenty-one lots), and Benjamin D. Wilson and Montgomery Martin, who together spent $728 on 5.58 acres (or thirteen lots).[48]

In the next few years, Euro-American men, including European-born men, acquired even more property through the donation system. Between 1852 and 1854, while the system operated, the city distributed 8,249 acres. Of that total, Euro-American men obtained 4,964 acres (60 percent) and Californio-Mexican men 2,834 acres (34 percent). Californio-Mexican women secured 414 acres (5 percent) and Euro-American women got only 37 acres (less than 1 percent of the total). Most city land went to Euro-American men, enabling them to build at a relatively low cost a new commercial center, located south and west of the plaza and Mexican barrio, the traditional heart of Los Angeles. Thus emerged a new social and economic elite.[49]

Table 5.3

Los Angeles City Property Values ($) by Gender and Ethnicity, 1857–1874

| Year | Spanish-speaking | | Euro-American | | |
	Women	Men	Women	Men	Totals
1857	79,850	243,055	7,200	363,835	686,740
1860	88,380	179,863	4,670	558,897	831,810
1861	68,200	191,035	3,100	522,741	785,076
1867	61,382	99,959	32,425	466,948	660,714
1870	126,150	203,114	55,075	1,093,603	1,477,942
1874	258,677	238,136	189,980	1,092,163	1,778,956

Sources: Tax Roll, 1857, and Assessment Rolls, 1860, 1861, 1867, 1870, 1874, Los Angeles City Archives.

Not only were incoming Euro-American and foreign-born men acquiring land at rates that outpaced those of Californio-Mexicans, the value of their properties—land and improvements, such as structures or buildings—would rise substantially during the 1870s, following a city-wide economic depression in the mid-1860s.[50] In the town's early years, property values had risen primarily as a result of the distribution and improvement of the donation lots. That mild real estate boom soon subsided, and by the early to mid-1860s property values had fallen sharply as a result of natural disasters—the same droughts and floods that left many rancheros bankrupt. Property values decreased significantly as a result of torrential rains in 1862 and 1863 and a smallpox epidemic (see the last column of table 5.3). Euro-American men weathered the city's socioeconomic disasters better than did the Spanish-speaking inhabitants. The 1857 city tax roll, the earliest extant record, indicates that 128 Euro-American men (42 percent of property holders) held 52 percent of the city's real estate, assets valued at $363,835. By 1860, 218 Euro-American men (49 percent of property holders) held 67 percent of the city's real estate assets valued at $558,897. (See table 5.3 and table 5.4.)

In contrast, Californio-Mexicans were hit hardest by the depression and smallpox epidemic, suffering losses in property and lives. The storms washed away adobe homes and fences as well as vineyards and gardens, which were important sources of subsistence for the community. The epidemic struck in winter 1863, killing at least 500 people and further wracking the ailing economy.[51] In 1857, 177 Californio-Mexicans (58 percent of property holders)—117 men and sixty women—owned

Table 5.4

Los Angeles City Property Holders by Gender and Ethnicity, 1857–1874

| Year | Spanish-speaking | | Euro-American | | |
	Women	Men	Men	Women	Totals
1857	60	117	128	2	307
1860	83	138	218	3	442
1861	70	133	195	3	401
1867	95	109	246	23	473
1870	124	115	443	41	723
1874	107	145	714	85	1,051

Sources: Tax Roll, 1857, and Assessment Rolls, 1860, 1861, 1867, 1870, 1874, Los Angeles City Archives.

47 percent of the city's real estate, assets valued at $322,905, with men holding $243,055 (35 percent) and women $79,850 (12 percent). By 1860, real property values for men and women had decreased substantially, whereas the number of property holders had increased slightly, from 177 in 1857 to 221 in 1860. That year, Californio-Mexicans owned land and improvements valued at $268,243 (32 percent of the city's real estate by value), a drop of almost $54,662, even though the number of property owners grew somewhat (see tables 5.3 and 5.4).

This indicates that the city-wide depression affected primarily the Mexican population of the pueblo. Californio-Mexicans, along with landless native peoples, not only made up the poorest segment of the population but also suffered the greatest loss of life during the winter of 1863, when smallpox took its heaviest toll. Initially, the epidemic severely impacted residents who lived north of the plaza, primarily Spanish speakers, though the disease later spread to other parts of the city. The inability to pay for medical care or vaccines, which arrived only intermittently by ship from San Francisco, worsened their prospects for a recovery.

As the city recovered from the epidemic and the natural disasters, residents and the recent arrivals witnessed marked improvements in the city's economy and society. The creation of new municipal services and formation of businesses, including a gas plant, an ice factory, two banks, and a local railway connecting Los Angeles to the port of San Pedro, signaled the renewal of economic life. The population also continued to expand, as the systematic foreclosure, subdivision, and sale of rancho land in the 1860s brought land-hungry migrants to the region. The newcomers, a significant number of whom settled in local townships, including El Monte, Santa Ana, and Los Nietos (all former ranchos), fueled the demand for municipal services, businesses, and, especially, property.[52] By the beginning of the 1870s, the records indicate that city property values—land and improvements—had climbed to nearly $1.5 million (table 5.3). The total number of real estate holders also increased, rising from 442 in 1860 to 723 in 1870 (table 5.4).

Real-estate values and the city's infrastructure continued to grow in the 1870s, but few Californio-Mexicans reaped the benefits of that prosperity. In 1874, city property values reached $1,778,956, more than double their 1860 levels. Californio-Mexican men and women combined held only 28 percent of land and improvements, valued at $496,813. In contrast, Euro-Americans held 72 percent, valued at $1.28 million, with almost $1.09 million of that held by men.[53] Euro-American women, whose population in the city had expanded, experienced dramatic increases. In four years, from 1870 to 1874, they more than tripled their real-estate worth, $55,075 to $189,980. The number of Euro-American real-estate owners and the value of their properties continued to increase following the arrival of the Southern Pacific Railroad in 1876, which brought thousands of Euro-Americans to the city, and the real estate boom of the 1880s. By the 1870s, the Californio-Mexicans, in contrast, held only a portion of real estate in the city, a miniscule amount in comparison to what they had held previously. By 1874, their holdings, particularly of the men, had dipped close to levels found in the 1850s (table 5.3).

Californio-Mexicans struggled not only to hold onto real estate but also to personal property. The tax records indicate that, in the 1870s, on average, a Californio-Mexican man and woman held less in personal wealth—cash, bank notes, or other movable goods—than he or she did in the 1850s (table 5.5). In 1857, a man owned, on average, $719 in personal goods, but by 1874, he possessed only $449 worth of such items. Californio-Mexican women, on average, suffered even greater losses. In 1857, an average woman had $716 in personal wealth, but by 1874, she had only $145, a decline of more than $500 (table 5.5). Comparing Californio-Mexicans' personal property values to those of Euro-American men reveals the decreasing economic power of Californio-Mexicans vis-à-vis Euro-American men. The data reveal that, whereas Californio-Mexican

Table 5.5

Average Personal Property Values ($) among Californio-Mexicans, 1857–1874

| Year | Spanish-speaking | |
	Women	Men
1857	716	719
1860	889	448
1861	889	436
1867	128	477
1870	166	230
1874	145	449

Sources: Tax Roll, 1857, and Assessment Rolls, 1860, 1861, 1867, 1870, 1874, Los Angeles City Archives.

men and women's personal property values remained nearly the same or declined between 1857 and 1874, Euro-American men holdings increased nearly 400 percent in that same period. Their net worth of personal property climbed from $364,734 in 1857 to $1,221,476 in 1874 (table 5.6).

The indisputable point is that the Californio-Mexican residents of Los Angeles were losing their personal wealth and real estate. They included María Armenta, a mid-strata woman, who lost her home because she was unable to repay a loan. In 1851, Rafael Guirado, a merchant, sued her in civil court for overdue bills of $350 on household items bought on store credit. To cover the debt, the judge ordered the sale of her house as well as some agricultural goods (sacks of beans, wheat, and corn). The sale resulted in $100 and partial payment of the debt. Whether she paid the balance is unknown, but there is no indication that Guirado later asked the court for additional compensation.[54]

María Antonia Tapia, like María Armenta, found herself having to sell her property in 1860 in order to pay a debt owed to Jonathon Scott, an attorney and real-estate investor. Two years earlier, in June 1858, she had borrowed $220 from Scott at 3 percent interest per month, with the balance and accrued interest due in eighteen months. Four months after her failure to meet that obligation, Scott sued for the money. The judge ordered the sheriff to seize and sell Tapia's home at public auction.[55]

Within the first decade and a half of American rule, Californio-Mexican women and men lost property. Even the few who managed to hold onto it for some years in the end succumbed to financial pressures.

Table 5.6

Personal Property Values ($) by Gender and Ethnicity, 1857–1874

| | Spanish-speaking | | Euro-American | | |
Year	Women	Men	Women	Men	Totals
1857	10,750	52,500	2,500	364,734	430,484
1860	14,220	31,373	2,195	546,745	594,533
1861	11,265	29,675	2,390	429,471	472,801
1867	7,530	42,012	10,585	475,689	535,816
1870	9,170	28,637	6,560	546,510	590,877
1874	11,158	36,812	32,259	1,221,476	1,301,705

Sources: Tax Roll, 1857, and Assessment Rolls, 1860, 1861, 1867, 1870, 1874, Los Angeles City Archives.

Dolores Buelna, who inherited her home and lot from her mother, Encarnación Buelna, retained her property for more than twenty years. However, she was also accumulating a heavy debt. In 1874, Buelna borrowed $1,470 at 1.5 percent per month interest from J. E. Hollenbeck. To secure the loan, she mortgaged the property that her family had held since the Mexican era. Four years later, she had not repaid the loan or the interest (the latter had accumulated to $1,058), nor had she paid taxes on the property. Before she defaulted because of the taxes, Hollenbeck obtained a court judgment, ordering the sheriff to sell her property at public auction to pay the $2,767 she now owed him. The highest bid came from Hollenbeck, who promptly paid the $68 owed in taxes, enabling him to get title to the property. Buelna, meanwhile, had lost her home.[56]

Tax liens caused other foreclosures. Nicolasa Carreaga owned two 10 acre lots on Main Street, which she had acquired through the donation system. When she could not pay city and county taxes in 1853, the sheriff seized and sold her property at public auction.[57] Francisco Ballestreros, a mid-strata man who owned a home on a lot and a vineyard, lost everything. The vineyard went first in 1852 to cover monies owed to Louis Lamoreau, John Chapman, and two other unnamed creditors. Two years later, the lot was seized and sold to cover unpaid city taxes.[58]

Typical, too, was the experience of Julian Chávez. In 1878, he went to court seeking permission to break a trust that he had created five years earlier "in order to secure [the] future" of his wife, Luisa Machado, and their children. The trust had placed 57 acres in their names, but in recent years the land "gave them nothing" and the "onerous" overdue city taxes compelled him to sell the property. The judge approved the request, enabling Chávez to subdivide and sell the land. How much he garnered from the sale is unknown, but the outcome left him and his family landless.[59]

The sale and loss of land, homes, vineyards, and small gardens resulted in the leveling of social classes among Californio-Mexicans, leading them to cluster in the central area of town, near the plaza. By the 1880s, the locale housed 83 percent of Los Angeles's Spanish-speaking population, which had become the most economically marginalized and ethnically segregated sector of society. Residents of the barrio, including recently arrived immigrants from Mexico and an increasing number of Chinese immigrants, who resided near the "*callejon de los negros*" or "Negro Alley," lived in dilapidated housing underserved by public facilities. As late as 1879, according to the annual health department report, the area lacked a proper sewage and drainage system.[60] Also crowding into that area of town, increasingly designated a "slum" by outsiders, were unsavory business establishments—brothels, saloons, and gambling halls—and their clientele.[61]

Notwithstanding the declining conditions of their homes and neighborhood, Californio-Mexicans found ways to survive impoverishment and adapt to the changing economy. The federal censuses of the 1860s, 1870s, and 1880s, though incomplete, reveal that Californio-Mexican men and women increasingly drifted into manual or domestic jobs in the growing urban and agriculture economy. By the 1870s, nearly 80 percent of the men were in unskilled jobs, toiling as day laborers, laying bricks, repairing city structures, or picking crops. Women also took on unskilled jobs, working as seamstresses, washerwomen, housekeepers, and farm laborers, enabling them, alongside their spouses, brothers, and fathers, to eke out an existence for themselves and their families.[62]

Within a relatively short period after the American conquest, a Euro-American-dominated, Protestant, capitalist society had emerged in Los Angeles, displacing and transforming the world of the original residents. Owners of town property easily confirmed their titles, but the increase in land values in the late 1860s and 1870s, high-interest loans, and taxes strained the resources of the original residents—women as well as men—and led to widespread property loss and impoverishment of both the well-to-do and mid-strata residents. They joined the poor in the barrio, struggling to survive as unskilled laborers.

Rancho owners, men and women, once considered the elite, as well as the handful of Native Americans, faced similar destitution. For the rancheros, it came as a consequence of time-consuming and costly legal proceedings to confirm their land titles as well as from natural disasters that decimated cattle and crops between 1857 and the mid-1860s. Here, too, men and women, regardless of ethnicity, shared the loss. As for the landless Native Americans, their scattering into the rural countryside, which had begun in the 1830s and 1840s, and population decline due to disease and abuse accelerated as the newly impoverished Californio-Mexicans displaced them as laborers in the towns and on the ranchos. Some established themselves in small, isolated communities or they survived by working in the expanding commercial farming industry. Those survivors, like natives elsewhere, remained the most culturally and socially marginalized people in California.

The experiences of Spanish-speaking and native property owners varied little across gender, ethnic, and social-class lines: Californio-Mexican and Native American men and women of all social levels lost their land and became impoverished. By examining and analyzing the experiences of Californio-Mexican and Native American women—separate from and in relation to men—we have seen that women also bore the brunt of the conquest. For the single, widowed, separated, or divorced women (whose numbers were on the rise in the post-conquest period), the loss of personal wealth had a direct and severe impact on their families, who depended upon them for support. With the rise of female-headed households—as the next chapter will describe—women had to find innovative ways in which to deal with the social, economic, and cultural upheaval of their rapidly changing world. Their solutions, however, were not always welcomed and, in many ways, challenged the values espoused by the Californio-Mexican community.

Chapter 6

Illegitimacy and Social Dislocation
after the American Conquest

In 1873, Delfina Varelas, a Mexican, and Bernard "Bernardo" Cohn, a Jewish Euro-American, took their newborn son, Matias Bernardo José, to the Los Angeles Plaza Catholic Church for his christening.[1] During the ceremony, the priest learned that Varelas and Cohn were unmarried, and so he identified Matias as an hijo natural (a child born to unmarried parents who were eligible to marry in the Catholic Church).[2] Cohn, however, was a married man. Sixteen years earlier, in 1857, he had wed Esther (whose maiden name is unknown), a Jewish Euro-American, in a civil ceremony in Los Angeles.[3] Under California common law, adopted in 1850, marriage was a civil contract entered into by two consenting adults. Any judge, justice of the peace, clergyman, or licensed preacher could perform the ceremony as long as they kept a written record of the marriage and filed a certificate with the proper authorities. Civil marriages, although not recognized by the Catholic Church, were lawful.[4] Hence, in the eyes of the law, Cohn was married to Esther, and he had an obligation to support their three children—Julius, Casper, and Carrie.[5]

Since Cohn was lawfully married to Esther and not to Delfina, he had no legal obligation to support or make provisions for her or Matias. However, Cohn was a prominent philanthropist, successful businessman, and owner of town property (valued at over $30,000 in 1876), so he supported both families. Despite Esther's insistence that he leave Varelas or else face divorce and a suit for support for her and their children, he and Delfina continued to see each other. They had two additional children, Eduardo in 1874 and Marcos in 1877. After Esther's death in 1885, the relationship with Delfina continued until Cohn's death in 1889, but the couple never married. Cohn's extramarital relationship produced no social outcry, and he was even elected to the city council in 1888.[6]

This case was part of a general increase in illegitimacy in post-conquest Los Angeles. Beginning in the 1850s, the percentage of children born outside of a marriage recognized by California law began to rise dramatically among Spanish-speaking and Native American peoples in the greater Los Angeles region. This was in sharp contrast to the low proportion of illegitimate children born in the Spanish and Mexican eras. By the late 1850s, only one decade after the conquest, the rate of children born out of wedlock had increased significantly among the Spanish-speaking population, and it continued to grow, only leveling off in the 1870s. The rate increases were even more dramatic among Native Californians.[7]

The dramatic rise in illegitimacy was not a consequence of changing attitudes towards sexuality in and outside of marriage. Rather, it can be traced to transformations already underway in the late Mexican period, which accelerated with the social dislocation following the American conquest.[8] Primary among the destabilizing elements were the impoverishment and marginalization of the Spanish-speaking population and the rapid decline of the indigenous community; the migration of Spanish-speaking men to other parts of the state and to Mexico; the increasing abandonment of Spanish-speaking women by their husbands; the decision of abandoned women to cohabit with men who would support them and their children; the increasing number of Euro-American, European, and Sonoran men, who migrated to the region as a consequence of the Gold Rush; and the "Americanization" of the Catholic Church, and the alienation of the Spanish-speaking community from it.

In the post-conquest period, Spanish-speaking and Native Californian women who bore children out of wedlock lived in a society undergoing rapid cultural and institutional change. Among the most profound of those transformations was the impoverishment and marginalization of the Californio-Mexican population in the three decades following the American takeover. This group was subjected to onerous legal requirements and violence. Land policies that violated the spirit of the Treaty of Guadalupe Hidalgo (1848) dispossessed most Spanish-speaking landowners—the mid-strata and the poor, as well as the elite. These losses did not occur immediately nor did they affect all property holders equally, but they were ultimately devastating to most Spanish-speaking Californios.

By the 1880s, nearly half of the rancho owners in the vicinity of Los

Angeles had sold their property or had lost significant parts of their holdings due to legal delays, financial pressures, and natural disasters, among other things. The elite, mid–strata, and poor property holders in Los Angeles, in contrast, acquired their land titles more quickly, but they soon also lost their holdings due to debts, taxes, and increased land values brought on by the emerging Euro-American-dominated capitalist society. By the 1860s and 1870s, the Spanish-speaking Californios found themselves overrun by Euro-Americans, who sought and acquired much of the rancho land as well as the most valuable city property. The end result was that most Californio residents sold, transferred, or in other ways lost their property and were reduced to living in an ethnically segregated and economically marginalized barrio.[9]

The indigenous community suffered even more dramatic losses in the post-conquest period because of diseases and environmental changes that were already underway. The decline of the native population in California, from about 300,000 prior to European contact to about 150,000 in the mid-nineteenth century, began with Spanish conquest and colonization and accelerated under the mission system. The close quarters at the missions hastened the spread of infectious diseases, such as syphilis, smallpox, measles, dysentery, pleurisy, and pneumonia, to which the indígenas had little resistance.[10] Women and children, in particular, had less resistance and suffered high death rates.[11] Destruction of the natural environment and land takeovers by Spaniards and, later, Mexicans and Americans also strained the traditional food resources of California's indigenous peoples.

Native Californians also suffered with the outright theft of their land, discriminatory legal policies and practices, and violence aimed at eradicating the "Indian problem." With the secularization of the missions in the 1830s, heads of native families were to receive land, livestock, and supplies so that they could settle with their families in communities or pueblos. In reality, however, the administrators of the missions—most of whom were Californios—appropriated much of the property that was earmarked for the neófitos, leaving the latter with few options: petition the government for land, migrate to the pueblos in search of work, or flee inland and rejoin kin who were already living there.[12] When several hundred of native Californians migrated to Los Angeles rather than remain at the missions, local leaders passed laws designed to regulate their movements. As a result, those native people who were found drinking, gambling, or unemployed were often arrested and forced to labor on the city's public works or for private individuals.[13]

In the American period, lawmakers passed even more stringent laws regulating the movements of indigenous peoples. In 1850, in the first session of the California legislature, legislators enacted a vagrancy law that required that "any Indian able to work and to support himself . . . [and] who shall be found loitering or strolling about, or frequenting public places where liquors are sold, begging, or leading an immoral . . . life, shall be . . . arrested on the complaint of any citizen." In Los Angeles, the city council passed a similar ordinance. If arrested, Native Americans were made to labor on public works. When the city had no projects in progress, the law stated that prisoners were to be "auctioned off to the highest bidder for private service" and compelled to work for their "employer" until they completed their sentence or paid a fine for their offense.[14] According to Horace Bell, a resident, "Los Angeles had its slave mart as well as New Orleans or Constantinople—only the slave at Los Angeles was sold fifty-two times a year as long as he lived, which did not generally exceed one, two, or three years. . . ."[15] Indians were also subject to other discriminatory and abusive state and local laws. For instance, the state decreed that if abused by their "white" employers, native peoples could not testify against them in a court of law.[16] Many Euro-Americans disliked the practice of forced Indian labor, complaining that the free work drove "white" wages down.[17]

Outside of the courtrooms and jails, indigenous peoples had to deal with an increasing population of Euro-Americans who had little tolerance for racial and cultural differences. This led to one of the bloodiest chapters in Los Angeles history. Violence plagued the town, especially in the 1850s, when vigilantes regularly took the law into their own hands, dealing harshly with suspected murderers, thieves, and rapists. Native Americans as well as "half-breed Mexicans," who were despised and viewed as a degraded race by Euro-Americans, bore the brunt of the vigilantism and racial violence. By the 1880s, the native population had dwindled in Los Angeles and elsewhere in the state, including the mining areas of northern California, where native peoples had suffered from even more extreme forms of hostility and brutality. California censuses demonstrate that the native Californian population declined from about 100,000 in 1850 to about 20,500 in 1880.[18] In Los Angeles county, which encompassed present-day Los Angeles, Orange, and parts of Riverside counties, the population fell from 2,014 in 1860 to 219 in 1870, and then increased slightly to 316 in 1880. Despite that small increase and the census's exclusion of native peoples living on their traditional lands or reservations, the native Californian population was, at that point, only a fraction of the size it had been in the Mexican and Spanish eras and, especially, prior to European contact.[19]

The few native peoples who managed to survive continued to reel from diseases and forced relocation to poorly managed federal Indian reservations. The smallpox epidemic of the early 1860s took a heavy toll on the native population of the southern California area. Removal to the reservations also had disastrous effects. In the early 1850s, Benjamin Wilson, the Indian agent in southern California, proposed a system of fifteen state-funded reservations, to feed and house native peoples on their own lands. California legislators, however, refused to support the idea, arguing that the public had no obligation to maintain Native Americans. Instead, indigenous peoples were left to fend for themselves in a hostile environment.

Several years later, the federal government established a reservation system run by the U.S. military. In southern California, the government established Fort Tejón, north of Los Angeles where native Californians lived under the harshest conditions. Government officials staffed the reservation with corrupt agents, whose malfeasance contributed to the deaths of many indígenas because of the poor conditions and malnutrition. Native peoples who refused to live within the reservation system had no choice but to flee to other parts of the state or continue living on their own lands until government officials, squatters, or vigilantes expelled them at gunpoint.[20]

While native peoples found few ways to survive in the hostile environment, impoverished and landless Spanish-speakers turned to agricultural labor or migrated in search of employment and subsistence. Between 1850 and 1870, the number of laborers in Los Angeles nearly doubled, from 18 percent to 30 percent of the total population, whereas the percentage of farmers increased only slightly. This would indicate that land ownership was being concentrated in the hands of a small, increasingly Euro-American group, while the numerically larger Spanish-speaking population was undergoing proletarianization.[21] To cope with diminishing economic opportunities, especially with the collapse of the cattle industry and devaluation of land in the late 1860s and 1870s, Spanish-speaking men migrated to other parts of the state in search of seasonal employment.[22] Some worked on distant ranchos, in the mines, or in the railroad industry in Arizona, while those who had remaining livestock went in search of cattle markets.[23] These trips were grueling, dangerous, and lengthy, and female family members were usually left behind to fend for themselves.

The migration of Californio-Mexican men to Mexico and other parts of California and their extended absence from their families and households contributed to an increase in the number of female-headed households. In 1850, Spanish-speaking women in Los Angeles headed nearly 29 percent of households, most of which were extended family units.[24] By 1860, the female-headed households had decreased slightly, to 27 percent, but in the following decade, a sharp reversal occurred. By 1870, women headed 38 percent of the households, most of which were now single-parent, nuclear families rather than extended-family units.[25] Although that decreased to 31 percent in 1880, a significant proportion of Spanish-speaking women were heads of household and responsible for supporting themselves and their dependents. Census records confirm that most them did so by working outside the home, as washerwomen, seamstresses, and housekeepers.[26]

Women were not only working to support themselves and family members but also forming relationships with men who were not their spouses. The records indicate that in the three decades following the American conquest, 954 Spanish-speaking women and 231 native women (20 to 30 percent of the women in those ethnic groups) formed intimate relationships with men of various ethnic backgrounds and social classes to whom they were not married.[27] For some, taking up with men who had the ability to support them was their only means of survival. As a consequence, they bore children out of wedlock. The evidence demonstrates that 189 of the 954 Spanish-speaking women (20 percent) had long-term, extramarital liaisons.[28] These unions suggest that, even though no marriage ceremony took place, some of the women and their partners probably formed, for all intents and purposes, family units, in which they fulfilled their roles and obligations as "husband" and "wife." Under California law, such unions constituted "common-law marriages"—in which a couple lived together and acknowledged each other as "husband" and "wife." According to a state Supreme Court decision in 1852, as long as a couple made "an open avowal" of the intent to contract marriage and took on the "relative duties, which it impose[d]," the union was "valid and binding." The 1872 Civil Code reiterated that point when it stated that "consent alone does not constitute marriage; it must be followed by a solemnization, or by a mutual assumption of marital rights, duties, or obligations."[29] If the existence of a common-law union could be demonstrated in court, the offspring of that relationship would be considered legitimate. In contrast, in Spanish and Mexican civil law, *uniones libres* (informal relationships), although common and tolerated, were not deemed to be legitimate marriages.[30]

Ramona Alvarado was among the women who had long-term relationships and likely lived in unions that would have been considered common-law marriages. She spent ten or more years in the 1860s and 1870s with Jesús Bilderrain, a European who served as a Los Angeles police officer in the early 1870s. Alvarado and Bilderrain had four children, one of whom died shortly after birth.[31] Jesús Tapia also spent thirteen years living in a consensual union with Ramón Paco, with whom she had six children.[32] Altagracia Sierra spent at least fourteen years with Luis Soto and bore him six children, and Hilaria Domínguez had four children during a more-than-ten-year relationship with Francisco Johnson, who was the son of the English trader, James "Santiago" Johnson, and a Californio, Carmen Guirado.[33]

Women also had short-term relationships that lasted, on average, less than five years. María de los Angeles Argüello spent at least three years with Ben "Vicente" McLoughlin, a Euro-American who settled in Los Angeles in the 1850s and set up shop building and repairing carriage wheels. They had two children, one in 1859 and the other in 1861.[34] From 1863 to 1869, Timotea Ybarra had a short-term relationship with Santiago Johnson, another son of the English trader of the same name. It appears they acknowledged this relationship publicly, for they named their only son "Santiago."[35]

A few native women also formed long-term consensual relationships. The records indicate that fourteen (6 percent) of the 231 native women who had children outside of marriage lived with men for periods lasting from four to over fifteen years. They included Escolástica, a woman from Misión San Luis Rey, who had an extramarital relationship with Gerónimo Ochoba, a native Californian from the mission. Their union lasted for at least four years, during which time they had two children, one in 1856 and the other in 1858.[36] María Crisanta, also a neófita, had a more-than-twelve-year relationship with a Mexican man, Juan Braca-montes, with whom she had four children, with their youngest son, Santiago, being born in 1867.[37]

Native Californians women also had long-term relations with Euro-American men. María Palma and Harvey Rhodes, a Los Angeles money-lender, maintained a relationship for at least ten years, during which time they had six children.[38] Nicolasa Triunfo, another single native woman, had a six-year relationship with Cyrus "Cy" Lyons, a Euro-American from Maine who came to Los Angeles in 1849 to try his luck at sheep raising. Lyons and Triunfo had three children, with the youngest, José Enrique, born in 1858. When their relationship ended is unknown, but it is known that he took up with a Californio-Mexican woman, Luisa Espinoza, sometime in 1864, who bore a child out of wedlock with him that year. Eventually, twelve years later, in 1876, he married Ynéz Cota, another Californio-Mexican woman.[39]

Native American and Spanish-speaking women not only formed long-term consensual unions that sometimes qualified as common-law marriages, but they also lived in "extended engagements" that ultimately resulted in civil or religious marriages.[40] The records in Los Angeles and San Gabriel for the thirty years following the American conquest indicate that a handful of women—thirty-one Californio-Mexicans and one Native American of the 1,185 Californio-Mexican and Native American women who bore children out of wedlock—eventually married the fathers of their children, legitimizing these offspring in the process. Marina García, for instance, married Pedro Stone, the father of her two children, several months after the birth of their second child in 1863.[41] Anselma Escobar and Ramón Miranda also married that same year, following the birth of their daughter, María Josefa de los Angeles.[42] Although Escobar and García waited only a short period to marry, other women took much longer to do so. Ygnacia Arias, for example, had a relationship with José María Dávalos that began in 1857. They finally celebrated their nuptials in the Catholic Church after the birth of their seventh child in December 1867.[43] Only after six years and five children did Luisa Bojorquez marry Alexandro Nelson in a civil ceremony in 1865. The Church did not recognize civil marriages as valid, so the four children born after the civil ceremony were identified as hijos naturales, just as were the five born before. In the eyes of American common law, however, all nine children were legitimate.

Most women who lived in long-term relationships or common-law marriages were single or widowed and did not formally marry. However, a smaller, yet significant, number—twenty-nine (15 percent) of the 189 Spanish-speaking women who lived in consensual unions—were already married, but to other men. These women shared a common characteristic: They were either separated from or had been abandoned by their lawful husbands. The common-law relationships were maintained despite social and cultural mores that condemned adulterous relationships. In 1852, María Catarina Verdugo, for instance, left her spouse, Teodoro Navarro, for another man because of the intolerable living conditions resulting from Teodoro's inability to support her and their five children. She took along their three youngest children when she moved in with José Apodaca on Rancho Palos Verdes. Verdugo remained with Apodaca, a recent immigrant from Sonora, for at least five years, and they had one son, José Francisco, in 1856.[44]

Similarly, Gumecinda Cruz, the woman in chapter four who lost a divorce suit, took up with another man because her husband failed to support the household. In 1865, after fourteen years of living with Andrés Elias, she left him for Ygnacio Reyes. During their five or more years together, they had three children. Their union would not have been considered a common-law marriage since she remained legally married to Elias.[45] Tomasa Cosio cohabited with Adolfo "Younge" Junge, a successful businessman who owned a drugstore in town, in part because her husband, Antonio Journeaux, had abandoned her a few months after their marriage in 1861.[46]

The result of these extramarital relationships was an increasing out-of-wedlock birth rate in the post-conquest period. In the Spanish era, from settlement in the 1770s to Mexican Independence in the 1820s, illegitimacy among gente de razón and neófitos was infrequent, less than 8 and 2 percent of the children born to Mexicans and Christian natives, respectively.[47] In the 1830s and 1840s, with the increasing population and the weakening of the Catholic Church, the percentage of Mexican and Native Californian offspring born outside of marriage increased to 13 and 9 percent, respectively. These figures pale in comparison to rates in the American era, however. The illegitimacy rate among Californio-Mexicans nearly doubled, reaching 19 percent in the 1850s and 24 percent in the 1860s. It leveled off in the 1870s, at 22 percent (table 6.1). Figures among Christianized Indians rose even more significantly and

Table 6.1
Illegitimacy Rates (%) at Misión San Gabriel and the Los Angeles Plaza Church, 1800s–1870s

	1800–1820s	1830s–1840s	1850s	1860s	1870s
Spanish-surnamed couples	7.6	13.7	19	24	22
Neófito couples	1.7	8.7	27	43	28
Euro-American men & Neófitas		44	52	64	74
Spanish-speaking men & Neófitas		24	61	73	86
Euro-American men & Spanish-speaking women		14	12	26	20

Note: Figures for the 1800–1820s and 1830s–1840s are averages. No record of illegitimacy was found prior to 1800.
Sources: Los Angeles Plaza Church, Baptisms, Books 1–5, 1826–1920, Family History Center; and Misión San Gabriel, Baptisms, Books 1–3, 1771–1855, and Book 6, 1868–1908 (Books Four and Five, 1855–1868, are missing), Family History Center.

remained higher than those found among Californio-Mexicans. The percentage of illegitimate neófito children climbed to 27 in the 1850s and 43 percent in the 1860s, decreasing to 28 percent only in the 1870s.

Among ethnically mixed couples—particularly those consisting of indigenous women and Euro-American or Spanish-speaking men—the rate of illegitimacy was even higher than among couples made up of a man and a woman from the same or similar ethnic backgrounds. In the Mexican period, 44 percent of the children born to Euro-American men and native women that were baptized were illegitimate, that is, their parents were not married in the Catholic church; the remainder were born to parents who had married. This was the highest of any ethnic group. This reveals that Euro-American men were unlikely to marry neófitas with whom they had had sexual relations. In the American period, those figures climbed dramatically to 52 percent, 64 percent, and 74 percent, in the 1850s, 1860s, and 1870s, respectively (table 6.1). However, the increase in illegitimacy rates among couples consisting of indigenous women and Spanish-speaking men were even more dramatic, substantially exceeding those for indigenous–Euro-American couples. In the late Mexican period, 24 percent of children born to indígenas and Spanish-speaking men were illegitimate, but in the 1850s, 1860s, and 1870s, that rate rose to 61, 73, and 86 percent, respectively (table 6.1). Native Californian women and Mexican, Californio, or Euro-American men engaged in sexual relations but seldom married in either religious or civil ceremonies, even though California law permitted marriages between these groups.[48] Doubtless, indigenous women's low socioeconomic status and racial and ethnic marginalization made them unattractive marriage partners.[49]

Couples consisting of Spanish-speaking women and Euro-American men also had children out of wedlock, but the rates were far lower than for other ethnically mixed couples. In the 1830s and 1840s, rate was 14 percent, and it decreased slightly to 12 percent in the 1850s. In the 1860s, however, the rate climbed to 26 percent, decreasing only in the 1870s, to 20 percent (table 6.1). Those figures suggest that Euro-American and Spanish-speaking men who had relations with Spanish-speaking women were more likely to marry them than indigenous women. Spanish-speaking women, unlike native women, were more likely to have family networks with access to property, political position, and social status that made them attractive mates to unattached Euro-American and Spanish-speaking men, including the recently arrived Sonorans, who hoped to establish themselves in town.

Standing in stark contrast to illegitimacy rates for all ethnic groups in American California are the rates in seventeenth-, eighteenth-, and nineteenth-century America. In colonial and early modern New England, for example, illegitimacy rates among the "white" population remained relatively low, ranging from 3 to 5 percent, though they briefly increased slightly in the late colonial period as a result of increased geographic mobility and the lessening of social and parental control.[50] The infrequency of children born out of wedlock in the early American colonial period is explained, in part, by the colonists' desire to maintain a homogenous white society, by their "anti-assimilationist mentality," and their limited social interaction with indigenous and African slave communities.[51] In Los Angeles, on the other hand, people of different ethnic backgrounds—Euro-Americans, Mexicans, and Native Americans—regularly interacted, socialized, and, as the records reveal, sustained intimate sexual relations in and outside of marriage. Ethnic prejudices and hostilities, although present and causing antagonism and violence, did not prevent members of one ethnic group from intermingling with others. An imbalanced gender ratio appears to have contributed to an increase in the formation of ethnically mixed relationships and the birth of children out of wedlock.

The imbalance in the gender ratio arose in the 1850s, with the arrival of Euro-American men between the ages of twenty and fifty, who generally came to California without family members.[52] These new settlers worked in unskilled and skilled mercantile trades. In 1850, 38 percent of these newcomers lived in households with which they had no family or kinship ties.[53] Because few Euro-American women came to the region, men outnumbered women and thus would be more likely to form relationships with Spanish-speaking and Indian women than with those of their own ethnic background. The 1850 census reveals that only about fifty Euro-American women over the age of eighteen resided in the greater Los Angeles region. Contemporary accounts of mid-nineteenth-century California corroborate that.[54] Harris Newmark, a European who immigrated to California in 1853, remarked on the absence of women, particularly in San Francisco, his port of entry. "I was amazed," he would later recall in his memoirs, "at the comparative absence of women."[55]

The Euro-American men who formed relationships with Spanish-speaking and native women and had children in and out of wedlock were part of a larger group of men who migrated to Los Angeles in the 1850s, 1860s, and 1870s. The major initial impetus bringing these newcomers to the region was the discovery of gold at Sutter's Mill in 1848.[56] The 1849 gold rush triggered a mass migration of men (and a few women) from other parts of the United States, northern Mexico, Central and South America, Europe, and Asia.[57] In 1848 and 1849, nearly 10,000 Sonorans went to the placer mines, with several thousand California-born Mexicans and California Indians eventually joining them.[58] At the height of the gold fever, between 1849 and 1854, some 80,000 to 300,000 fortune-seekers entered the state, with many passing through Los Angeles, which functioned as a way station to the mines.[59] Earnings in the first five years after the discovery of gold were calculated at more than several hundred million dollars, and some miners made small fortunes. With the end of the gold rush, the miners, and those who had sold goods to them, settled throughout the state. Most professional men and skilled workers went to urban areas, such as San Francisco, Sacramento, and Stockton, whereas small shopkeepers, traders, merchants, and semi- and unskilled workers went to Los Angeles and nearby ranchos. There they hoped to take advantage of land-based activities, such as agricultural and livestock production, the primary industries in the region. Later, in the 1860s, 1870s, and especially 1880s, many more Euro-Americans came to southern California and invested in real estate and other attractive businesses.[60]

The impact of Euro-American migration to Los Angeles was especially dramatic. In 1850, Euro-Americans and foreign-born individuals numbered only 365, or 25 percent of the city's population of 1,610 (see table 5.2). During the next three decades, in response to the stream of migrants from northern California and from the eastern half of the United States, the percentage of Euro-Americans increased significantly, eventually surpassing that of the Spanish-speaking population. In 1860, Euro-Americans constituted 53 percent of the population, whereas in 1870, they accounted for 62 percent, and in 1880, 81 percent of the city's residents.[61]

The increasing Euro-American population, the gender-ratio imbalance, and the rising rates of illegitimacy coincided with the weakening of an already troubled Catholic Church and the alienation from it of the Spanish-speaking and native population, which had begun with secularization in the 1830s and had accelerated in the 1840s and thereafter. The Church in Mexico suffered from weak leadership, insufficient personnel, lack of funds, and low morale among the priests.[62] California had no resident bishop throughout the Spanish era and most of the Mexican period. Ecclesiastical authority over Alta California lay with the Diocese of Sonora. Thus, distance, infrequent communication, and the absence, for over twelve years, of a prelate assigned to California meant virtually no contact or guidance. Leadership rested with the president of the missions, but whoever held that position was absorbed by wrenching problems, distractions, and the struggle for survival that accompanied secularization. Only in 1840 did Ambas Californias acquire a bishop, Fray Francisco García Diego y Moreno, a Mexico-born Franciscan from the College of Zacatecas. However, the enormous size of his diocese, the difficulties faced by his congregants, and his lack of supplies and manpower rendered him nearly powerless. In 1843, he complained to the Minister of Justice in Mexico about his lack of "population, clergy, income, and, in fine, all resources."[63] Matters only worsened. Three years later, Alta California had only five secular priests, a handful of Franciscan friars, and no hope for attracting clergy from the interior and urban centers of Mexico, where priests were also in heavy demand. Inadequate personnel and resources doomed Bishop García y Moreno's attempt to establish a seminary that might otherwise have created a cadre of native-born clergy.[64]

Also undermining the effectiveness of the clergy in California was the church-state struggle in Mexico, which was about clerical privileges and wealth. In the 1820s, the Mexican government abolished compulsory tithing, which had obligated people to contribute one-tenth of their income to the Church. Then, in 1842, the government expropriated the Pious Fund, a private benefice designed to support the California missions. The impact devastated an already crippled diocese. Catholic Californians, as they had been accustomed to doing during the heyday of the missionary era, provided little financial support to their local parishes.[65] Bishop García Diego y Moreno attempted to resurrect tithing, by asking for contributions of 10 percent of the people's earnings and a portion of their livestock, but the congregants were indifferent. "All peoples," he wrote to his superiors in Mexico, "even the pagans, have honored, sustained, and looked after their priests. . . . Only this diocese has yet to comply with that sacred duty."[66] Nor did the Church raise much from *aranceles* or "stole fees," the payments derived from the administering of sacraments, such as baptisms, marriages, and last rites. Poverty and the sparse number of inhabitants meant almost no revenue for the Church. Its destitution in California was not unique in borderland settlements. In New Mexico, for example, parishioners often found the aranceles onerous, preferring to forego the sacraments to avoid the costs. In California, Bishop García Diego y Moreno, frustrated with the meager returns and disappointed with the protests from congregants, eventually eliminated the aranceles, though the Church later reintroduced them.[67]

The Catholic Church in California also had difficulty in maintaining the loyalty of the neófito population. Its alienation began in the 1830s, when most neófitos fled from the missions rather than claiming the land and property that rightfully belonged to them.[68] Many went to Los Angeles or to nearby ranchos, where they worked as servants and manual laborers, and others fled to the interior where few "whites" lived. Mexican priests, however, clung to the hope that the newly established Mexican government would reestablish a quasi-mission system and restore their control over their former wards. In 1846, for example, Tomás Esténega, the priest at Misión San Gabriel, complained to Abel Stearns, the prominent Los Angeles resident, about his mayordomo at Rancho Los Alamitos: Antonio Bermudez was hiding two Indian women, Matilda and Josefa, who had left the mission in the company of other Indians. The women "are under my charge," Esténega informed Stearns, and will remain so "until the [Mexican] government decide[s] what to do with the mission and the women." Despite the priest's demands, the two women never returned to San Gabriel, and Esténega died the following year.[69]

A weakened Church in California resulted in declining morale and, apparently, morals of the remaining Franciscans friars and the recently arrived secular priests. Impoverishment, advanced age, and ill health made it all but impossible for them to carry out their duties.[70] The scant attention paid to them may have led certain of them to commit excesses, as contemporaries reported that some of them "behaved scandalously."[71] Residents of Monterey accused Father Cajetan Sorrentini of sexual indiscretions and eventually drove him from town by burning him in effigy.[72] Locals and travelers in New Mexico and Texas also accused padres there of violating their vows.[73] The clergy denied these accusations, and in turn, accused their critics of lacking spirituality and harboring "irreverence" for the Church.[74]

After the American conquest, the Church's effort to revitalize and "Americanize" Catholicism only accelerated the alienation of the Spanish-speaking and Indian populations. These reforms began with the Seventh Provincial Council of Baltimore, the seat of the Catholic Church in the United States, which met in 1849 to address the future spiritual welfare of California. A year later, the council appointed Spanish-born Joseph Sadoc Alemany as the bishop of Monterey. He reported directly to Rome until jurisdictional issues with Mexico were resolved in 1853. That year, the Pope gave authority over Alta California's Catholic community to the U.S. Church and put the Church in Baja California under the Archbishop of Mexico City. The Pope appointed Alemany as Archbishop of San Francisco and Thaddeus Amat, a Spanish-born Vicentian, as bishop of the newly created Diocese of Monterey and Los Angeles, whose jurisdiction extended from Santa Cruz south to the Mexican border, a region that was still almost exclusively Spanish-speaking.[75]

Soon after arriving in California, Alemany imposed tithing and aranceles to raise funds for the financially strapped Church. Most Mexicans reacted angrily.[76] He ordered local priests to refuse the sacraments to the dissenters until "they mend their ways."[77] Estevan Muñoz learned first-hand the consequences of that policy. In 1856, a priest at Misión San Gabriel, Jaime Lestrade, refused to administer the last rites to Muñoz, the former administrator of the mission, because he owed the Church almost $1,800.[78] Meanwhile, at the Los Angeles Plaza Church, a priest began charging high rates for sacraments—$300 for a funeral and $50 for a wedding.[79] According to Francisco Ramírez, editor of Los Angeles's *El Clamor Público,* the exorbitant charges forced "many Catholics to opt for civil marriages, for [which] they pay reasonable fees."[80] A group of citizens who opposed the onerous costs petitioned the bishop to lower them.[81] He eventually acquiesced, but his actions had clearly rankled the laity, who were already under the stress of accommodating to a new government and legal system.[82] Most Mexican Catholics, although perhaps opting for a civil marriage, persisted in baptizing their children, for the Church taught that unbaptized children who died would be refused entry into heaven. If the parents or *padrinos* (godparents) could not afford a baptism, the Church usually waived those costs. Neófitos and gentiles were also explicitly exempted from the fees.[83]

Like Alemany, Amat also sought to redefine the relationship between the Church and the laity. Soon after becoming bishop, Amat set out to cleanse the Catholic Church of ideas and practices, including Mexican folk practices, that, he believed, lacked decorum and which might offend the growing Euro-American population and Protestant sensibilities. His concern for public opinion emerged early in his career. As the superior of Saint Charles Seminary in Philadelphia in the 1840s and 1850s, he witnessed anti-Catholic riots firsthand.[84] He shared the American Catholic hierarchy's belief that the best way to overcome prejudice was to conform to popular American social and cultural norms.[85] When he arrived in California and saw the practices of Franciscan friars, he reprimanded them severely, and he accused them of fostering superstitious practices and displaying a careless attitude in administering the sacraments to "public sinners" and "untutored children."[86] Several secular priests supported Amat, voicing their concern over a "high level of corruption and immorality among the upper-class Catholics of Santa Bárbara who served as a bad example to the rest of the populace."[87]

In Amat's first pastoral letter, issued in 1856 in Santa Bárbara, the bishop reprimanded the laity for failing to follow religious observances. In 1862, 1869, and 1876, Amat issued a series of religious regulations aimed at bringing his flock into conformity with Catholic Church law and teachings. In all, he issued over 140 regulations dealing with marriages, concubinage, baptisms, funerals, and other rites and customs. In his view, the Mexican Catholics had become lax as a result of poor Franciscan pastoral care. For example, in 1862, he directed parish priests to persuade those parishioners who committed the "most serious crime, concubinage" to "shrink" and "abstain" from the practice or face excommunication.[88] Amat also instructed the padres to "admit no person into matrimony who is ignorant of Christian doctrine" and to discourage marriage between Catholics and non-Catholics, such as Euro-Americans, as those

Catholics who married non-Catholics were also subject to excommunication.[89] In effect, these laws discouraged partaking of the Catholic sacraments and made it more difficult for people to practice the Catholic religion.[90] To the Spanish-speaking population, who had to deal with the social, economic, political, and cultural changes wrought by the American conquest, Amat seemed "judgmental."

In contrast to Amat, Alemany made some effort to establish congenial relations with the Spanish-speaking population, allowing them, among other things, to request a priest of their own ethnic background to perform marriages.[91] Amat, in contrast, was less inclined to accommodate Mexican or Indian Catholics. In the mid-1850s, Pablo de la Guerra, a member of a prominent family in Santa Bárbara, pled for the bishop's patience with the Californio-Mexican population. It is difficult for them, he told Amat, to transfer their loyalties from Mexican friars to recently arrived clergy who are "avaricious even to the point of stealing in order to obtain wealth." Amat responded unsympathetically. "Don Pablo, Don Pablo," Amat declared, "the older priests [Franciscans] robbed still more."[92] Such condescending remarks undoubtedly did not quell de la Guerra's anxieties about the alienation of the Spanish-speaking community from the American Catholic Church.

However, the prelate seemed unconcerned, and he persisted in his criticism of the Mexican-born Franciscan friars, accusing them of being "proud, undisciplined, ignorant, lazy, and superstitious."[93] In his communications to Rome, Amat often belittled the friars' work in California and accused them of "discrediting the bishop, absolving the unworthy and unrepentant, neglecting the salvation of souls [ex-mission Indians], and fomenting absurd [beliefs] among the people."[94] The friars, Amat declared, were "no longer useful . . . in this country, for its most ancient institution [the mission] does not accommodate itself to the present age."[95] He especially scorned the friars for begging for money and sustenance in the streets, a practice that they had begun in the late Mexican period as a result of impoverishment. He feared the "ridicule of the Church by American Protestants."[96] Amat's vision for the Catholic Church, according to historian Francis J. Weber, was "gradually taking on a structure that set it apart from the earlier concepts of the friars."[97]

In Santa Fe, New Mexico, Nuevomexicanos also witnessed the transformation of the Catholic Church from local and autonomous governance to centralized control under new and foreign leadership. When the Frenchman Jean Baptiste Lamy was appointed to vicar apostolic in 1851, he set out to modernize the Church in New Mexico by reforming and, if necessary, excommunicating priests who failed to carry out their duties. Lamy also targeted the laity: He denounced women who bore children out of wedlock as "immoral," and he refused to hear their confession.[98]

In California, Amat's attempt to transform the California Catholic Church by eliminating Mexican folk practices and appeasing Euro-American Protestants did not go unnoticed by the Spanish-speaking populace. His denunciations of the laity caused the Mexican populace to distance itself from him. Daniel Hill, a "Mexicanized" Euro-American, who settled in southern California in the 1820s, noted in 1859 that the "laity, unaccustomed to censure or disapproval, assumed a menacing attitude and . . . proclaimed the Bishop heretical, . . . preaching doctrine different from that which they had been taught . . . by the friars." Amat, Hill concluded, "was too American in his principles of decorum and too much opposed to the promulgation of reverence for . . . Mexican innovations."[99] These "innovations" included celebrations of holy days not only with religious services but also with secular events, such as bull and bear fights and dances.[100]

In the late 1860s and early 1870s, the construction of a new cathedral, Saint Vibiana's, highlighted the cultural and religious isolation and "segregation" of Mexican Catholics from the Catholic Church. The privately funded cathedral was built to meet the growing population of Catholics in the city, particularly the increasing Euro-American population. It was constructed at Main and Second streets, a fashionable, Euro-American section of Los Angeles, which placed the cathedral considerably south of the central plaza area, where most Mexicans resided.[101] The cathedral was dedicated in 1876 and finished in 1880, but the Spanish-speaking population continued to attend the Plaza Church, their traditional place of worship. They also practiced religious folk customs at home. By the late 1850s and 1860s, few Spanish-speaking Catholics attended religious services, partook of the sacraments, or followed the teachings of the Catholic Church. The records indicate that an increasing number of couples turned to the civil authorities for marriage and, as noted earlier, bore children outside of a Church-sanctioned marriage.[102]

Like Californio-Mexicans, the Christianized Indians, or neófitos, also became alienated from the American Catholic Church, but their separation was more dramatic and complete. In the American period, neófitos found an increasingly indifferent church hierarchy, which made little real effort to minister to them. The neglect reflected, in part, the financial and personnel difficulties faced by the Church. This was nowhere more apparent than at the defunct missions, where many neófitos lived and eked out an existence. Some 3,000, for example, lived at the former Misión San Luis Rey, by that point, in serious disrepair. Amat instructed four elderly friars from Santa Bárbara to go to San Luis Rey to set up a mission-like institution to provide spiritual guidance and the sacraments to the Indians. The friars, aware of the undesirable conditions at San Luis Rey, refused to comply with his orders.[103] The Native Americans at San Luis Rey continued living there until pressure from the growing Euro-American population forced them to relocate to the recently established reservations or to retreat to the inland areas.

As a result of the Church's neglect, the numbers of Indians who maintained ties to the Church or observed the sacraments diminished considerably. Catholic Church records indicate that in the 1850s, 475 neófito children were baptized in Los Angeles and at San Gabriel. In the 1860s, those figures dropped dramatically to 147 and then fell again in the 1870s to only 81. In the same period, the Church baptized even fewer gentile children: 101 in the 1850s, 15 in the 1860s, and 11, in the 1870s.[104] Those figures not only reveal the extent to which the population was dying from diseases and violence in the post-conquest period, they also underscore the alienation of Native Americans (Christian and non-Christian) from the Catholic Church.

The alienation of the Californio-Mexican and Native American populations from the Church, though telling, obscures the intimate details and personal circumstances surrounding the increasing illegitimacy rates and the relationships that engendered those children. A close examination of the records indicate that the Californio-Mexican and Native American women who had illegitimate offspring in the post-conquest period faced a host of legal and economic consequences that made it difficult for them to raise their children. According to California law, fathers of illegitimate children had no obligation to provide for the education and maintenance of their offspring. That burden fell on the mother alone. A father's lack of responsibility was made clear in an 1870 California Supreme Court Case that ruled that illegitimate children, unlike those of divorced parents who were entitled to paternal support, had no similar privileges, "however strong may be the [father's] moral obligation." "The law," the court held, "for reasons of public policy, does not impose on him any obligation."[105]

Since California had no system of social welfare or poor laws, mothers were forced to find ways to make ends meet. Although some worked, others sought charity from friends, family, or orphanages.

Unlike American common law, Spanish and Mexican civil law obligated fathers to provide a minimal measure of support for hijos naturales, though how often those men complied with that duty is unknown. On the other hand, fathers of hijos espurios—those born as a result of adultery—were under no such obligation.[106] Mothers of illegitimate offspring, in contrast, had to support and educate their children, whether naturales or espurios. Frequently, those mothers turned to relatives, extended family networks, or to the civil or ecclesiastical authorities for help. Far less often, they resorted to begging or stealing.[107]

Thus, the women who bore illegitimate children out of wedlock in the American period faced harsh legal and economic consequences, and although it was diminishing with the transition from Mexican to American culture, they also endured social disdain. In the Mexican period, cultural and social mores taught that extramarital sexual relations threatened marriage, the family, and a stable society. Consequently, an illegitimate birth brought shame and dishonor to a woman and her family. Hijos naturales, children born to unmarried parents who were eligible to marry, carried less social stigma than hijo espurios, the children of an adulterous relationship. Couples with hijos naturales could marry in the Catholic Church at any time and legitimize their children. In general, however, and especially among the elite, illegitimate children were socially dishonored persons whose parentage remained in question and whose marital choice, occupation, and social mobility were often limited.[108] On the northern frontier, many illegitimate Californios and Mexicans nevertheless ascended to influential political posts and social positions because in the frontier region, social status and mobility were more dependent on ethnicity, property holding, and family ties than on legitimacy.[109]

The shame that illegitimacy brought to a family or to an individual appears to have eased in the American era, for almost all fathers of illegitimate children in the post-conquest period acknowledged the paternity of their sons or daughters. Given that American law failed to obligate fathers of illegitimate children to provide them with financial support, it may have made it easier and less risky for those fathers to claim paternity. In contrast, in the Mexican period, fathers of hijos naturales were obligated to provide some support. It is clear that in Spanish and Mexican

Los Angeles, fathers, especially among the elite, admitted paternity only infrequently. Mexican men who fathered illegitimate children benefited from a sexual double standard that condemned, and sometimes publicly humiliated, women for sexual impropriety yet often merely reprimanded culpable men. Men faced little, if any, public humiliation, for they could and often did remain anonymous participants in the birth of an illegitimate child. The records indicate that in Los Angeles, fewer than 5 percent of those men who fathered illegitimate children in the Spanish and Mexican eras acknowledged paternity. Fathers often escaped shame and dishonor through the intervention of the clergy, who, rather than giving the individual's name, usually identified such a man in the baptismal registers as a *padre no conocido* (unknown father).[110]

On the rare occasion that a woman named the father of her child during the Spanish and Mexican periods, he often denied it. In 1822, for example, when the widow María Antonia Valenzuela named Antonio Elizalde as the father of her child, he challenged her declaration. The priest at Misión San Gabriel reported that "[Elizalde] doubts his role as the father."[111] When mothers refused to identify the father of their children, family members or close friends sometimes disclosed that information. When Gertrudis Moreno took her child to be baptized at Misión San Gabriel in 1822, she did not name the father of her child, stating simply that he was "unknown." The child's *madrina* or godmother had no qualms about revealing his identity. "If we believe what the godmother said," the priest noted in the margin of the baptismal record, the father is "Ysidro Guillen."[112]

In contrast, in the American period, fathers (as well as mothers) routinely informed the priest of the identity of the child's father. The records indicate that from the end of the 1850s through the 1870s, more than 85 percent of the men who had a child outside of marriage acknowledged their offspring. Mexican men, such as Francisco Machado, who, in 1868, had a child with Ysidora Talamantes, a married woman, and Carlos Vasquez, who fathered a child with Luisa Valenzuela in 1874, disclosed their identities to the priests.[113] The men who fathered children out of wedlock with Indian women in the post-conquest period also almost always claimed paternity, whereas in the Mexican period, fewer than 10 percent did so, indicating that attitudes towards children born outside of marriage were changing across ethnic lines.[114]

Though fathers regularly acknowledged paternity, and their role in the birth of the child thus became common knowledge, the shame associated with illegitimate children did not disappear overnight. Some people clung to the belief that children born out of wedlock, and the relationships leading to those births, were shameful and immoral. On occasion, a few Spanish-speaking and Euro-American men denied paternity, and family members sometimes ostracized the women who bore illegitimate children. The father of Lugarda Rubio's daughter, for instance, denied his role in the birth of the child. In 1850, approximately two years after Rubio had baptized her daughter and revealed that Stephen "Esteban" Foster was the father, Foster lodged a formal denial with the priest. In all likelihood, Foster's recent marriage to the widow María Merced Lugo, who belonged to a socially, economically, and politically prominent family, prompted him to make the disclaimer.[115] Two decades later, in 1878, Luis Odignot, another Euro-American, went before the Catholic priest at Misión San Gabriel to reject the claim of Juana, a native woman, that he was the father of her son, José Eusebio. The priest supported not only his denial—"I believe him, for the child bears no resemblance [to him]," but also his contention that someone else was responsible: "Don Luis says Adolfo Ayo is the father."[116]

Although many fathers acknowledged their children born out of wedlock, there is evidence that some people felt tainted by illegitimacy when it occurred in their own household or in their extended family. In 1870, Martín Olvera proclaimed his embarrassment because his cousin, María Lugarda Reyes, had left her husband, George Whitehouse, and was living with a younger man, Felipe Valenzuela. She lived with Valenzuela for ten years, and they had several children. "It made me feel ashamed to see her living as she was," Olvera said, "because she was a relative, and he [Whitehouse] was such a good man."[117] The stepfather of Gumecinda Cruz, a married woman, also admitted a sense of vergüenza and dishonor after hearing rumors about her living out of wedlock and having children with Ygnacio Reyes.[118]

The social, economic, political, demographic, and cultural changes brought about by the American conquest had a far-reaching effect, altering the most intimate aspects of Californio-Mexican and Native American women's lives as well as family and community life in Los Angeles and the larger region. In the aftermath of the American takeover, an increasing number of Californio-Mexican and Native American women bore children out of wedlock. There were many reasons for this: increased landlessness and impoverishment, leading to marginalization of the Spanish-speaking population and the decimation of the Native American population; the migration of men into and out of the region; the consequent abandonment of women, which, coupled with the general economic impoverishment, led them to live out of wedlock with men who could afford to support them; and the alienation of the Spanish-speaking and Native American populations from the Catholic Church.

Although the increasing rate of illegitimacy affected men and women alike, it created special burdens for unmarried or abandoned women, who had to find a means to support themselves and their offspring. Some, living in common-law marriages, had the support of their partners. Others were forced to find employment outside the home in unskilled and labor-intensive jobs, working as washerwomen, seamstresses, or housekeepers. Some were even forced to resort to begging or stealing to make ends meet.

Women's increasing responsibility for caring, often single-handedly, for children reveals that Californio–Mexican and Native American women's status underwent profound changes in the American period. Yet, despite the social dislocation, women adapted to the new social, economic, political, and cultural order. Whether or not everyone in the barrio approved of women taking on new roles—working for a living or living with a provider who was not a spouse—remains largely unknown, but it is clear that necessity and determination compelled these women to pursue new avenues in order to survive. In the process of building and crafting a better future for themselves and their families, they became agents of cultural change by redefining and expanding women's roles and relations in the Mexican community at the end of the nineteenth century.

Legacies: An Afterword

In 1885, María Amparo Ruiz de Burton published *Squatter and the Don*, a novel that dramatically depicted the loss of land and impoverishment suffered by Mexican rancheros in nineteenth-century California. Focusing on the fictional Alamar family as representative of the collective experiences of the once land-rich Mexican elite, Ruiz recounted the injustices endured under the new legal, economic, and political systems imposed by the United States. She singled out for special criticism the federal laws that established the process for confirming titles to the vast lands that had been granted during the Spanish and Mexican eras. She saw those laws as the product of a diabolical conspiracy among legislators, corporations, capitalists, and monopolists. The hero of her novel, the once proud and powerful patriarch, Don Mariano Alamar, epitomized the people who were brought down by that conspiracy.[1]

Looking back on the federal land laws that violated the promises made in the 1848 Treaty of Guadalupe Hidalgo, which had guaranteed the protection of property, Don Mariano offered a corrective: "If the law had obliged us to submit our titles to the inspection of the land commission but had not opened our ranchos to settlers *until it had been proved that our titles were not good,* and if, too, taxes were paid by those who derived the benefit from the land, then there would be some color of equity in such laws."[2] Sadly, when the U.S. Congress passed the legislation, it never considered Don Mariano's remedy, nor did it do so later, after the law's devastating effects had become apparent to all. As the novel ends, the old don lies on his deathbed, broken in spirit and penniless, and he lashes out for the last time at the merciless enemy: "The sins of our legislators brought me to this!"[3]

The American conquest in 1846 brought legal, economic, political, cultural, demographic, and social transformations that undermined Mexican society and culture and that left its people impoverished and landless. The takeover also affected intimate aspects of personal life, including gender relations, marriage, and the family. In the Spanish and Mexican eras, patriarchal authority figures—husbands and fathers, civil and religious leaders—had ruled at home and in the community, wielding authority over Spanish-speaking women and Native American men and women. Women who transgressed socio-sexual codes of behavior faced serious consequences, including physical harm and public denigration. Men who similarly violated sexual mores suffered few, if any, repercussions. Instead, they benefited from a sexual double standard that allowed them to engage in extra-marital relations while preserving their honor and social standing.

Despite that double standard and patriarchal constraints, Californio-Mexican and Native American women of different economic circumstances took advantage of legal and extralegal means to challenge men who failed in marital, family, or social obligations. Although some turned to the civil and ecclesiastical courts for redress, others took matters into their own hands, often fleeing from unhappy homes even at the risk of severe punishment imposed by the law and cultural norms. Women also took advantage of their property rights to seek control over their lives and to achieve a measure of economic independence from husbands, fathers, and men, in general. Understandably, those women who possessed personal wealth achieved a greater degree of freedom. That was especially true of single women and widows, whom Mexican law protected from male interference in property matters. The less fortunate women tended to be the poor, whether Californio-Mexican or Native American.

The American conquest had radical implications for male and female relations in marriage, family, and community life. The emergence of a predominant Euro-American, Protestant, and capitalist society and, in particular, land legislation enacted under the new regime undermined the ability of nearly all Mexican and native property holders—men and women alike—to retain their property. Impoverishment forced Spanish-speaking men to migrate in search of work and women to find employment as wage laborers. Men's migration led to the abandonment of women, many of whom then took up with men of different ethnicities and social classes. For some, a woman's decision to live out of wedlock with a man who could support her was her only means for economic survival.

Consequently, a growing number of Californio-Mexican women bore children out of wedlock and, if their partners could not or did not maintain them and the children, the women had to find a means to do so. These women increasingly turned to wage labor in as domestics and to family members for sustenance.

These challenges notwithstanding, the transition from Spanish and Mexican civil law to U.S. common law increased Mexican women's leverage in their personal relationships with men. Women's right to divorce and the opportunity to gain support, community property, and custody of children enabled some of them to break with cultural norms, leave intolerable marriages, and, in a few cases, form new, supportive relationships. Nevertheless, in reality, most spouses were insolvent and unable to pay alimony or child support. As most divorced women learned, the opportunities for financial and personal freedom promised by the dissolution of their marriages gave way to the grim reality of economic destitution and, for those without extended family networks, personal isolation.

Although the American conquest brought dramatic transformations for California's indigenous peoples, they were already in the throes of major change. In the Spanish era, they had faced violence and had seen their way of life threatened. Soldiers assaulted native women, sometimes killing the native men in the process. Contagious diseases, violence, starvation, and land depletion led to enormous population loss. In the Mexican era, the native Californians were promised land but never received it. In the American era, they faced perhaps their most dangerous enemy: the Euro-Americans, who had little tolerance for racial difference, generally, and for native peoples, in particular. Armed conflicts, violence, and legal and extralegal policies and practices aimed at dealing with the "Indian problem" decimated the Native American population in California. It dwindled from approximately 300,000 at the time of European contact to 150,000 at the close of the Mexican era, and with the American conquest, it declined even further, to fewer than 20,000. The Native American "holocaust" in the American era remains a disgraceful chapter in U.S. history.

The American conquest of the present-day southwestern United States touched nearly all aspects of Californio-Mexican and native women's lives and irrevocably altered their existence. Despite staggering challenges, these women adapted to their changing environment and took advantage of the opportunities available to them. Women used the new legal system to their advantage. When necessary, they headed their own households and found employment doing domestic wage labor. Some turned to family and friends for support, and others formed beneficial relationships with recently arrived migrant men, who were often of different ethnicities and social classes. And even though women challenged cultural norms, cultural identity remained strong as the Spanish-speaking community in Los Angeles drew closer together under the onslaught of the increasing Euro-American presence. Women's strategies, though unconventional, attest to women's desire to preserve their families, communities, and self-respect in a hostile world.

Like the post-conquest nuevomexicanas that Deena González has described, Californio-Mexican and Native American women helped to rebuild families, homes, and barrios out of the rubble of the war. They also fought to reclaim their property, challenged cultural norms, and, in the process, left an indelible mark in history for their families and for future generations to cherish. They are a testament to the legacy of Mexican and native women's history of survival and resistance against all odds.

The stories of the women in nineteenth-century California are also the stories of our California, Mexican, and native grandmothers and great-grandmothers, who, in the twentieth century, faced multiple responsibilities and challenges in their homes, churches, and communities. Our *abuelas* (grandmothers) and *bisabuelas* (great-grandmothers) living in México and the United States often had to deal with physical and emotional abuse, dire poverty, the birth and death of many children, as well as judgmental members of the community, including priests. Such experiences parallel those of my paternal grandmother, whose life history in Aguascalientes, Mexico, inspired the research for and writing of this book. My abuelita "Jilda" (short for Leobijilda), as I learned as a young child, had to support six children with meager earnings that she gained through the sale of candies and other treats. At the same time, as I learned later in life, she also had to contend with a physically and verbally abusive husband. Though the onset of a degenerative disease relegated him to a wheelchair, and later to a bed, she encountered no letup in the burdens placed on her by his anger and frustration. I often wondered how she managed to accomplish all of the familial responsibilities while she cared for an ailing man who treated her with little regard.

My grandmother, like the women in this study, employed creative and resourceful strategies to deal with and overcome her burdens. Mexican and native women of the nineteenth century took on those challenges and usually met with success, as did my grandmother in the twentieth century. Yet, they often did so at a high price: They sacrificed their personal freedom and security to maintain their children and families. We must remember that these women made choices based on their personal and familial circumstances–on what was at their disposal economically and materially.

In remembering the Mexican and native women who preceded us, let us not romanticize the sacrifices they made nor neglect to appreciate the challenges they endured, survived, and resisted on a daily basis. We owe them our lives and our history. In carving out our future as mexicanas, Chicanas, and mestizas residing in the United States, we often turn to them and their stories for sources of inspiration, strength, and guidance. In essence, we are building upon a tradition of strength they laid out in the past. Let us continue to build upon on that legacy.

Notes

Abbreviations Used in the Notes

Cal   Reports of Cases Determined in the Supreme Court of the State of California, 1872. California State Law Library, Sacramento

HSSCQ   *Historical Society of Southern California Quarterly*

LAACR–CC   Los Angeles Area Court Records–Criminal Court. Henry E. Huntington Library, San Marino, California

LAACR–DC   Los Angeles Area Court Records–District Court. Henry E. Huntington Library, San Marino, California

LACA   Los Angeles City Archives. Records Management Division, City of Los Angeles

LAPC   Los Angeles Plaza Church, baptismal records. Family History Center, Church of Jesus Christ of Latter Day Saints, Davis, California

LC   U.S. District Court, Land Cases, Southern District. Bancroft Library, Berkeley, California

SA   Spanish Archives. California State Archives, Sacramento, California

SC   Abel Stearns Collection. Henry E. Huntington Library, San Marino, California

SCQ   *Southern California Quarterly*

SGM   Misión San Gabriel, baptismal records and marriage records. Family History Center, Church of Jesus Christ of Latter Day Saints, Davis, California

WHQ   *Western Historical Quarterly*

Preface

1. For the purposes of this preface, my discussion of Malintzin has been brief. The main points come from: Kartunnen, "Rethinking Malinche"; Del Castillo, "Malintzin Tenépal; and Lanyon, *Malinche's Conquest*. Dozens, perhaps hundreds, of Mexican, U.S., European, and Australian studies exist on Malintzin or La Malinche, all with divergent viewpoints. For one of the most popular views of Marina in colonial Mexico, see Díaz del

Castillo, *Historia verdadera de la conquista de la Nueva España*; and Paz, *The Labyrinth of Solitude*.

2. See, for example, Paz, *The Labyrinth of Solitude*.

3. Kartunnen, "Rethinking Malinche," 312. For recent studies that seek to reinterpret her role as a "traitor" and see her as a shrewd woman, see del Castillo, "Malitzin Tenepal"; Sweeney, "Chicana History: A Review of the Literature"; Alarcón, "Chicana's Feminist Literature: A Re-Vision through Malintzin/or Malinche"; Phillips, "Marina/Malinche: Masks and Shadows"; Soto, "Tres modelos culturales: La Virgen Guadalupe, La Malinche y la Llorona"; González, "La Chicana: Guadalupe or Malinche"; Pérez, *The Decolonial Imaginary*; Candelaria, "La Malinche, Feminist Prototype"; Gutiérrez, "Chicano History: Paradigm Shifts and Shifting Boundaries"; and Gutiérrez, "Unraveling America's Hispanic Past."

4. For recent studies on gender in colonial Mexico, see, for example, Arrom, *The Women of Mexico City*; Lavrin, *Sexuality and Marriage*; Twinam, *Public Lives, Private Secrets*; Seed, *To Love, Honor, and Obey in Colonial Mexico*; Gutiérrez, *When Jesus Came, The Corn Mothers Went Away*; Boyer, "Women, La Mala Vida, and the Politics of Marriage." For similar studies on Mexico's northern frontier, see, for example, Castañeda, "*Presidarias y pobladoras*"; Bouvier, *Women and the Conquest of California*; and González, *Refusing the Favor*.

5. I recognize that the term or concept of "gender" is used by scholars in a variety of ways. I employ it to mean the social and cultural values associated with and attributed to biological differences between males and females. The meaning I employ comes from several sources, including Bouvier, *Women and the Conquest of California*, ix–xvii; Scott, "Gender: A Useful Category of Historical Analysis"; and Johnson, " 'A Memory Sweet to Soldiers'."

6. Bouvier, *Women and the Conquest of California*, xv.

7. González, *Refusing the Favor*, 256.

8. For legal studies that examine the influence of Spanish and Mexican civil law on American common and statutory law, particularly on women's property rights in California, see Prager, "The Persistence of Separate Property Concepts in California's Community Property System"; and Schuele, "Community Property Law."

9. Several works were useful in developing this methodology. See, for example, Arrom, *Women of Mexico City*; and Erickson, *Women and Property in Early Modern England*.

10. Pérez, *The Decolonial Imaginary*, 3–27.

11. Ibid., 7.

12. Theoretical works on feminist scholarship consulted for this study include De La Torre and Pesquera, "Introduction," in *Building with Our Hands*; Castañeda, "Women of Color and the Rewriting of Western History"; Burkett, "In Dubious Sisterhood"; Scott, "Introduction," in *Feminism and History*; and Scott, *Gender and the Politics of History*.

13. For recent work on the blurring of "private" and "public" spheres, see, for example, Kierner, *Beyond the Household*; Ryan, *Women in Public*; and Goodman, "Public Sphere and Private Life."

14. Numerous studies have explored the theme of patriarchy across time and space.

For general works, see, for example, Lerner, *The Creation of Patriarchy*; Pateman, *The Sexual Contract*; Murray, *The Law of the Father?*; and Brown, *Good Wives, Nasty Wenches, and Anxious Patriarchs*. For works on colonial Spanish America, see, for example, Arrom, *Women of Mexico City*; Stern, *The Secret History of Gender*; Lavrin, *Sexuality and Marriage*; Kymm Gauderman, "Father Fiction"; and Pescatello, *Power and Pawn*. For those in Spanish, Mexican, and early American California, see Hurtado, *Intimate Frontiers*; Griswold del Castillo, "Patriarchy and the Status of Women," 85–99; and Monroy, "They Didn't Call Them 'Padre' for Nothing."

Chapter 1. Gender and the Conquest and Colonization of California

1. For the full transcript of this case, see Archivo General de la Nación, Californias, vol. 2, file 6, Bancroft Library, Berkeley, California, fols. 243–83. For Carrillo's investigation, see Mariano Carrillo, San Diego, April 10, 1773, ibid., fols. 244–93. For insightful analyses of this case, see Bouvier, *Women and the Conquest of California*, 47–48; and Beilharz, *Felipe de Neve*, 27–30.

2. Bouvier, *Women and the Conquest of California*, 47–48; Beilharz, *Felipe de Neve*, 27–30.

3. Bouvier makes the point that Attorney General José Antonio Areche found the overlooked file fifteen months after Pedro Fages sent it from Alta California to Mexico City. *Women and the Conquest of California*, 197, n. 68.

4. For more on the provincias internas, see Gutiérrez, *When Jesus Came, the Corn Mothers Went Away*, 299–306; and for more on the office of the commandant general, see Haring, *The Spanish Empire*, 80.

5. Bouvier, *Women and the Conquest of California*, 48; and Beilharz, *Felipe de Neve*, 30.

6. The term *gente de razón* originated in Spain during the Inquisition and differentiated between Spanish subjects and recently converted infidels, *gente sin razón*, "people lacking in reason," or neófitos (neophytes). Hispanic peoples throughout the Spanish Borderlands used these terms primarily as ethnic signifiers, that is, to differentiate between Spanish subjects and native peoples. See Gutiérrez, *When Jesus Came, the Corn Mothers Went Away*, 195.

7. Of the many studies on Spain's effort to fortify New Spain's northern provinces, this book relies on Bancroft, *The Works of Hubert Howe Bancroft*, vol. 18, 13–69, 111–14; Bouvier, *Women and the Conquest of California*, 3–53; and Beilharz, *Felipe de Neve*, 8–44. For other studies that explore this topic in detail, see Weber, *The Spanish Frontier in North America*; and Bannon, *The Spanish Borderlands Frontier*.

8. This discussion on the Spanish crown draws from Haring, *The Spanish Empire*, 3–5, 94–97, 100–101, 166–67; Phelan, "Authority and Flexibility," 50–54; Góngora, *Studies in the Colonial History of Spanish America*, 68–77; and Gutiérrez, *When Jesus Came, the Corn Mothers Went Away*, 95–101.

9. For more on the patronato real, see *Recopilación de las leyes de las indias*, vol. 1.; and above, note 8.

10. Haring, *The Spanish Empire*, 94, 188; and Phelan, "Authority and Flexibility," 48–50. For more on the jurisdictional conflicts between secular and religious officials in Alta

California, see Bouvier, *Women and the Conquest of California*, 36; and in New Mexico, see Gutiérrez, *When Jesus Came, the Corn Mothers Went Away*, 96–101.

11. Bancroft, *The Works of Hubert Howe Bancroft*, vol. 18, 115–29; and Avilez, *Population Increases*, 1–4.

12. Serra, San Diego, to Francisco Palóu, April 16, 1770, in Tibesar, *The Writings of Junípero Serra*, vol. 1, 165. For more about these trips and the hardships endured, see Diary by Serra of the Expedition from Loreto to San Diego, March 28 to July 1, 1769, in ibid., 97, 103; Serra, San Diego, to Palóu, February 10, 1770, ibid., 159; Bancroft, *The Works of Hubert Howe Bancroft*, vol. 18, 130–36, 140–65; Avilez, *Population Increases*, 1–4; Bouvier, *Women and the Conquest of California*, 40; and Teggart, *The Portolá Expedition*.

13. Serra, Monterey, to Juan Andrés, June 12, 1770, in Tibesar, *The Writings of Junípero Serra*, vol. 1, 171; Bancroft, *The Works of Hubert Howe Bancroft*, vol. 18, 168–71, 175; and Avilez, *Population Increases*, 4–5.

14. Before the arrival of European and Spanish-speaking women, Spanish explorers and conquerors used the image of the Virgin Mary to subdue the native peoples and convince them that they had come in peace. Bouvier develops this idea in chapters 1, 2, and 3 of *Women and the Conquest of California*. For more on the role of patriarchy in Alta California, see Castañeda, "*Presidarias y pobladoras*," 96–98; and chapter 2 of this book.

15. For more on Mexican women's roles in colonial Mexico, see Arrom, *The Women of Mexico*, 53–97.

16. Bouvier, *Women and the Conquest of California*, 54; and Serra, San Diego, to Father Guardian, Mexico City, March 31, 1774, in Tibesar, *The Writings of Junípero Serra*, vol. 2, 43. On page 54, Bouvier notes that Sebastián and his wife fled with a companion from Baja California, but Bancroft states that Sebastián and his wife were in the company of his parents (*The Works of Hubert Howe Bancroft*, vol. 18, 221, n. 3).

17. Castañeda develops these ideas in her dissertation, "*Presidarias y pobladoras*," 130–35; see also "Sexual Violence," 25–26. Bouvier also addresses these themes in *Women and the Conquest of California*, 52. For more on the sexual exploitation of native women in the Spanish conquest, see Hurtado, *Intimate Frontiers*; Gutiérrez, *When Jesus Came, the Corn Mothers Went Away*; and Trexler, *Sex and Conquest*.

18. Quotation cited in Geiger *Letter of Luís Jayme*, 26–27; Geiger, "Instructions Concerning the Occupation of California," 212; and Bouvier, *Women and the Conquest of California*, 37.

19. Serra, Mexico City, to Antonio María de Bucareli y Ursúa, Mexico City, May 21, 1773, in Tibesar, *The Writings of Junípero Serra*, vol. 1, 361. For a thorough analysis of this incident, see Castañeda, "Sexual Violence," 15–33. For other accounts of this incident, see Engelhardt, *San Gabriel Mission*, 3–16; Priestly, *A Historical, Political, and Natural Description of California by Pedro Fages*, 18–19; and Bancroft, *The Works of Hubert Howe Bancroft*, vol. 18, 180–82.

20. Serra, Monterey, to Fr. Rafael Verger, Mexico City, August 8, 1772, in Tibesar *The Writings of Junípero Serra*, vol. 1, 257.

21. Castañeda, "*Presidarias y pobladoras*," 78.

22. For Serra's comments, see Serra, Monterey, to Verger, Mexico City, August 8, 1772, in Tibesar, *The Writings of Junípero Serra*, vol. 1, 261; and Bouvier, *Women and the Conquest of California*, 51. For Jayme's comments, see Geiger, *Letter of Father Luis Jayme*,

38. The five missions established in Alta California were San Diego (1769), San Carlos de Borromeo (1770), San Antonio de Padua (1771), San Gabriel (1771), and San Luis Obispo (1772).

23. Geiger, *Letter of Father Luis Jayme*, 40.

24. Serra, Mexico City, to Bucareli, Mexico City, April 22, 1773, in Tibesar, *The Writings of Junípero Serra*, vol. 1, 339, 341.

25. Serra, Mexico City, to Bucareli, Mexico City, May 21, 1773, ibid., 363.

26. Serra, Guadalajara, to Verger, Mexico City, November 11, 1773, ibid., vol. 2, 3.

27. Serra, Monterey, to Bucareli, Mexico City, April 22, 1773, ibid., vol. 1, 341.

28. Scholars dispute the reasons for the 1775 assault against the San Diego Mission. Some writers say the attacks against Indian women played a role, whereas others argue that the native peoples' general disdain for the Spanish led to the rebellion. In a recent study, Richard L. Carrico has argued that several factors—including the Spaniards' weakening of shamans' power, the rape and murder of native women, the exploitation of native food sources, and the forced labor at the missions—led to the assault. See Carrico, "Sociopolitical Aspects of the 1775 Revolt," 144–46. I would like to thank George H. Phillips for bringing Carrico's study to my attention. Bancroft, in *The Works of Hubert Howe Bancroft*, vol. 18, 181, says that there was "little doubt" the soldiers' indiscretions led to the native people's assaults. Scholars also dispute the number of rancherías involved in the uprising. Carrico identifies fifteen, whereas Phillips, *Chiefs and Challengers*, 23–24, says forty rancherías and eight hundred Indians attacked the San Diego Mission. For more details of the incident, see Geiger, *Letter of Luis Jayme*, 44–49; and Bouvier, *Women and the Conquest of California*, 47–48. For a first-hand account of the assault, see Father Vicente Fuster, San Diego, to Serra, Monterey, November 28, 1775, in Tibesar, *The Writings of Junípero Serra*, vol. 2, 449–58; Serra, Monterey, to Antonio María de Bucareli y Ursúa, Mexico City, December 15, 1775, ibid., 410; and Bolton, *Font's Complete Diary*, 186–235.

29. California Archives, Bancroft Library, Berkeley, California, vol. 15, 24–25; Bouvier, *Women and the Conquest of California*, 49–50, 140–41; Forbes, *Native Americans*, 33, and Carrico, "Sociopolitical Aspects of the 1775 Revolt," 149.

30. Quotation cited in Temple, "Toypurina the Witch," 148.

31. For more on Toypurina, see Forbes, *Native Americans*, 34; Castañeda, "*Presidarias y pobladoras*," 87, especially n. 70; Bouvier, *Women and the Conquest of California*, 141; and Jackson and Castillo, *Indians, Franciscans, and Spanish Colonization*, 76. For more on neófitos who planned assaults at and escaped from other missions, see Forbes, *Native Americans*, 33–40; and Bancroft, *The Works of Hubert Howe Bancroft*, vol. 18, 709–11. For those who poisoned and killed priests, see Forbes, *Native Americans*, 34; Bancroft, *The Works of Hubert Howe Bancroft*, vol. 19, 345, 388–89; and Asisara, "The Assasination of Padre Andrés Quintana," 116–25, 50–52.

32. Geiger, *Letter of Luis Jayme*, 40.

33. Serra, Mexico City, to Bucareli, Mexico City, May 21, 1773, in Tibesar, *The Writings of Junípero Serra*, vol. 1, 361, 363.

34. Castañeda, "*Presidarias y pobladoras*," 81; and Bancroft, *The Works of Hubert Howe Bancroft*, vol. 18, 180, n. 29.

35. Geiger, *Letter of Luis Jayme*, 42–44.

36. Ibid., 83; and Bouvier, *Women and the Conquest of California*, 130–31.

37. Serra, Mexico City, to Bucareli, Mexico City, May 21, 1773, in Tibesar, *The Writings of Junípero Serra*, vol. 1, 363.

38. Bouvier, *Women and the Conquest of California*, 51–52; Engelhardt, *San Gabriel Mission*, 8; and Bancroft, *The Works of Hubert Howe Bancroft*, vol. 18, 181.

39. Engelhardt, Father Serra's staunch supporter, blamed the soldiers of De Anza's first expedition in 1774 for the introduction and spread of venereal diseases. Sherburne F. Cook, however, argues that all of the expeditionary forces had a role in the spread of the disease. See, Engelhardt, *San Gabriel Mission*, 82, 90, 109; Geiger, "Introduction," in *Letter of Luís Jayme*, 30; Cook, *The Conflict between the California Indian and White Civilization*, 14–33, 207–9; and Monroy, *Thrown among Strangers*, 80–81.

40. Cook, *The Conflict between the California Indian and White Civilization*, 19–33; and Jackson and Castillo, *Indians, Franciscans, and Spanish Colonization*, 44, 48–49.

41. Geiger, *As the Padres Saw Them*, 71–74.

42. Ibid., 74.

43. For Lorenzana's observation, see Sánchez, Pita, and Reyes, "*Memorias* de doña Apolinaria Lorenzana," 5.

44. Quotation cited in Cook, *The Conflict between the California Indian and White Civilization*, 27.

45. Jackson and Castillo, *Indians, Franciscans, and Spanish Colonization*, 45, 57.

46. Serra, Mexico City, to Bucareli, Mexico City, March 13, 1773, in Tibesar, *The Writings of Junípero Serra*, vol. 1, 299, 301; and Bancroft, *The Works of Hubert Howe Bancroft*, vol. 18, 191.

47. Serra, Mexico City, to Bucareli, Mexico City, May 21, 1773, in Tibesar, *The Writings of Junípero Serra*, vol. 1, 361, 363; Castañeda, "*Presidarias y pobladoras*," 83–84; Bancroft, *The Works of Hubert Howe Bancroft*, vol. 18, 191, n. 16.

48. Serra, Monterey, to Father Guardian, Francisco Pangua, Mexico City, July 18, 1774, in Tibesar, *The Writings of Junípero Serra*, vol. 2, 107–9.

49. Geiger, *Letter of Luís Jayme*, 39.

50. Bouvier argues that the "incidents became the central issue of concern in the internal tensions between the church and the military" (*Women and the Conquest of California*, 48). Scholars, including Castañeda, Beilharz, and Bancroft, argue that not all of Father Serra's accusations had a basis in fact. Contrary to Serra's accusations, Fages routinely apprehended, prosecuted, and punished offenders and in other ways enforced the law.

51. Beilharz, *Felipe de Neve*, 52.

52. Ibid., 132.

53. Quotation cited in ibid., 52. For more on quarrels over Indian labor at the missions, see ibid., 72–73. For an example of a dispute between Fages and Serra over authority in the region, see Fages, San Diego, October 11, 1772, to Serra, San Diego, in Tibesar, *The Writings of Junípero Serra*, vol. 1, 420, n. 124; and for Father Serra's response, see Serra, San Diego, October 13, 1772, to Pedro Fages, San Diego, ibid., 287.

54. For Father Serra's thirty-two recommendations, see Serra, Mexico City, to Bucareli, Mexico City, March 13, 1773, ibid. 295–329. Quotation cited in ibid., 307; Cas-

tañeda, "*Presidarias y pobladoras*," 83–84; and Bancroft, *The Works of Hubert Howe Bancroft*, vol. 18, 208–16.

55. Serra, Mexico City, to Bucareli, Mexico City, March 13, 1773, in Tibesar, *The Writings of Junípero Serra*, vol. 1, 307.

56. Costo and Costo, "Interview," in *The Missions of California*, 224; and Guest, "An Inquiry into the Role of the Discipline in California Mission Life," 28.

57. Bouvier, *Women and the Conquest of California*, 53. According to several authors, Father Serra was the first to suggest the colonization of Alta California by women and families.

58. Serra, San Diego, to Francisco Palou, July 3, 1769, in Tibesar, *The Writings of Junípero Serra*, vol. 2, 143. Serra also recommended the colonization by additional neófito families from Baja California, who could provide much-needed labor and set good examples for the newly converted neófitos at the Alta California missions. See Serra, Mexico City, to Bucareli, Mexico City, March 13, 1773, ibid., vol. 1, 311; and Castañeda, "*Presidarias y pobladoras*," 85.

59. Serra, Mexico City, to Bucareli, Mexico City, March 13, 1773, in Tibesar, *The Writings of Junípero Serra*, vol. 1, 325; and Castañeda, "*Presidarias y pobladoras*," 84–85.

60. Serra, Monterey, to Melchor de Peramas, Mexico City, June 14, 1774, in Tibesar, *The Writings of Junípero Serra*, vol. 2, 65, 67, 87; Serra, Monterey, to Bucareli, Mexico City, August 24, 1774, in ibid., vol. 2, 139; and Bouvier, *Women and the Conquest of California*, 39, 55.

61. Castañeda, "*Presidarias y pobladoras*," 86.

62. Engelhardt, *San Gabriel Mission*, 16.

63. Castañeda, "*Presidarias y pobladoras*," 121.

64. The women included Ana María Hurtado, the wife of Fernando Chamorro, a blacksmith, and their two daughters, Cipriana Chamorro, aged twenty, and María del Carmen, aged eighteen; María Theresa de Ochoa, single and orphaned; María Josefa Davila, also single and a servant; Doña Josefa, the wife of Don Rafael de Pedro y Gil, a storekeeper bound for the presidio at San Diego; Josefa María Góngora, the wife of a surgeon, Don José Davila, also on board; and María Arroyo Herrera, married to José María Arroyo, another blacksmith. Names are identified in ibid., 117–24.

65. Ibid., 118–19.

66. Ibid., 120–21. For more on the practice of "joyas," see Bouvier, *Women and the Conquest of California*, 41–43; Priestly, *A Historical, Political, and Natural Description*, 33, 48, 59; and Boscana, *Beliefs, Usages, Customs, and Extravagancies of the Indians*, 227–34; and Hurtado, *Intimate Frontiers*, 6–9. For more on the practice of polygamy among chiefs, see Priestly, *A Historical, Political, and Natural Description*, 11; and among the Yuma, see Bouvier, *Women and the Conquest of California*, 43–44, 73–74; and Forbes, *Warriors of the Colorado*.

67. Bouvier, *Women and the Conquest of California*, 56–57, for a more thorough description of these women and the difficulties of maintaining artisan families, see Castañeda, "*Presidarias y pobladoras*," chapter 3; Tibesar, *The Writings of Junípero Serra*, vol. 2, 11, 29; and Bancroft, *The Works of Hubert Howe Bancroft*, vol. 18, 615–16.

68. Castañeda, "*Presidarias y pobladoras*," 141.

69. Castañeda notes that little is known from the extant documents about the families who came to Alta California with Rivera y Moncada. See ibid., 16–17, 142–43; Bouvier, *Women and the Conquest of California*, 57; Tibesar, *The Writings of Junípero Serra*, vol. 2, 468, n. 15; and Bancroft, *The Works of Hubert Howe Bancroft*, vol. 18, 217–29.

70. Bouvier, *Women and the Conquest of California*, 58.

71. Castañeda, "*Presidarias y pobladoras*," 144.

72. Ibid., 145–52.

73. Mason, *Census of 1790*, 30.

74. Serra, Monterey, to Bucareli, Mexico City, January 8, 1775, in Tibesar, *The Writings of Junípero Serra*, vol. 2, 203; Castañeda, "*Presidarias y pobladoras*," 153–59; Bouvier, *Women and the Conquest of California*, 58–67; and for first-hand accounts of de Anza's expeditions, see Bolton, *Anza's Expeditions*; and Bolton, *Font's Complete Diary*.

75. Bouvier, *Women and the Conquest of California*, 115–16.

76. For their marriage, see Catholic Church, Misión San Gabriel, Family History Center, Church of Jesus Christ, LDS, Davis, California (hereafter cited as SGM), Marriages, book 1, 1774–1855, entry no. 551, Martín Reyes, María Celia (1795). For Reyes' status as a soldier, see Mason, *Census of 1790*, 26.

77. For the number of soldiers at San Gabriel and Monterey in the 1770s, see Mason, *Census of 1790*, 26–28, 22–24, For those at San Gabriel and Los Angeles in the 1790s, see Bancroft, *The Works of Hubert Howe Bancroft*, vol. 18, 647–48, n. 6; for those at Monterey in the same decade, see ibid., 677–78; for estimates of those at San Gabriel and Los Angeles in 1810, see ibid., vol. 19, 101, 110–12; for those at Monterey in the same decade, see ibid., 141–42; and for estimates of the guards at San Gabriel and Los Angeles in 1820, see ibid., 349, 357; and Geiger, "Six Census Records of Los Angeles," 316–22. Bouvier suggests that in addition to the lack of incentives, the "strong bonds between neophyte women and their families and the poor quality of the prospective husbands (according to the friars) also seem to have inhibited greater intermarriage" (*Women and the Conquest of California*, 116).

78. Los Angeles had few active soldiers but a large population of retired soldiers, mostly from San Diego, upon whom the authorities called when needed. In the 1790s, half of the households were headed by retired soldiers. See Mason, *Census of 1790*, 82–86; and Bancroft, *The Works of Hubert Howe Bancroft, vol. 18*, 732–44.

79. According to Bancroft, only twenty-four mixed marriages between Spanish-speaking men and neófitas were celebrated from 1769 to 1800. See Bancroft, *The Works of Hubert Howe Bancroft*, vol. 18, 610, n. 20.

80. For statistics for Monterey, see Castañeda, "*Presidarias y pobladoras*," 138.

81. For the names of the three couples who married at Monterey, see Bouvier, *Women and the Conquest of California*, 115; and Mason, *Census of 1790*, 23–24.

82. Serra, Monterey, to Bucareli, Mexico City, 24 August 1775, in Tibesar, *The Writings of Junípero Serra*, vol. 2, 149. For more on mixed unions or intermarriage, see Castañeda, "*Presidarias y pobladoras*," 136–38; and Bouvier, *Women and the Conquest of California*, 115–16.

83. For evidence that Butrón received the land, see Bancroft, *The Works of Hubert Howe Bancroft*, vol. 18, 608. According to Bancroft, Butrón later abandoned it. Neither

Castañeda nor Bouvier state whether any of the other men at Monterey and their families received land. No similar petition or record for the man at San Gabriel has been located.

84. Castañeda, *"Presidarias y pobladoras,"* 159.

85. Ibid.

86. Ibid., 159–62; Neve, *Reglamento para el gobierno*; Lummis, "Felipe de Neve, Regulations and Instructions for California," 156–88; Guest, "Municipal Government in Spanish California," 307–11; and Bancroft, *The Works of Hubert Howe Bancroft*, vol. 18, 307–52.

87. Beilharz, *Felipe de Neve*, 97.

88. Serra, Monterey, to Teodoro de Croix, Mexico City, August 22, 1778, in Tibesar, *The Writings of Junípero Serra*, vol. 3, 253.

89. Costo and Costo, "Interview," in *The Missions of California*, 224.

90. Serra, Monterey, to Teodoro de Croix, Mexico City, August 22, 1778, in Tibesar, *The Writings of Junípero Serra*, vol. 3, 255.

91. Ibid., 155–56, 390.

92. Bancroft, *The Works of Hubert Howe Bancroft*, vol. 18, 606–7, n. 13.

93. Castañeda, *"Presidarias y pobladoras,"* 114–17.

94. For more on the Híjar-Pádres colony, see Hutchinson, *Frontier Settlement in Mexican California*; and González, "Searching for the Feathered Serpent," 35–82.

95. Bancroft, *The Works of Hubert Howe Bancroft*, vol. 18, 355; Temple, "Se fundarón un pueblo de españoles"; Ríos-Bustamante and Castillo, *An Illustrated History of Mexican Los Angeles*, 24–25, 33.

96. Castañeda, *"Presidarias y pobladoras,"* 125. See also Temple, "Soldiers and Settlers of the Expedition of 1781," 99–116; Garr, "A Rare and Desolate Place," 134; Campbell, "The First Californios," 594; Moorhead, *The Presidio: Bastion of the Spanish Borderlands*, 178–200; McAlister, *The "Fuero Militar" in New Spain*.

97. Haas, *Conquests and Historical Identities*, 9–44; Castañeda, *"Presidarias y pobladoras,"* 91–102; and Monroy, *Thrown among Strangers*, 18–50.

98. These points on women's roles in the missions, presidios, and pueblos are drawn from Castañeda, *"Presidarias y pobladoras,"* 190–237.

99. Ibid., 90–91.

100. Ibid., 200; Mason, *The Census of 1790*, 44.

101. Castañeda, *"Presidarias y pobladoras,"* 205–6; for fertility rates, see Miranda, "Hispano-Mexican Child Rearing Practices," 307–11. Scholars disagree on fertility rates in Spanish and Mexican California. For instance, Lockhart finds that in colonial San José, on average, a woman gave birth to about eight children. See Lockhart, "A Demographic Profile of an Alta California Pueblo," cited in Osio, *The History of Alta California*, 264, n. 12.

102. Castañeda, *"Presidarias y pobladoras,"* 196–97, 208–9.

103. Ibid., 190–91.

104. Ibid., 219–23; and Forbes, *Native Americans*, 30.

105. Sánchez, Pita, and Reyes, *"Memorias de doña Apolinaria Lorenzana,"* 5.

106. Such examinations took place occasionally. See California Archives, vol. 17, 307–19. Juez Fiscal, Ignacio Martínez, San Francisco, September 18, 1819, "Causa criminal

contra un individuo por estrupo de sus entenadas"; and California Archives, vol. 18, 127–28, in which Governor Sola had Bernardina Alvarez, the wife of Cosme Venegas, inspect a young woman suspected of sexual indiscretions at Santa Bárbara in 1820.

107. Castañeda, "*Presidarias y pobladoras*," 221. For an example of women assisting women in childbirth, see Raymundo Carrillo, Santa Bárbara, to Pedro Fages, Monterey, October 25, 1785, in California Archives, vol. 3, 169. Carrillo requests permission for his wife to travel to Los Angeles to give birth in the company of her mother. For Eulalia Pérez's work, see Sánchez, Pita, and Reyes, "Eulalia Pérez, Una Vieja...," 33–41.

108. For more on Amador, see ibid., 35; for more on Lorenzana's duties, see Sánchez, Pita, and Reyes, "*Memorias* de doña Apolinaria Lorenzana," 3–5, 14; for the measurement of a league, see Pérez, *Land Grants in Alta California*, 240–41.

109. Cook, *The Conflict between the California Indian and White Civilization*, 33.

110. Many examples appear in the baptismal records of San Gabriel Mission and the Los Angeles Plaza Church. For the Ruiz baptisms, see SGM Baptisms, book 3, 1820–1855, entries no. 6633 "María Ruiz" (1821) and 6634 "Romualdo Ruiz" (1821).

Chapter 2. Patriarchs, Power, and Sexuality

1. Francisca Peréz's case is contained in the Alcalde Court Records (hereafter cited as ACR), Seaver Center for Western History, Natural History Museum of Los Angeles County, Los Angeles, California, vol. 4, 892–914 (1844). The court cases that make up this nine-volume collection spanning the 1830s and 1840s are not arranged chronologically. For clarity, dates are given for each court case and volume cited.

2. For examples of other women who brought and then rescinded criminal complaints after their husbands agreed to their demands, see ibid., vol. 3, 690–712 (1842) and vol. 7, 1028–32 (1850).

3. For more on honor, see Gutiérrez, *When Jesus Came, the Corn Mothers Went Away*, 176–226.

4. For more on gente de razón, see Sánchez, *Telling Identities*, 56–61; Haas, *Conquests and Historical Identities*, 29–32; and Weber, *The Spanish Frontier in North America*, 327–29.

5. Arrom, *The Women of Mexico City*, 57–77.

6. For official ecclesiastical statements regarding marriage and the family in the Californias, see Weber, *The Writings of Francisco García Diego y Moreno*. ACR and the Los Angeles Prefecture Records, Los Angeles City Archives, Los Angeles Records Management (hereafter cited as LAPR) also contain religious decrees. For a summary of the Church's views on marriage, annulment, and divorce in colonial Mexico, which applied to Alta California, see Arrom, *Women of Mexico City*, 65–66, 206–58; and Lavrin, "Introduction," *Sexuality and Marriage*.

7. Arrom, *Women of Mexico City*, 208–9.

8. This observation results from my reading of the sources for Alta California, which contain numerous references to the *Laws of the Indies*, a seventeenth-century compilation of laws for governing New Spain, as well as to ordinances and decrees issued by the governors of Alta California. Historian Charles R. Cutter and legal scholar Joseph W.

McKnight have noted similar findings for colonial New Mexico and Texas. See Cutter, *The Legal Culture of Northern New Spain*, 34–43, 83–99; McKnight, "Law Books on the Hispanic Frontier," 74–84; and McKnight, "Law without Lawyers on the Hispano-Mexican Frontier," 51–65.

9. For more on the *Siete Partidas* and *Leyes de Toro*, see Arrom, *Women of Mexico City*, 55, 59, 68, 73–79; also see Lavrin, "Introduction."

10. Under the law, an "hijo natural" was defined as a child born to an unmarried couple that had no impediment to marriage. The child was entitled to support but not able to claim an inheritance from the father, unless the father made special provisions in a testament or other legal document. The discussion of hijos naturales and hijos espurios is drawn largely from Twinam, *Public Lives, Private Secrets*. For more on illegitimacy, see chapter 6 of this study.

11. In colonial Mexico, a man also had the power to castigate his spouse and offspring. See Stern, *The Secret History of Gender*, 77, 210–11.

12. This meaning of a *casa de honor* (honorable home) derives from my reading of the sources. See ACR, vol. 5, 1–20 (1845), and vol. 4, 557–698, 892–914 (1844); and LAPR, vol. 2, 572–77 (1847).

13. Stern, *The Secret History of Gender*, 14 21; Arrom, *Women of Mexico City*, 65–70; and Lavrin, "Introduction," in *Sexuality and Marriage*, 6–21.

14. For more on the Court of the First Instance (juzgado de primera instancia), see Grivas, "Alcalde Rule," 11–19; and MacLachlan, *Criminal Justice in Eighteenth Century Mexico*. Another work, Langum, *Law and Community*, especially chapters 2, 3, and 4, provides useful material on the tribunal system in California. For more on conciliation trials in colonial Mexico, see Arrom, *Women of Mexico City*, 211.

15. See, for example, ACR, vol. 1, 914–17 (1843) and vol. 6, 178 (1844).

16. For Domínguez's complaint in the conciliation court, see ibid., vol. 1, 900–902 (1843). For similar complaints made by other Mexican women in the conciliation court, see vol. 1, 914–17 (1843) and vol. 6, 66–70 (1846); for those complaints heard in the criminal court, see vol. 4, 892–914 (1844); vol. 3, 168–79 (1842), vol. 7, 465–92 (1849), and vol. 9, 1186–91 (1843); and California Archives, Bancroft Library, Berkeley, California, vol. 35, 355 (1843).

17. For Pérez's complaint of adultery in the conciliation court, see ACR, vol. 4, 892–914 (1844).

18. For García's complaint of adultery in the criminal court, see ibid., vol. 5, 20–34 (1845).

19. For Reyes's complaint of adultery in the conciliation court, see ibid., vol. 1, 893–95 (1843); and for other complaints of adultery in the criminal court, see vol. 3, 127–67, 690–712 (1842).

20. For the second and third incidents between Vejar and Urquides, see ibid., vol. 3, 127–67, 690–712 (1842). No record of the first incident is extant, but in Vejar's second complaint, she and the judge summarized the earlier court appearance. For evidence of Valenzuela's presence in Los Angeles, see Newmark and Newmark, *Census of the City and County of Los Angeles*, 82.

21. ACR, vol. 7, 465–92 (1849).

22. For Figueroa's conflicts with Riera in the American period, see Los Angeles Area Court Records, Criminal Court, Huntington Library, San Marino, California (hereafter cited as LAACR-CC), Criminal Case No. (8–14) "Reia [sic], Assault and Battery," (1850).

23. In Monterrey, young women also contested paternal authority. David J. Langum has found that in 1835 the local alcalde granted Dolores Vasquez permission to leave her father's home after she complained about his abusive behavior. How frequently women successfully contested a father's perogative is unknown. See, Langum, Law and Community, 241.

24. Sepúlveda's case is contained in ACR, vol. 9, 146–51 (1842); and LAPR, book 1, part 2, 465–67, 632, 635, 650, 654, 685 (1842). Also see García Diego y Moreno to Santiago Argüello, May 3, 1842, in Weber, The Writings of Francisco García Diego y Moreno, 120; García Diego y Moreno to Argüello, May 18, 1842, ibid.; García Diego y Moreno to Argüello, August 22, 1842, ibid., 121; García Diego y Moreno to Tomás Esténega, May 3, 1842, ibid., 122; García Diego y Moreno to Esténega, May 21, 1842, ibid., 123; and García Diego y Moreno to Esténega, August 22, 1842, ibid., 124. The original record of Casilda Sepúlveda's last appearance in court is not extant in the ACR, but a reproduced copy of her complaint is found in California Archives, vol. 35, 245 (1842). For other instances when priests intervened in women's marital troubles, see ACR, vol. 4, 142–48 (1843), vol. 5, 1–20 (1845), and vol. 7, 465–92 (1849).

25. Gutiérrez, When Jesus Came, the Corn Mothers Went Away, 228, 315–18. For evidence that the Royal Pragmatic on Marriage was extended to California, see Teodoro de Croix, Arispe, Sonora, to Felipe de Neve, Monterey, December 29, 1779, California Archives, vol. 1, 337–45.

26. Following the ascendancy to power of the Centralists in Mexico, the national government in 1837 established prefectures in local jurisdictions as a means of extending federal authority over local affairs. For more on the prefecture system, see Langum, Law and Community, 35–55.

27. Tomás Esténega, San Gabriel, to Abel Stearns, Los Angeles, May 7, May 8, May 9, May 10, May 15, June 2, June 9, and July 9, all box 24, Stearns Collection, Huntington Library, San Marino, California (hereafter cited as SC).

28. Gutiérrez, When Jesus Came, the Corn Mothers Went Away, 213. For more on depósito, see Penyak, "Safe Harbors and Compulsory Custody," 83–99. For cases in which women are placed in depósito with their family members, see, for example, the case of Tomasa Ruiz, LAPR, book 1, 621 (1842). She was charged with prostitution and placed with her cousin, Servulo Varela, who agreed to watch over her. Native women were also put in seclusion. For a case in which a young woman was kept in depósito for more than a year, see LAPR, 422 (1841).

29. Arrom, Women of Mexico City, 69, 208, 211–13.

30. Sepúlveda and Duarte's household is listed in the 1844 census. For the original census, see "Padrón 1844," Los Angeles City Archives, Records Management Division, Los Angeles, California (hereafter cited as LACA), vol. 3, 666–801. The 1844 census in Northrop's "The Los Angeles Padrón of 1844," 360–417, is incomplete and excludes, among other things, the native female and male population enumerated in the original census. For more on the Sepúlveda and Duarte family, see Northrop, Spanish-Mexican Families, vol. 2, 75, 320.

31. ACR, vol. 4, 142–48 (1843).

32. For gentiles taking their complaints to the priests, see Nelson, *Marriage and Divorce Practices*, 36.

33. Geiger, *As the Padres Saw Them*, 65, 113–15; Nelson, *Marriage and Divorce Practices*, 24–25; Boscana, *Beliefs, Usages, Customs, and Extravagancies of the Indians*, 26; and Phillips, *Chiefs and Challengers*, 10. For more on marital and conjugal relations among the Quechans, see Forbes, *Warriors of the Colorado*, 25, 55–57.

34. ACR, vol. 2, 659–78 (1841). Most other cases of violence involving neófitas and gentiles were reported by family members or local officials. For those instances of abuse brought to the attention to the court by local officials, see ibid., vol. 2, 499–530 (1841), vol. 5, 303–31 (1845), vol. 6, 448–73 (1837), vol. 7, 411–36 (1849).

35. For cases of complaints brought on behalf of Mexican and Native American women by family members, see, for example, ibid., vol. 2, 1172–76 (1842), vol. 6, 36–38 (1846), vol. 4, 299–348 (1843); California Archives, vol. 35, 172–73 (1841), and vol. 35, 213 (1842).

36. Arrom, *Women of Mexico City*, 63.

37. For more on Aguilar, see Bancroft, *The Works of Hubert Howe Bancroft*, vol. 19, 688. For the court case, see ACR, vol. 1, 506–62 (1840).

38. Langum, *Law and Community*, 57–58.

39. The case can be found in ACR, vol. 1, 506–62 (1840).

40. Ibid., vol. 4, 1170–88 (1844).

41. Ibid., vol. 5, 1–20 (1845).

42. Ibid., vol. 2, 531–65 (1841).

43. Ibid., vol. 7, 763–93 (1847).

44. Ibid., vol. 6, 541–83 (1837). For evidence of their continued relationship, see Los Angeles Area Court Records, District Court, Huntington Library, San Marino, California (hereafter cited as LAACR-DC), case no. 862 *Jacob Elias v. Francisco Arzaga et al.* (1862). In this case, the children were unaware that their parents never married. For other examples of cases involving women who sought to escape from their households, see ACR, vol. 1, 810–37 (1842) and 906–8 (1843).

45. Pegui's case can be found in ACR, vol. 1, 506–62 (1840). For more on Durán, see Bancroft, *Register of Pioneer Inhabitants of California*, 786.

46. In a contemporary petition to the governor, a group of *angeleños* (residents of Los Angeles) said that the neófitos "steal all neighboring fences and on Saturdays celebrate and become intoxicated to an unbearable degree, thereby resulting in all manner of venereal diseases." Quotation cited in Robinson, "The Indians of Los Angeles," 523.

47. For more on the case, see LAPR, vol. 1, 447, 451 (1840). For another interpretation of the case, see Langum, "Sin, Sex, and Separation in Mexican California," 44.

48. For more interpretations of the incident, see Bancroft, *The Works of Hubert Howe Bancroft*, vol. 20, 417–19; González, "Searching for the Feathered Serpent," 138–49.

49. LACA, vol. 1, 81–91; ibid., vol. 4, 186–88; and Victor Prudon, "Vigilantes de Los Angeles, 1836."

50. For Zúñiga's public shaming, see Governor, Monterey, to Capitan José de la Guerra, Santa Bárbara, October 3, 1818, in California Archives, vol. 17, 205–6; and Engelhardt, *San Gabriel Mission*, 122. For similar episodes where the authorities shaved

the heads of women who transgressed sociocultural norms of behavior, see Bancroft, *The Works of Hubert Howe Bancroft*, vol. 19, 559, n. 3, and 678, n. 47.

51. LACA, vol. 3, 666–801. It is unknown, with certainty, who carried out the 1836 and 1844 censuses. One scholar believes that Narciso Botello, a local leader and scribe, completed the 1836 census (Layne, "The First Census of Los Angeles," 82).

52. For her seven children, see Los Angeles Plaza Church, Family History Center, Church of Jesus Christ of Latter Day Saints, Davis, California (hereafter cited as LAPC), Baptisms, book 1, 1826–1848, entries no. 234 "Theresa Varelas" (1830), 379 "Petra Hilaria Domínguez" (1833), 558 "Prudencio Varelas" (1835), 1283 "José María López" (1844), 1619 "José Antonio del Refugio López" (1846), and 1636 "María Manuela de Jesús López" (1847), and SGM, Baptisms, book 3, 1820–1855, entry no. 8237 "Juan Nepomuceno Varelas" (1838). For Varelas' mother's death, see Northrop, *Spanish-Mexican Families*, vol. 1, 56.

53. ACR, vol. 6, p 179 (1844). For reference to her "taberna," see ibid., vol. 7, 22–69 (1845). For evidence of her relationship with Sánchez and their children, see LAPC, Baptisms, book 1, entries no. 1132 "María Antonia Sánchez" (1842) and 1564 "José Antonio Sánchez" (1846).

54. Illegitimacy rates were calculated using baptismal registers from Misión San Gabriel (1771–1912) and Los Angeles Plaza Church (1826–1920). For the baptismal records, see LAPC, Baptisms, book 1, book 2, 1848–1858, book 3, 1858–1864, book 4, 1865–1872, and book 5, 1872–1900; SGM Baptisms, book 1, 1771–1795, book 2, 1795–1819, book 3, 1820–1855, book 6, 1868–1908. SGM Baptism books 4 and 5 are missing.

55. For illegitimacy rates in Mexico City, see Arrom, *Women of Mexico City*, 123; and for the most comprehensive discussion available about illegitimacy in Spanish America, see Twinam, *Public Lives, Private Secrets*.

56. For illegitimacy rates in Cuba, see Martínez-Alier, *Marriage, Class, and Colour*, 58. In Cuba, the "coloured" had a much higher rate of illegitimacy, 75 percent.

57. For more on these stereotypes, see Castañeda, "The Political Economy of Nineteenth Century Stereotypes." My findings refute those of David J. Langum, who writes, "The Mexican California judicial records reveal a considerable instance of bastardy" ("Sin, Sex, and Separation," 46). My examination of church records demonstrates the contrary. Langum also reinforces the idea that "bastardy" was common among the lower classes: "Members of the upper economic class conducted carefully sheltered courtships during which young women were not permitted to be in the company of suitors without the presence of *dueñas*, their chaperones. *These matters could not be as rigidly structured among the lower classes*" (ibid., emphasis added).

58. It is possible that the illegitimacy rates were slightly higher in the Los Angeles-San Gabriel region in the Spanish and Mexican period, for it is likely that some men and women lied about or hid the status of an illegitimate child. However, this possibility does not change in any significant way the low rates of illegitimacy identified in the pre-American conquest period. In Cuba, Martínez-Alier has found that people often lied—committed fraud—about the racial classification of their children. See *Marriage, Class and Colour*, 83.

59. Several scholars have suggested that these women were prostitutes. See Layne,

"The First Census of Los Angeles," 81; and Robinson, *Lawyers of Los Angeles*, 18; Robinson, *Tarnished Angels*, 7.

60. On the sexual double standard, particularly as it was upheld in Hispanic law, see Arrom, *Women of Mexico City*, 64–65.

61. My evidence indicates that Sepúlveda and Domínguez had at least two children. See LAPC, Baptisms, book 1, entries no. 7818 "José María Damaso Domínguez" (1832) and 966 "José Dolores Domínguez" (1840). Northrop finds that they had at least four children. Northrop, *Spanish-Mexican Families*, vol. 1, 308, 310. Men who fathered illegitimate children include: Eulogio Celis, Demetrio Villa, Rafael Carbajal, Juan De Dios Padilla, Ireneo Pérez, Bernardo Sepúlveda, José María Cota, Eulogio Celis, Manuel Arzaga, Juan Ribas, Antonio [E]lisaldi, José de la Luz Linares, José Antonio Nieto, Hilario Ybarra, Rafael Cañedo, Rafael García, José María Navarro, Joséph Antonio Yorba, Teodosio Yorba, Joaquin Carrillo, Juan Pérez, Vicente Domínguez, Domingo Olivas, Mariano Olivera, José E. Rodriguez, Julian Rendon, José Silvas, José Antonio Sánchez, Antonio Rocha, Felipe Valenzuela, Pedro Romero, Yanuario Avila, Vicente Sotelo, Manuel Peña, Geronimo Higuera, Luis Altamirano, José Guillermo "Bosque" [Wolfskill], Francisco Duarte, Guillermo Weetle/Huittle "Bruno," José María Domínguez, and José López.

62. For Reyes's illegitimate children, see LAPC, Baptisms, book 1, entries no. 556 "Ynocencia Reyes" (1835), 1216 "Margarita Primitiva de la Trinidad Yorba" (1843), and 1968 "José Antonio Felipe Yorba" (1848); SGM Baptisms, book 3, 1820–1855, entries no. 8382 "José de la Asunción Reyes" (1840), 8830 "María Trinidad de los Angeles Reyes" (1845), 8894 "Juan Bautista del Espiritu Santo Yorba" (1846), and 8196 "Andrés Reyes" (1837). Northrop also documents Reyes and Yorba's relations (*Spanish-Mexican Families*, vol. 1, 371–72). For more on American common law and divorce, see chapter 5.

63. For more on Williams' relationships with the three women, see LAACR-DC, case no. 539 *Stephen C. Foster and wife v. Heirs of the estate of Isaac Williams, Merced Williams de Rains et al.* (1858–1888); and for a general history of Isaac Williams and his daughters, see Black, *Rancho Cucamonga and Doña Merced*.

64. For statistics on illegitimacy among neófitos, see LAPC, Baptisms, books 1–5; and SGM Baptisms, books 1–3, 6; and chapter 6 of this book.

Chapter 3. Family, Property, and Economic Independence

1. One square league of land measured 5,000 square *varas*, or 4,440 acres. See Becker, *Diseños of California Ranchos*, xi; and Pérez, *Land Grants in Alta California*, 240–41.

2. For Valdez and the Vejares' dispute with Luciano Valdez, see ACR, vol. 7, 284–306 (1840).

3. María Rita Valdez, as well as a number of other women in this discussion, not only owned ranchos but also property in town. For Valdez's property in town, see Spanish Archives, California State Archives, State Library, Sacramento, California (hereafter cited as SA), vol. 8, 112–22 (1845).

4. For more on the Plan de Pitic, see Engstrand, "The Legal Heritage of Spanish California," 220–23.

5. *Recopilación de leyes de las indias*, vols. 1–3. The general principles of the *Recopilación* are reproduced and discussed in several works on land in California. This book has relied extensively on: Dwinelle, *The Colonial History of the City*; Robinson, *Land in California*; Meyer, *Water in the Hispanic Southwest*; Cutter, *The Legal Culture of Northern New Spain*; United States Congress, "Report on the Laws and Regulations," 113–16; Engstrand, "California Ranchos," 282–86; Livingston, "Earliest Spanish Land Grants," 195–99; and Baker, "Mexican Land Grants in California," 236–43. Robert G. Cowan's *Ranchos of California*, 2–11, though useful, is incomplete. Women's ownership of ranchos, in particular, is omitted because of his over-reliance on U.S. government reports, which invariably list the men (the heads of households) as the owners of ranchos. This practice ignores women who acquired and brought the property into the marriage. For more on Cowan's discrepancies, see Lothrop, "Rancheras and the Land," 68.

6. Arrom, *The Women of Mexico City*, chapters 1 and 2; Lavrin and Couturier, "Dowries and Wills," 283; Bernal de Bugeda, "Situación Jurídica de la Mujer," 21–40; and Iduarte, "Condición Jurídica de la Mujer," 41–54.

7. ACR, vol. 8 (1847), 137–66. For more on Carrillo, see Bancroft, *Register of Pioneer Inhabitants of California*, 745.

8. In the 1840s, at least fifteen women gave men power of attorney to conduct many of their business transactions. For an example, see LAPR, book A, 777 (1849), where María Dolores de Serrano gives power of attorney to Francisco R. López.

9. The records make numerous references to women's inability to write, use of scribes who could do so for them, and use of "verbal petitions." For instance, see LAPR, 337 (1847). Narciso Botello was a well-known scribe in Los Angeles. For Botello's profession as a scribe, see LACA, vol. 3, 671.

10. See chapter 2.

11. For the allocation of lands and other natural resources in the pueblo, see Neve, *Reglamento para el gobierno*. For the regulations and procedures of the town council, see LACA, vol. 2, 1064–75 (1846); and for an example of a council decree, see ibid. 1061 (1846).

12. Montoya, *Translating Property*, 163–64.

13. The 1824 and 1828 colonization laws reflected principles in the *Recopilación de las leyes de las indias*. Earlier recommendations to distribute ranchos were promulgated in Viceroy Antonio Bucareli's "Instrucción que debe observer el Comandante" as well as the Spanish Cortes of 1813. For a translation and reproduction of the colonization laws, see Dwinelle, *Colonial History*, addenda, 23–26. For the Spanish-language original, see Plan de colonización extrangera; and Reglamento de los territorios de ambas Californias. For studies on colonization in the Spanish and Mexican eras, see Castañeda, "*Presidarias y pobladoras*"; Hutchinson, *Frontier Settlement in Mexican California*; and González, "Searching for the Feathered Serpent."

14. Of the 148 people who received ranchos, 121 were men and 27 were women.

15. For more on Avila's father, see Bancroft, *The Works of Hubert Howe Bancroft*, vol. 19, 705. For more on rural judges, see Langum, *Law and Community*, 43.

16. For Asención (also known as Concepción) and Juan Avila's Rancho El Nigüel, see SA, vol. 4, 111–19 (1842). For more on the Avilas' El Nigüel and the conflicts surrounding that rancho, see Haas, *Conquests and Historical Identities*, 45, 47, 83.

17. For Casilda Soto's Rancho La Merced, see SA, vol. 4, 598, 604 (1844). See also Northrop, *Spanish-Mexican Families*, vol. 1, 54, 307.

18. It is unlikely that any other women—save Manuela Nieto—inherited ranchos in the Spanish period, as no other female landholder in the Mexican era traced her acquisition of property to the colonial era. While California historians have found that most of the men who received land grants had family connections to military and political leaders or were, themselves, political leaders, few scholars have examined the role of family links in women's ability to obtain land. For an example of a scholar who does explore those relationships, see Lothrop, "Rancheras on the Land," 69–84; and Bowman, "Prominent Women of Provincial California," 149–66. For studies that examine men's family links, see, for example, Monroy, *Thrown among Strangers*, 134; and Eversole, "Towns in Mexican Alta California," 323–47. For studies that examine marital alliances among families in colonial Mexico, see, among others, Kuznesof and Oppenheimer, "The Family and Society in Nineteenth-Century Latin America," 215–34; and Ladd, *The Mexican Nobility at Independence*.

19. Northrop, *Spanish-Mexican Families*, vol. 1, 237.

20. SA, vol. 2, 288–96 (1833).

21. Northrop, *Spanish-Mexican Families*, vol. 1, 149.

22. SA, vol. 4, 412–19 (1843), and vol. 7, 529–31 (1840–1843).

23. The SA suggest that, although Spanish law favored those who married Mexican or neophyte women, only one male Mexican citizen married a neófita. Why this was so will require additional research. The low rate of inter-ethnic marriages among landholders in the Mexican era applies to the general population in the Spanish era. Castañeda finds a low rate (15 percent) of intermarriage between Spanish soldiers and neophyte women in Monterey, and she notes that this pattern "is consistent with the marriage pattern in Spain's American frontiers" (*"Presidarias y pobladoras,"* 254–58). For more on this, see chapter 6.

24. SA, vol. 4, 443–67 (1840); and Northrop, *Spanish-Mexican Families*, vol. 1, 309.

25. The figures for men's ranchos in the Spanish era come from Bancroft, *The Works of Hubert Howe Bancroft*, vols. 18–19, and those for the Mexican era come from SA; Bancroft, *The Works of Hubert Howe Bancroft*, vols. 18–22; and Pérez, *Land Grants in Alta California*, 52–104.

26. See SA and note 25 above.

27. SA, vol. 4, 11–21 (1842); Northrop, *Spanish-Mexican Families*, vol. 2, 285, 287.

28. SA, vol. 5, 230–34 (1845); for more on Forster, see Bancroft, *The Works of Hubert Howe Bancroft*, vol. 20, 744.

29. Lugo, *"Vida de un ranchero,"* 202. For the Williams' land grant, see SA, vol. 5, 617–19 (1843). For the governor's grant of Rancho Santa Ana del Chino, see SA, vol. 3, 419–26 (1840). For more on the latter rancho, see Black, *Rancho Cucamonga and Doña Merced*; and for Williams' Indian servants in the 1840s, see "Padrón 1844," LACA, vol. 3, 666–801.

30. SA, vol. 5, 234–38 (1845).

31. Ibid., vol. 6, 13–15 (1843). For the other Indian men who received similar grants of land—from 200 to 1,000 square varas, see ibid., vol. 5, 186–87 (1842), 207–9 (1845),

249–55 (1845), 266–68 (1845), and 458–61 (1845); ibid., vol. 6, 1–2 (1843), 25–27 (1843), and 144–47 (1846).

32. For Rancho El Encino, see ibid., vol. 5, 313–20 (1843); for its sale to Vicente de la Osa, see LAPR, 774–76 (1849); and for the other similar grant, which went to three desperate heads of neófito families, see SA, vol. 5, 326–33 (1845).

33. Of the twenty-three grants, one was carved out of land formerly belonging to Misión San Fernando, fifteen were from Misión San Gabriel, and seven from Misión San Juan Capistrano. These findings, as well as the figures for rancho grants, come from the SA; Bancroft, *The Works of Hubert Howe Bancroft*, vols. 18–22; and Pérez, *Land Grants in Alta California*, 52–104.

34. For more on Antonio María Lugo's Rancho San Antonio, see Bancroft, *The Works of Hubert Howe Bancroft*, vol. 18, 565. For the governor's grant of Rancho Santa Ana del Chino, see SA, vol. 3, 419–26 (1840). For more on the latter rancho, see Black, *Rancho Cucamonga and Doña Merced*.

35. These figures come from the SA, ACR, and LAPR.

36. For an example of a civil dispute over boundaries, see SA, vol. 1, 452–63 (1833).

37. The SA, ACR, and LAPR indicate that Mexican women participated in at least thirteen civil suits over ranchos, ten of which involved inheritances and the remainder dealing with conflicts over boundaries and denouncements. Men participated in thirty-one property disputes, seventeen involving boundaries and denouncements, and the remainder centered on various other conflicts.

38. For María Cleofas Nieto's case, see SA, vol. 2, 288–96 (1827–1833), vol. 6, 546 (1849), and vol. 7, 445–46 (1841); ACR, vol. 9, 1136–39 (1843); and LAPR, book A, 809 (1849). For Joaquín Ruiz's request for Rancho La Bolsa Chiquita, see SA, vol. 3, 506–17 (1839).

39. For the sale of Rancho Las Bolsas in the early 1860s, see LAACR-DC, case no. 746 *Abel Stearns v. María Cleofas Nieto et al.* (1860).

40. For more on Tomás Antonio Yorba, see Bancroft, *The Works of Hubert Howe Bancroft*, vol. 22, 782.

41. SA, vol. 6, 63–73 (1845); "Will of Tomás Antonio Yorba" (1845), trans. Haydee Nora, Huntington Library, San Marino, California. For other court disputes over inheritances among family members, see ACR, vol. 8, 706–81 (1848); LAPR, book A, 911–25, 871–80 (1849); and LACA, vol. 1, 597–601 (1837).

42. For the concession of Rancho San Pascual to Juan Mariner, Perez's spouse, see SA, vol. 2, 263–40 (1833). For the concession of San Pascual to Enrique Sepúlveda and José Pérez, see SA, vol. 3, 326–29 (1840). For the authorities' assessment of Eulália Pérez's weak financial situation, see LAPR, book 1, 335, 341, 350 (1840). For more on Mariner's acquisition of Rancho San Pascual, see Robinson, *Land in California*, 83.

43. Cutter, *Legal Culture of Northern New Spain*, 34–43.

44. For Cota's dispute, see SA, vol. 4, 361–62 (1837); and LACA, vol. 2, 397 (1837). For evidence that Cota sold her land to Carpenter, see LAACR-DC, case no. 48, *Heirs of Antonio María Nieto v. Samuel Carpenter* (1851); and Bancroft, *The Works of Hubert Howe Bancroft*, vol. 19, 742. For other disputes over ranchos and rancho property, such as livestock, see SA, vol. 2, 555–56 (1837), 507–8 (1841); ACR, vol. 2, 733–73 (1841); ACR, vol. 3, 545–

637 (1842); ACR, vol. 6, 133–35 (1845); and 140–41 (1845); and ACR, vol. 7, 284–306 (1840).

45. Robinson, *Land in California*, 54.

46. Lugo, *"Vida de un ranchero,"* 216. The 1836 and 1844 censuses show all of the ranchos employed skilled and unskilled workers; see LACA, vol. 3, 666–801; and González, "Searching for the Feathered Serpent," 62–64; and Nelson, "The Two Pueblos of Los Angeles," 1–11.

47. For Yorba's workers, see LACA, vol. 3, 704–5. Of the eighteen ranchos identified in the 1836 census, only five claimed to have any skilled workers, and of the twenty-one ranchos identified in the 1844 census, only four had skilled workers. For more on the skilled workers in Los Angeles and the surrounding region, as enumerated in the 1836 and 1844 censuses, see LACA, vol. 3, 666–801.

48. González, "Searching for the Feathered Serpent," 60–65.

49. Lugo, *"Vida de un ranchero,"* 217.

50. Ibid., 216–19.

51. For more on haciendas in Mexico, see Lockhart and Schwartz, *Early Latin America*, 327–31; and Van Young, *Hacienda and Market in Eighteenth-Century Mexico*.

52. Lugo, *"Vida de un ranchero,"* 191.

53. For Uribes's property, see ACR, vol. 6, 140–41 (1845); for more on Leandry, see Bancroft, *The Works of Hubert Howe Bancroft*, vol. 21, 709.

54. For Victoria Higuera's inheritance, see LAPR, book A, 597–603 (1849). See also Northrop, *Spanish-Mexican Families*, vol. 1, 307; and Bancroft, *The Works of Hubert Howe Bancroft*, vol. 21, 711.

55. For reference to the deal, see LACA, vol. 2, 1180–86 (1845).

56. Records of loans are found throughout LAPR.

57. Domínguez to Stearns, San Fernando, April 2, 1840, SC, box 21.

58. For Cota's loan, see LAPR, book A, 205 (1845).

59. For Vicenta Sepúlveda's purchase, see ibid., book A, 269–71 (1847); for Tomasa Pico's purchase, see Tomasa Pico to Abel Stearns, August 7, 1834, SC, box 1. The business records of Stearns and other local merchants indicate that women such as Pico, Sepúlveda, and Cota had the means—cash, hides, *aguardiente* (a local brandy), and credit—to purchase luxury items such as silk shawls, stockings, and dresses made of fine fabrics. They also bought household items, such as furniture, kitchenware, and imported fine crystal glasses.

60. Doc. No. 1149 "Dalton Account Book of Store" (1844–1845); Doc. No. 1150 "Account Book" (1845–1856); and Doc. No. 1151 "Cash Book" (1845–1856), Henry Dalton Collection, Huntington Library, San Marino, California.

61. For petitions for solares and suertes, see LACA. Los Angeles property records in LACA indicate that at least fifty-five Mexican women held property, including houses, solares, suertes, huertas, and viñas.

62. For Cota's request, see LACA, vol. 1, 120–22 (1836); for Machado's request, see ibid., vol. 2, 1172–78, 1274 (1845).

63. For more on the women identified as leading *mala vidas*, see chapter 2.

64. For more on Carreaga, Villa, and Valencia, see chapter 2. For their petitions for,

and concessions made to them of, pueblo land, see LACA, vol. 2, 900, 909 (1844) and 1138, 1145 (1846), and LACA, vol. 4, 170–72 (1847) and 515, 654 (1847).

65. LAPR, book A, 1063, 1840. Geiger, "Six Census Records of Los Angeles," 317.

66. For the division of Espinosa and Verdugo's estate, see LACA, vol. 1, 598–601 (1831). For Espinosa's property holdings, see ibid.; and "Report," De la Guerra y Noriega Collection, Huntington Library, San Marino, California.

67. That same year, in 1822, an act of the *diputación* (the California provincial legislature) at Monterey established Los Angeles's town council, extinguishing de la Guerra y Noriega's office. Bancroft, *The Works of Hubert Howe Bancroft,* vol. 19, 560–61. For more on the *comisionado's* office, see Guest, "Municipal Government in Spanish California," 307–35.

68. "Luisa Varelas to José Antonio de la Guerra y Noriega, February 1, 1822," De la Guerra y Noriega Collection, Huntington Library, San Marino, California.

69. ACR, vol. 1, 890–93, 895–97 (1843). For another case where a mid-strata woman brought her husband to civil court, see, for example, ibid., 920–22 (1846).

70. SA, vol. 3, 184–87 (1839).

71. LACA indicates that at least thirty-two individuals requested extensions of time.

72. SA, vol. 4, 530 (1847).

73. LACA, vol. 2, 176, 484 (1836). For other disputes with similar outcomes, see LACA, vol. 1, 619, 620 (1837), 403 (1844), 457–59 (1844), 470–73 (1844); and SA, vol. 3, 184–87 (1839).

74. On mission land tenure policies, see Dwinelle, *Colonial History,* 19–21; Robinson, *Land in California,* 23–32. For more on the mission system, see Weber, *The Spanish Frontier in North America,* 92–121; Castañeda, *"Presidarias y pobladoras,"* 63–113, 190–237; and Monroy, *Thrown among Strangers,* 66–68, 74.

75. For more on the problems in implementing secularization plans, see González, "Searching for the Feathered Serpent," 37–42; and Dwinelle, *Colonial History,* 39, addenda, 20–23, 31–35.

76. Phillips, "Indians in Los Angeles," 436. For examples of native women who fled from the missions to ranchos after secularization, see Tomás Esténega to Abel Stearns, June 6, 1846, box 24, SC. The 1836 and 1844 censuses also list hundreds of former neófitos and gentiles from various missions and regions, who labored at ranchos within Los Angeles's district. For more on the censuses, see chapter 3, notes 46 and 47.

77. For the petition to relocate the native settlement and subsequent action by the governor and town council, see LACA, vol. 1, 527–35 (1846); for more on this incident, see Phillips, "Indians in Los Angeles," 438–50.

78. SA, vol. 5, 417–19 (1845).

79. Bancroft, *The Works of Hubert Howe Bancroft,* vol. 20, 633–34, indicates that she obtained Rancho Cuati in 1830. This date, however, is a typographical error. SA, vol. 6, 545 (1838), indicates that she obtained it in 1838, and Bancroft, *The Works of Hubert Howe Bancroft,* vol. 22, 691, also dates Victoria's grant in 1838. For more on Victoria's second husband, Hugo Reid, see ibid., 691; and Dakin, *A Scotch Paisano.* For Reid's grant, see SA, vol. 3, 480–86 (1839). For the inventory of her estate, see "Inventario de los bienes de la propiedad de Victoria de Reid," Thomas Workman Temple Collection, Seaver Center for Western History, Natural History Museum of Los Angeles County.

80. For this dispute, see SA, vol. 4, 111–19 (1842). For more on the Avilas' Rancho El Nigüel and the conflicts surrounding it, see Haas, *Conquests and Historical Identities*, 45, 47, 83.

81. For the Indians' petition, see LACA, vol. 1, 640–43 (1838). For an additional discussion of this incident, see Phillips, "Indians in Los Angeles," 437.

82. Haas, *Conquests and Historical Identities*, 38–44. For more on native labor policies in Los Angeles, see Bell, *Reminiscences of Ranger*; Phillips, "Indians in Los Angeles"; González, "Searching for the Feathered Serpent," 179–211; and Monroy, *Thrown among Strangers*, 127–28. For dozens of examples of native men and women put to labor for failure to pay fines, see ACR, especially vols. 1–7.

83. For a critical and insightful analysis of the writings of nineteenth-century Euro-American and foreign travelers, see Castañeda, "The Political Economy of Nineteenth Century Stereotypes," 213–36. Also see Langum, "Californio Women and the Image of Virtue," 245–50, though he largely accepts the judgments made about upper- and lower-class women: "The issue of virtue may indeed be a function of social and economic class" (247).

84. Quotation cited in ibid., 246.

85. For more on Manifest Destiny, see Horsman, *Race and Manifest Destiny*, especially chapters 11–12. For more on the U.S.–Mexico War, see Haas, "War in California," 331–55, and Harlow, *California Conquered*.

86. Richard White, "*It's Your Misfortune*," 64–69.

87. Haas, "War in California," 333.

88. Doc. No. 618, "José María Flores to Antonio de Haro y Tamariz, December 29, 1846," Henry Dalton Collection, Huntington Library, San Marino, California.

89. Haas, "War in California," 331–55.

90. Quotation cited in Saunders, "An Examination of the Legal Transformation," 25; for the original document, see U.S. Senate, 29th Cong., 2d Sess., Senate Executive Document 1, Serial No. 493 at 644–45.

91. Saunders, "An Examination of the Legal Transformation," 37.

92. Ibid., 41.

93. Ibid., 42–48.

94. Doc. No. 617, "Certification of Property Stolen from Dalton by US Naval Forces, Nov. 27, 1846," Henry Dalton Collection, Huntington Library, San Marino, California.

95. For Cota's claims, see Miscellaneous Legal Papers, Doc. No. 10, "Josefa Cota," January 27, 1847, SC, box 73.

96. For Villalobos' claim, Doc. No. 16, "María Villalobos," January 22, 1847, SC, box 73.

97. For Alvarado's claim, see LACA, vol. 4, 121–25, 392 (1847); and for Rendon's claim, see ibid., 619, 630 (1847).

98. For Juana Ballestreros claim, see "Miscellaneous Legal Papers," Doc. No. 35, "Juana Ballestreros," January 19, 1847, SC, box 73.

99. For Urquides's claim, see ibid., Doc. No. 21, "Dolores Urquides," January 25, 1847, SC, box 73.

100. For the losses sustained at the port of San Pedro, see Unnumbered Doc., "San Pedro, April 27, 1847," SC, box 73.

Chapter 4. Divorce, Culture, and the Family

1. LAACR-DC, case no. 1830 *Rubio v. Rubio* (1870).

2. Arrom, *The Women of Mexico City*, 57–77.

3. *El Clamor Público*, Los Angeles, July 24, 1855, no. 6, 3.

4. Arrom, *Women of Mexico City*, 208–10; Nizza Da Silva, "Divorce in Colonial Brazil, 313–14.

5. Riley, *Divorce*, 3–55.

6. Ibid.; Basch, *Framing American Divorce*, 20–44; Ford, "Women, Marriage, and Divorce"; and Riley, *Building and Breaking Families*, 113–44.

7. Basch, *Framing American Divorce*, 6–7, 46–60.

8. Ibid.

9. California. *Statutes and Amendments to the Codes of California, Passed at the First Session of the Legislature (hereafter cited as California Statutes)* 140 (1850), cited in Langum, *Law and Community*, 252, n. 82; Basch, *Framing American Divorce*, 48, 65–68.

10. For the statute limiting California natives in testifying, see California *Statutes* 133, sec. 6 (1850), 409. For more on Native Californians' lack of legal rights, see Fernández, "Except a California Indian," 161–75; and Ellison, "The Federal Indian Policy in California," 37–67. The literature on Native Americans and divorce in nineteenth-century California is scant. See, for example, Riley, *Building and Breaking Families*, 114, 120; and Hurtado, *Indian Survival on the California Frontier*, 18. More recently, scholars have examined divorce and property in other regions of the United States. See, for example, Osburn, "'Dear Friend and Ex-Husband,'" 157–75.

11. In the District Court records examined for this book, no native women or men petitioned for divorce. Sherburne F. Cook, however, notes that in at least three California cases, a "white tribunal" divorced Native Americans who had been married by "Indian custom." Cook does not provide detailed information on those cases. See *The Conflict between the California Indian and White Civilization*, 372. Also see Riley, *Building and Breaking Families*, 114. According to Riley, years later, in the 1880s and 1890s, some native peoples in other regions, particularly, the Oklahoma Territory, obtained divorces through American Indian Councils, such as the Cherokee National Council, which had passed statutes granting "white-style" divorces. Ibid., 120.

12. Ibid., 114; and Cook, *The Conflict between the California Indian and White Civilization*, 367–69.

13. *California Statutes* 20, sec. 1–4 (1851), 186–87. In the 1850s and 1860s, a number of statutes and Supreme Court decisions defined "extreme cruelty" to include mental suffering and defamation of character, and they stipulated that actionable desertion occurred after two years rather than three. Basch, *Framing American Divorce*, 48, 65–67; Griswold, *Family and Divorce in California*, 19–20; *Morris v. Morris*, 14 in *Reports of Cases Determined in the Supreme Court of the State of California, 1872* (hereafter cited as Cal.), 76–81; *Eidenmuller v. Eidenmuller*, 31 Cal., 364–66 (1867).

14. *California Statutes* 188 (1869–1870), 291; Griswold, *Family and Divorce in California*, 18.

15. Deering, *Civil Code of the State of California*, sec. 92–107 (1872), 143.

16. Riley, *Building and Breaking Families*, 59.

17. *California Statutes* 33 (1850), 93–96. For more on the jurisdiction of the district courts, see ibid., chaps. 1–3 (1851), 2–15. In 1869, the state reorganized the districts and renamed Los Angeles's First Judicial District Court as the Seventeenth Judicial District Court. In 1880, with the approval of a new state constitution, the district courts were abolished and their jurisdiction transferred to the local county Superior Courts. Robinson, *Lawyers of Los Angeles*, 318.

18. On defaults, see *California Statutes* 20, 187 (1851); and *Civil Code*, sec. 130, 47 (1872).

19. Robinson, *Lawyers of Los Angeles*, 318; Bancroft, *The Works of Hubert Howe Bancroft*, vol. 20, 769; ibid., vol. 21, 758–59; Griswold del Castillo, *The Los Angeles Barrio*, 156.

20. For the provisions on English and Spanish in the courts, see *California Statutes* (1853), 304–5. For district court cases in which sheriffs affirmed having no knowledge of Spanish, see, for instance, LAACR-DC, case no. 1485 *Godey v. Godey* (1869) and case no. 1223 *Verdugo v. Carvajal* (1866).

21. Demographic data on Mexican, Euro-American, and European women in Los Angeles County for the first three decades of American rule can be found in the following census compilations: Newmark and Newmark, *Census of the City and County of Los Angeles*, United States, *Population Schedules of the Eighth Census of the United States, 1860*; United States, *Population Schedules of the Ninth Census, 1870*; United States, *Population Schedules of the Tenth Census, 1880*.

22. The records, though incomplete, reveal that of 69 Spanish-speaking women who filed for divorce, 29 owned property valued between $1,000 to $5,000; 12, property valued over $5,000; and 9, property valued under $1,000; and 19 gave no indication of their socioeconomic status. My research indicates that 22 of the 69 women were born in California, 2 were born in Mexico, and 45 provided no indication of regional origin.

23. The records, though incomplete, indicate that of 213 Euro-American women who sought divorces, 72 belonged to the mid-stratum or elite; 10 were impoverished; and 131 provided no indication of their real property values.

24. For the 396 divorce cases—as well as all data and figures tabulated—used in this discussion, see LAACR-DC; and "Index to the Los Angeles Area Court Records," vols. 1–3, 5 (vol. 4 is missing), Huntington Library, San Marino, California.

25. Hurtado, *Indian Survival*, 172; and Bouvier, *Women and the Conquest of California*, 112.

26. Quotation cited in ibid.

27. For findings on Contra Costa and Santa Clara counties, see Griswold, *Family and Divorce in California*, 30. Griswold, however, does not account for ethnic differences among "whites"—which likely includes California-Mexicans, Europeans, and Euro-Americans. For findings in Sacramento, see Ford, "Women, Marriage, and Divorce," 9, 164, 244. Griswold and Ford's results on the propensity of women to file for divorce dovetail with earlier evidence for New England and central Mexico. See Nancy F. Cott, "Eighteenth-century Family and Social Life," 107–35; Riley, *Divorce*, 35, 90; and Arrom, *Women of Mexico City*, 206–7.

28. Arrom, *Women of Mexico City*, 210, 255; and Nizza Da Silva, "Divorce in Colonial Brazil," 314.

29. *California Statutes* 20, sec. 7 (1851), 186–87.

30. *Dupreuz v. Dupreuz*, 5 Cal., 387–89 (1855); *Perkins v. Perkins*, 18 Cal., 60–66 (1861); *Wilson v. Wilson*, 45 Cal., 403 (1873); and Ford, "Women, Marriage, and Divorce," 112.

31. *Eidenmuller v. Eidenmuller*, 31 Cal., 364–66 (1867).

32. *Civil Code*, sec. 138–50 (1872), 49–52.

33. Ibid., 48–49.

34. *Everett v. Everett*, 52 Cal., 384 (1877).

35. Ford, "Women, Marriage, and Divorce," 82, 111–12, 248.

36. For Rafaela Carrillo's divorce suit, see LAACR-DC, case no. 247 *Carrillo v. Carrillo* (1856).

37. LAACR-DC, case no. 841 *Gift v. Gift* (1862).

38. *California Statutes* 103, Sec. 2 (1850), 254–55. The larger implications of this statute, including the influence of Hispanic and Mexican civil law on it, are discussed in numerous works. See, for example, Arrom, *The Women of Mexico City*, 53–97, 206–58; Prager, "The Persistence of Separate Property Concepts"; Schuele, "Community Property Law"; De Funiak, *Principles of Community Property*, 535–661; Ford, "Women, Marriage, and Divorce," 1–49, 71–119, 235–40; Griswold, *Family and Divorce in California*; August, "The Spread of Community-Property Law," 35–66; and McMurray, "The Beginnings of the Community Property System," 359–80.

39. *California Statutes* 103, sec. 9 (1850), 254.

40. Ibid., chap. 489, sec. 1 (1863), 750.

41. *Lord v. Hough*, 43 Cal., 585 (1872).

42. *Civil Code*, sec. 167 and 172 (1872), 55–56.

43. *Beard v. Knox*, 5 Cal., 252–56 (1855); *Dueprez v. Dueprez*, 5 Cal., 387–89 (1855).

44. *Smith v. Smith*, 12 Cal., 216–26 (1859).

45. *Civil Code*, sec. 172 (1872), 56.

46. The Supreme Court upheld that statute in an 1862 decision. See *Mahone v. Grimshaw*, 20 Cal., 175–77 (1862).

47. *California Statutes* 103, sec. 12 (1850), 254.

48. *Galland v. Galland*, 38 Cal., 265–78 (1869); and *Godey v. Godey*, 39 Cal., 157–68 (1869).

49. For the 1869 Supreme Court decision, see *Godey v. Godey*, 39 Cal., 157–68 (1869); for the 1872 Civil Code statute, see *Civil Code*, sec. 148 (1872), 51–52; and De Funiak, *Principles of Community Property*, 650–53.

50. *California Statutes* 176, sec. 1 (1857), 199; and De Funiak, *Principles of Community Property*, 538–39.

51. Ibid., 623–49; and Arrom, *Women of Mexico City*, 209–16.

52. *Eslinger v. Eslinger*, 47 Cal., 62–64 (1873).

53. LAACR-DC, case no. 4112 *Pierce v. Pierce* (1877).

54. Ibid., case no. 4838 *Easton v. Easton* (1878). María Antonia's maiden name was recorded only as "R" in the divorce suit.

55. For the other four cases, see ibid., case no. 4296 *Jacobs v. Jacobs* (1878), case no.

4308 *Olsen v. Olsen* (1878), case no. 4929 *Osburn v. Osburn* (1879), and case no. 4935 *Jenkins v. Jenkins* (1879). Ford, "Women, Marriage, and Divorce," 100, 113, 248.

56. LAACR-DC, case no. 1485 *Godey v. Godey* (1869–1870).

57. *Godey v. Godey*, 39, Cal., 157–68 (1870).

58. *California Statutes* 103, sec. 1 (1850), 254–55.

59. Prager, "The Persistence of Separate Property Concepts," 26.

60. *California Statutes* 103, sec. 3–5 (1850), 254–55.

61. Arrom, *Women of Mexico City*, 68–69.

62. *Ingoldsby v. Juan*, 12, Cal., 576 (1859), cited in *Meagher v. Thompson*, 49, Cal., 191 (1874).

63. *O'Brien v. Foreman*, 46, Cal., 81–82 (1873); and *Meagher v. Thompson*, 49, Cal., 189–92 (1874).

64. *California Statutes* 161, sec. 1–2 (1870), 226–27.

65. Ibid., chap. 103, sec. 9 (1850), 254–55.

66. *Civil Code*, sec. 162 (1872), 54.

67. LAACR-DC, case no. 955 *Domínguez v. Chapman* (1863).

68. Ibid., case no. 1164 *Baltz v. Baltz* (1866).

69. For the criminal suit, see LAACR-CC, case no. 7-5 *People v. Felipe Rheim* (1850). For the three divorce suits, see LAACR-DC, case no. 440 *Dias v. Rheim* (1857), case nos. 455 *Rosario Dias de Rheim v. Phillipe Rheim* (1857) and 700 *Rosario Dias de Rheim v. Felipe Rheim* (1860).

70. LAACR-DC, case no. 363 *Shugg v. Shugg* (1856). For the other case, see ibid., case no. 1630 *Ranfi v. Ranfi* (1870).

71. For the divorce suit, see LAACR-DC, case no. 3891 *Merced Williams de Carrillo v. José C. Carrillo* (1877). See also, Black, *Rancho Cucamonga and Doña Merced*, 125.

72. LAACR-DC, case no. 1540 *Burnett v. Carrillo, Williams, et al.* (1869–1870).

73. Black, *Rancho Cucamonga*, 125–71.

74. Bridger's statement is found in LAACR-DC, case no. 1380 *Williams v. Williams de Carrillo et al.* (1868).

75. Black, *Rancho Cucamonga*, 132–38, 181. María Merced's married life is unclear after her attempt to divorce. According to Black, María Merced Williams separated permanently from Carrillo and eventually remarried a Mr. Fernández, whose identity is unknown. Carrillo's whereabouts are also unclear.

76. Fraijo falsely identified Méndez as his lawful spouse and their child as "*hijo legitimo*" (legitimate) in baptismal records, see LAPC, Baptisms, book 2, 1848–1858, No. 892 "Antonio Fraijo" (1854).

77. For the divorce suit, see LAACR-DC, case no. 442 *Soberanos v. Fraijo* (1857); for Fraijo's title to property in Los Angeles, see Los Angeles City Archives, City Records Management, Los Angeles, California, *Deeds from the City of Los Angeles*, vol. 2, Aug. 8, 1852–Sept. 11, 1856 (1854), 12, 300. For the transfer of those titles to Mendéz, see ibid. (1856), 435. For his outstanding loans, see LAACR-DC, case no. 224 *Mathew Keller v. Gregorio Fraijo* (1855), case no. 248 *Matthew Keller v. Gregorio Fraijo* (1855), case nos. 364 *Bernardo Giovani v. Gregorio Fraijo* (1856) and 402 *Matthew Keller v. Gregorio Fraijo* (1857). For his bankruptcy case, see ibid., case no. 256 *Gregorio Fraijo, an Insolvent Debtor* (1855).

78. For the thirteen criminal cases, see LAACR-CC. For the Olivera and Duarte case, see LAACR-CC, case no. 8-15 *Martín Duarte, Assault and Battery, María Juana Olivera* (1850).

79. De Funiak, *Principles of Community Property*, 623–49; Arrom, *Women of Mexico City*, 209–16; and Basch, *In the Eyes of the Law*, 20, 90–93.

80. Nine of 104 cases involving Euro-American men were not completed for reasons that remain unknown. A pattern similar to Los Angeles emerged in Sacramento, where adultery was the most frequent and successful accusation made by husbands against their wives. Ford, "Women, Marriage, and Divorce," 10–11.

81. *Conant v. Conant*, 10 Cal., 249–58 (1858).

82. For an example of a woman who was found guilty of adultery and was denied alimony, see LAACR-DC, case no. 1193 *Humboldt v. Humboldt* (1866); for an example of a guilty woman who lost her share of community property, see ibid., case no. 1266 *Guillory v. Morales* (1867); and, for an example of a guilty woman who was denied custody of her children, see ibid., case no. 907 *Vejar v. Cota* (1862).

83. Ibid., case no. 1668 *Elias v. Cruz* (1870).

84. Ibid., case no. 1642 *Swigart v. Swigart* (1870).

85. *Civil Code*, sec. 103–4 (1872), 42; and Basch, *In the Eyes of the Law*, 15–19.

86. LAACR-DC, case no. 1381 *Domínguez v. Felch* (1868). For the other three Mexican women who lost divorce suits and property as well, see ibid., case nos. 25 *Pérez v. Silvas* (1851), 2204 *Riesgo v. Mayet* (1873), and 2862 *Araecha v. Araecha* (1875).

87. Ibid., case no. 961 *Grabs v. Grabs* (1863). For the other seven Euro-American women who lost divorce suits and property, see ibid., case nos. 962 *Jenkins v. Jenkins* (1864), 1463 *Gray v. Gray* (1869), 2171 *Kraemer v. Kraemer* (1873), 3313 *Bailey v. Bailey* (1876), 3756 *Cottle v. Cottle* (1877), 4027 *Bec v. Bec* (1877), and 4463 *Lawrence v. Lawrence* (1878).

88. Guadalupe Villareal de González to Francisca Sepúlveda, January 27, 1858, Sepúlveda-Mott Collection, Seaver Center for Western History, Natural History Museum of Los Angeles County, Los Angeles, California; ibid., March 1, 1860.

89. For the divorce suit, see LAACR-DC, case no. 100 *Sepúlveda v. Carrillo* (1854); for Sepúlveda's remarriage, see Northrop, *Spanish-Mexican Families*, vol. 1, 312.

90. LAACR-DC, case no. 3891 *Carrillo v. Carrillo* (1877); and Black, *Rancho Cucamonga*, 132–38, 176–81. For others who turned to family members for support, see LAACR-DC, case no. 2258 *Patterson v. Patterson* (1873), 3496 *Fabre v. Fabre* (1876), 4488 *Lastre v. Lastre* (1878), and 4949 *Vittorino v. Vittorino* (1879).

91. Ibid., case no. 2170 *Parker v. Parker* (1873).

92. See, for example, ibid., case nos. 2709 *Fogle v. Fogle* (1875) and 5288 *Deguerre v. Deguerre* (1879).

93. Ibid., case no. 4203 *Finley v. Finley* (1877).

94. Ibid., case no. 2015 *Valenzuela v. Aguilar* (1872).

95. Ibid., case no. 2102 *Barter v. Barter* (1872). For more on the Sisters of Charity, see Engh, *Frontier Faiths*, 12, 105–6, 139–63.

96. LAACR-DC, case no. 1788 *Benavides v. Benavides* (1871).

97. LAACR-CC, case no. 5-23 *People v. Alfred E. Ferris* (1877).

98. Ford, "Women, Marriage, and Divorce," 29.

Chapter 5. Loss of Property and Economic Independence

1. *Statutes at Large of United States* 9 (1848), 929–30.

2. Robinson, *Land in California*, 100. Numerous studies have examined the promises and realities of the treaty. For a sample of those works, see Griswold del Castillo, *The Treaty of Guadalupe Hidalgo*; and Luna, " 'This Land Belongs to Me,' " 115–62. I would like to thank Kevin R. Johnson for bringing Luna's work to my attention.

3. *Statutes at Large of United States* 9, chap. 41 (1851), 631–34.

4. For more on the *Recopilación* and the colonization laws of 1824 and 1828, see chapter 3. See also Robinson, *Land in California*, 101.

5. Ibid., 100–101. For those who contend that the Land Act of 1851 was fair, see, for example, Bradfute, *The Court of Private Land Claims*; and Gates, "The California Land Act of 1851."

6. Robinson, *Land in California*, 105.

7. Ibid., 166–68.

8. For more on married women's property rights in California, see chapter 4; for the 1850 statute, see *California Statutes* 103 (1850), 254–55.

9. For the statute on sole traders, see ibid., 42 (1852), 101–2.

10. The First District Court of California, whose jurisdiction embraced Los Angeles and San Diego counties (and whose authority extended over probate, divorce, and other civil matters as well as cases appealed from county and municipal courts), was renamed the Seventeenth District Court in 1880. For more on the district court, see chapter 4.

11. For other studies on married women's property rights in California, see Prager, "The Persistence of Separate Property Concepts"; Schuele, "Community Property Law"; and De Funiak, *Principles of Community Property*. For married women's property in other parts of the United States, see Basch, *In the Eyes of the Law*; and Salmon, *Women and the Law of Property in Early America*.

12. These figures come from my investigation and tabulation of material in the U.S. District Court, Land Cases, Southern District, Bancroft Library, Berkeley, California (hereafter cited as LC). Numerous studies of the California ranchos were used to supplement the federal records. Those works include Robinson, *Land in California*; Robinson, *Ranchos Become Cities*; Cleland, *Cattle on a Thousand Hills*; Cowan, *Ranchos of California*; and Pérez, *Land Grants in Alta California*.

13. Quotation cited in LC No. 229 (El Cajon de los Negros Grant, William Workman, claimant).

14. LC No. 362 (Sierra, Vicenta Sepúlveda, claimant); and Cowan, *Ranchos of California*, 98.

15. For more on the alcalde and prefect's roles, see chapters 2 and 3.

16. LC No. 371 (San Antonio [Rodeo de las Aguas], María Rita [V]aldez, claimant); and Cowan, *Ranchos of California*, 68–69.

17. For conversion scales for acres, leagues, and varas, see Pérez, *Land Grants in Alta California*, 240–41.

18. LC No. 133 SD (Los Féliz Grant, María Ygnacia Verdugo, claimant); and Cowan, *Ranchos of California*, 36. For similar cases with vague boundaries, which the board nevertheless approved, see LC No. 130 (El Nigüel Grant, Juan Abila et al. claimants); LC

No. 135 (San Gabriel Grant, claimant); and LC No. 303 (San Francisco Grant, Jacoba Féli[z], claimant).

19. LC No. 46 (Azusa Grant, Andrés Duarte, claimant); and Cowan, *Ranchos of California*, 18.

20. LC No. 58 (Land, San Gabriel, José Domingo, claimant); and Pérez, *Land Grants in Alta California*, 90.

21. For the claim brought by Alexander and Mellus, see LC No. 52 (Tujunga Grant, David W. Alexander and Francis Mellus, claimants); and Cowan, *Ranchos of California*, 14. For the other claims submitted by Euro-Americans, see LC No. 183 (Los Alamos y Agua Caliente Grant, Agustín Olvera [and Lancaster Brent], claimant[s]); LC No. 30 (Providencia Grant, David W. Alexander, claimant); LC No. 235 (Lands, San Gabriel Grant, Daniel Sexton, claimant); LC No. 259 (Land near the Misión San Gabriel, Daniel Sexton, claimant); and LC No. 316 (La Cañada Grant, Johnathan Scott, Benjamin Hayes, claimants).

22. For the six cases rejected by the board of land commissioners, see LC No. 193 (Santa Gertrudes Grant, Concepción Nieto et al., claimants); LC No. 47 (Lands, San Gabriel, Victoria Reid, claimant); LC No. 116 (San Pascual Grant, María Merced Lugo de Foster et al., claimants); LC No. 87 (Paso de Bartolo Grant, Pío Pico et al., claimants); LC No. 182 (Santa Ana del Chino Grant, Isaac Williams, claimants); and LC No. 143 (San Vicente y Santa Monica Grant, Francisco Sepúlveda, claimant).

23. Quotation cited in LC No. 256 (Las Virgenes Grant, Heirs of Domingo Carrillo, claimants). For a claimant who offered compelling evidence for not improving the land, see, for example, LC No. 281 (Muscupiabe Grant, Michael White, claimant). White successfully argued that Indian raids had forced him to abandon his rancho and take refuge in Los Angeles for months at a time.

24. For Lugo's claim, see LC No. 116 (San Pascual Grant, María Merced Lugo de Foster et al., claimants); for Garfias's claim, see LC No. 173 (San Pascual Grant, Manuel Garfias, claimant); and Cowan, *Ranchos of California*, 86.

25. For Reid's rejected claim, see LC No. 47 (Lands, San Gabriel, Victoria Reid, claimant); for the affirmed cases, see LC No. 171 (Huerta de Cuati, Victoria Reid, claimant); and LC No. 135 (San Gabriel Grant, Rafaela Valenzuela, claimant).

26. LC No. 47 (Lands, San Gabriel, Victoria Reid, claimant).

27. County Assessment totals are found in Guinn, *A History of California*, 253–54. I have not located any of the original assessment records for county property.

28. *El Clamor Público*, August 22, 1857, 2.

29. Other scholars who have examined this case are also unsure as to why the court refused to confirm Tapia and Prudhomme's title. Robinson (*The Malibu*, 16) believes that they "r[a]n up against technicalities that usually were not raised when occupancy could be proved."

30. For Prudhomme's financial debts, see LAACR-DC, case no. 156 *Beaudry v. Prudhomme* (1854), 159 *Keller v. Prudhomme* (1855), and 189 *Beaudry v. Prudhomme* (1855).

31. For Prudhomme and Tapia's case, see LC No. 147 (Topango [sic] Malibu, Leon V. Prudhomme [and María Tapia], claimants); and Cowan, *Ranchos of California*, 104. For other women who sold their property during confirmation hearings, see, for example, LC No. 134 SD (San Gabriel Grant, Lugardo Aguila, claimant); LC No. 208 (Las Bolsas

Grant, Ramón Yorba et al., claimants); and LC No. 217 (Rancho de la Merced, F.P.F. Temple et al., claimants).

32. For evidence of those sales, see LC No. 46 (Rancho Azusa, Andrés Duarte, claimant); LC No. 122 (Rancho San Jose, Ygnacio Palomares, claimant); LC No. 86 (Rancho Santa Anita, Henry Dalton, claimant); and for other ranchos subsequently sold, see, for example, LC No. 290 (Ranchos Los Alamitos, Abel Stearns, claimant); LC No. 17 (Rancho Los Cerritos, Juan Temple, claimant); and Robinson, *Ranchos Become Cities*, 54–55, 190–92, 209.

33. For Reid's land case, see LC No. 171 (Huerta de Cuati, Victoria Reid, claimant); Cowan, *Ranchos of California*, 31; for evidence of Reid's sale, see LAACR-DC No. 562 *Victoria de Reid v. William M. Stockton* (1858).

34. For the Verdugo's claim, see LC No. 381 (San Rafael Grant, Julio Berdugo [*sic*] et al.); Robinson, *Ranchos Become Cities*, 32–48; Northrop, *Spanish-Mexican Families*, vol. 1, 353.

35. The mayor and members of the Common Council also represented the town's claim to four sitios. For a discussion of that process, see Harlow, *Maps and Surveys*, 18–19.

36. *Statutes at Large* 9, 634.

37. For the 1850 law on the incorporation of cities, see *California Statutes* 30 (1850), 87 90; for the incorporation of Los Angeles as a city, see ibid., 60, sec. 1–3 (1850), 155. Technically, Los Angeles did not qualify to be a city since it did not meet the required 2,000 or more inhabitants stipulated in the "act to incorporate cities." The legislature granted it the status of city anyway and, at the same time, it fixed the boundaries at 4 square miles, mistakenly believing 1 square league was equivalent to 1 square mile.

38. For the act that gave Los Angeles rights to land outside its boundaries, see *California Statutes* 78, sec. 3 (1851), 329.

39. Robinson, *Lawyers of Los Angeles*, (17, 28, 35–36, 62–63; Harlow, *Maps and Surveys*; and, for Los Angeles's claim to city lands, see L.C. No. 386 (City of Los Angeles, claimant).

40. The Mexican ayuntamiento (town council) never surveyed pueblo lands.

41. For the ordinance on the sale of city lots, see "Los Angeles City Council Records (Minutes)," City Records Management, Los Angeles, California, vol. 1, 114–16 (1850), and LACA, vol. 4, 894 (1850). For a subsequent ordinance allowing the sale of city lots, see City Records Management, 352 (1854). The full text of the petitions and other proceedings in the council's meetings are contained in LACA, vols. 4–7 (1835–1875). City Records Management and LACA are available in Spanish (original) and English (translation). Citations are to the Spanish-language records. For the ordinance "to provide for the collection of [county] taxes," see City Records Management, 217–19 (1852). For city ordinances passed during the first two decades of American rule, see *Revised Ordinances of the City of Los Angeles for the years 1855, 1860, and 1873*. Not all ordinances are available in those two sources. To locate all ordinances passed by the Common Council, one must consult LACA. For a good, general discussion of municipal organization in Los Angeles, see Hunter, *The Evolution of Municipal Organization*.

42. For more on the surveys and subdivision of pueblo lands, see Harlow, *Maps and Surveys*, 33–57; for the ordinance enacting the "donation" of city lots, see LACA, vol. 1,

222–25 (1852); *Los Angeles Star,* July 17, 1852, 2; and, for the repeal of the ordinance, see LACA, vol. 2, 32, 34 (1854).

43. LACA, vol. 1, 337–38 (1854).

44. Harlow, *Maps and Surveys,* 96–97.

45. *California Statutes* 33 (1850), 93–96; for more on Los Angeles's district court, see chapter 4; and Robinson, *Lawyers of Los Angeles,* 31–33, 318.

46. Population figures are cited in Griswold del Castillo, *Los Angeles Barrio,* 35; and Newmark and Newmark, *Census of the City and County of Los Angeles.* For the original censuses, see chapter 4, note 21.

47. Engh, *Frontier Faiths,* 56.

48. For sales and purchases of city lots, see "Deeds from [the] City of Los Angeles, vol. 1, Nov. 7, 1849–Feb. 24, 1852," Los Angeles City Archives, Records Management Division (hereafter cited as "Deeds, vol. 1"); for Temple's purchase, see ibid. 1–11; and for Wilson and Martin's purchase, see ibid. 6–8.

49. For the donation of city lots, see ibid.; and "Deeds from [the] City of Los Angeles, vol. 2, Aug. 8, 1852–Sept. 11, 1856," Los Angeles City Archives, Records Management Division, Los Angeles, California (hereafter cited as "Deeds, vol. 2").

50. City property values—land and improvements—are based on figures tabulated from city tax, or assessment, rolls for the 1850s, 1860s, and 1870s. See LACA, "Tax Records, 1857," "Assessment Roll, 1860," "Assessment Roll, 1860–1861," "Assessment Roll, 1870–1871," and "Assessment Roll, 1873–1874." No other records have been found, despite a thorough search of the Los Angeles City Archives, Records Management Division; City Assessor's Office (Los Angeles); and the Los Angeles County Recorder's Office (Los Angeles and Norwalk).

51. For more on the natural disasters and the 1863 smallpox epidemic, see Cleland, *Cattle on a Thousand Hills,* 111–12, 169–81.

52. There are numerous general works that deal with the changing social, ethnic, demographic, and economic dynamics of Los Angeles after the conquest. See, for example, Robinson, *Land in California,* 147–75; Robinson, *Ranchos Become Cities;* Fogelson, *The Fragmented Metropolis,* 5–42; and Engh, *Frontier Faiths,* 55–68. Also see the 1850, 1860, 1870, and 1880 censuses, cited in chapter 5, note 46, for evidence of the expanding population and changing ethnic composition of the city and the nearby towns.

53. This figure was arrived at by adding the 1874 value of property held by Mexican men and women to that of property held by Euro-American women ($686,793); that number was subtracted from the total 1874 value of city property ($1,778,956), resulting in $1,092,163.

54. LAACR-DC, case no. 43 *Rafael Guirado v. José Bermúdez* [*sic*] (1851).

55. Ibid., case no. 772 *Johnathon R. Scott v. María Antonia Tapia* (1860). For similar cases, see ibid., case nos. 78 *Luis Vignes v. María Figueroa Ballestreros et al.* (1852) and 337 *William A. Wallace v. María Candelaria Pollorena de Lazos, Manuel Lazos[,] and Pedro Lazos* (1855).

56. Ibid., case no. 4387 *J. E. Hollenbeck v. Dolores Buelna* (1878). For Buelna's loss of other property that she had mortgaged, see ibid., case no. 4821 *Jane E. Hunter v. Dolores Buelna et al.* (1879).

57. For Carreaga's name on the 1853 delinquent tax list, see *Los Angeles Star*, Feb. 11, 1854, 2. Unfortunately, that list provides no indication of how much delinquent tax payers owed; for the sale of Carreaga's property and evidence of her overdue loan, see ibid., 4.

58. For Ballestreros's losses, see ibid., June 26, 1852, 2; February 11, 1854, 2.

59. LAACR-DC, case no. 4448 *Julian A. Chávez v. Luisa Machado de Chávez et al.* (1878). For the earlier case, see ibid., case no. 3465 *Julian Chávez v. Luisa Machado de Chávez et al.* (1876).

60. "Annual Report of Health Officer of Los Angeles City," November 3, 1879, Los Angeles City Archives, Records Management Division, Los Angeles, California. The health officer noted, "The great need of the city is a sewer on Alameda Street that will drain First, Commercial, and Aliso Streets and China town [*sic*]." Residents who lived near the intersection of Los Angeles Street and First Street, close to the plaza and Negro Alley, he continued, complained that the main sewer emptied in their neighborhood. "Very soon it will be the city's imperative duty to either have the sewage disinfected or to extend the main sewer farther from the city," he recommended to the council. I thank Hynda Rudd for bringing this report to my attention.

61. For more on the process of ethnic segregation, see Griswold del Castillo, *Los Angeles Barrio*; for the process of "barrioization" in southern California, see Camarillo, *Chicanos in a Changing Society*; for northern California, see Sánchez, *Adaptation to Conquest*.

62. Camarillo, *Chicanos in a Changing Society*, 101–41.

Chapter 6. Illegitimacy and Social Dislocation after the American Conquest

1. For the child's christening, see LAPC, Baptisms, book 5, 1872–1880, entry no. 392 "Matias Bernardo José Cohn" (1873).

2. For more on hijos naturales and espurios, see Twinam, *Public Lives, Private Secrets*, 26, 38, 40, 77.

3. For evidence of Cohn's marriage and his wife, see LAACR-DC, case no. 3517 "Esther Cohn v. Bernard Cohn" (1876); and Vorspan and Gartner, *History of the Jews of Los Angeles*, 95.

4. For California laws on defining marriage, see *California Statutes* 140, sec. 1 (1850), 424; ibid., sec. 6 and 8 (1850), 424–25; and *California Statutes* 103, sec. 16 (1850), 255. Later, in 1862, the legislature passed a law requiring couples who wished to marry to obtain a license authorizing the judge, justice of the peace, or other person, to perform the ceremony. That license, along with the certificate, would then be filed with the county recorder. See *California Statutes* 183, sec. 7 (1862), 450. For more on the Catholic Church canon law and marriage, see chapter 2 and Twinam, *Public Lives, Private Secrets*; Martínez-Alier, *Marriage, Class, and Colour*; Arrom, *The Women of Mexico City*; and Lavrin, *Sexuality and Marriage*.

5. Vorspan and Gartner, *History of the Jews of Los Angeles*, 95.

6. For evidence that Cohn supported Varelas and the children, see *Los Angeles Times*, November 14, 19, 1891; for the birth of their children, LAPC, Baptisms, book 5, entries no.

992 "Eduardo Cohn" (1874) and 1965 "Marcos Cohn" (1877); for Esther Cohn's divorce suit, which she later dismissed, see LAACR-DC, case no. 3517 *Esther Cohn v. Bernard Cohn* (1876). For more on Cohn, see Newmark, *Sixty Years in Southern California*, 180, 383, 425, 508, 550, 595; and Vorspan and Gartner, *History of the Jews of Los Angeles*, 95–96. In 1889, the year of Cohn's death, Varelas filed a lawsuit claiming an interest in the estate for herself and her children, as the lawful inheritors of the estate. After a year-long trial, the court ruled that the couple had not fulfilled the marital rights and obligations of marriage. For details of the trial, see *Los Angeles Times*, June 19, November 14, 18, 19, 21, and 23, 1891; December 5, 8, 10, 11, 22, 23, 30, and 31, 1891; January 1, 7, 8, 9, 12, and 18, 1892; October 3, 1892. Source is found in Vorspan and Gartner, *History of the Jews of Los Angeles*, 318–19.

7. Illegitimacy rates and the frequency of consensual and non-consensual unions were calculated using baptismal registers from SGM (1771–1912) and LAPC (1826–1920) and Los Angeles County civil marriage records (1851–1877), from Clary, *Los Angeles County Marriages*.

8. The term "social dislocation" is borrowed from Tilly, Scott, and Cohen, "Women's Work and European Fertility Patterns." The authors use it to describe the social, economic, and demographic changes in the wake of industrialization in Europe. I use it to discuss changes in the social, economic, demographic, ethnic, and legal environment in Los Angeles and the greater southern California region following the American takeover in 1846. The following works were also useful in this analysis: Fairchilds, "Female Sexual Attitudes"; Laslett, Oosterveen, and Smith, *Bastardy and Its Comparative History*; Wells, "Illegitimacy and Bridal Pregnancy in Colonial America"; Smith, "The Long Cycle in American Illegitimacy"; and Borah and Cook, "Marriage and Illegitimacy in Mexican Culture." Discussions with Michael Engh, Donna Schuele, and Ann Twinam clarified many points raised in this chapter.

9. For more on this topic, see chapter 5.

10. Phillips, *The Enduring Struggle*, 6, 25; for population statistics, see Cook, *The Population of the California Indians*, 43.

11. For more on the demographic collapse of Indians, see Jackson and Castillo, *Indians, Franciscans, and Spanish Colonization*, 41–58; and Jackson, *Indian Population Decline*.

12 Phillips, *The Enduring Struggle*, 30–33.

13. González, "Searching for the Feathered Serpent," 181–83.

14. Phillips, *The Enduring Struggle*, 35.

15. Quotation cited in ibid., 36.

16. For early statutes governing native peoples in California, see *California Statutes* 133, sec. 1–20 (1850), 408–10.

17. Laslett, "Social Change and the Family," 280. Laslett's research shows that the contemporary newspaper, *The Semi-Weekly News*, complained that native peoples were driving down wages of non-Indian labor.

18. Cook, *The Population of the California Indians*, 44, 65.

19. Phillips, *The Enduring Struggle*, 41, 52; and Fernández, "Except a California Indian," 163.

20. For more on native peoples in American California, see Hurtado, *Indian Survival*

on the California Frontier; for a literary exposé on the California Indians' plight in the nineteenth century, see Jackson, *Ramona: A Story*.

21. Laslett, "Social Change and the Family," 275.

22. Camarillo, *Chicanos in a Changing Society*, 35.

23. Griswold del Castillo suggests that the increasing rate of unemployment in the 1870s and 1880s—23 percent in 1850, 6 percent in 1860, 12 percent in 1870s, and 11 percent in 1880—indicates that men were forced to find work in other places. Richard Griswold del Castillo, *La Familia*, 31–35.

24. Laslett, "Household Structure on an American Frontier," 124–25.

25. Laslett, "Social Change and the Family," 275.

26. For rates of female-headed households, see Griswold del Castillo, *La Familia*, 32. His numbers are higher than Laslett's. She found that female-headed households decreased over time from 18 percent of all households in 1850 to 14 percent in 1870. For more on female-headed households, see Griswold del Castillo, *La Familia*, 38; and Laslett, "Social Change and the Family," 285.

27. These figures—954 and 231—were obtained using SGM, Baptisms, books 1, 2, 5, and 6; LAPC, Baptisms, books 1, 2, 3, 4, and 5; and Clary, *Los Angeles County Marriages*, books 1, 2, 3, and 4.

28. For these figures—954 and 189—see ibid.

29. Deering, *Civil Code of the State of California*, chapter 1, art. 1, sec. 55, 24; sec. 71, 26. In the 1890s, the legislature outlawed common-law marriages. They may have proven to be too flexible and, therefore, too problematic in determining family relations and inheritance procedures.

30. For more on this issue, see Borah and Cook, "Marriage and Legitimacy in Mexican Culture," 960–65.

31. For their four children, see LAPC, Baptisms, book 4, entries no. 737 "Ygnacia Bilderaya [*sic*]" (1867), and 2008 "Antonio Fabiano Bilderain" (1871); ibid., book 5, entries no. 375 "José Bilderain" (1873) and 2020 "Encarnacion Bilderain" (1877). José Bilderain, their third child, died shortly after his christening. For more on Bilderain, see Newmark, *Sixty Years in Southern California*, 432.

32. LAPC, Baptisms, book 4, entries no. 642 "Blas Paco" (1867), 1504 "María Loreto Norberta Paco" (1869), and 2147 "José Guillermo Vaca [*sic*]" (1871); LAPC, Baptisms, book 5, entries no. 1601 "José Lauro Paco" (1876), 1810 "Francisco Paco" (1877), and 2692 "Emigdio Paco" (1879).

33. For Sierra and Soto's children, see LAPC, Baptisms, book 3, entry no. 1600 "Francisco Soto" (1863); ibid., book 4, entries no. 4 "Francisca Xavier Soto" (1865), 616 "Estevan Soto" (1867), and 2367 "María Dominga Soto" (1872); ibid., book 5, entries no. 1072 "Carlos Soto" (1875) and 1890 "María Bernabe Soto" (1877). For Domínguez and Johnson's children, see LAPC, Baptisms, book 4, entry no. 830 "Dolores Clara Johnson" (1867); ibid., book 5, entries no. 622 "Loreta Rafaela Johnson" (1873), 623 "Carlos Johnson" (1873), and 1815 "Feliciana Johnson" (1877).

34. Newmark, *Sixty Years in Southern California*, 153. For their children, see LAPC, Baptisms, book 3, entries no. 210 "Carlos McLoglin [*sic*]" (1859), and 704 "José Guadalupe McLoglin [*sic*]" (1860).

35. Bancroft, *Register of Pioneer Inhabitants of California*, 693. Other than saying that Johnson was the son of the Englishman and Guirado, Bancroft provides no information about him. For Ybarra and Johnson's children, see LAPC, Baptisms, book 3, entry no. 1636 "María Paulina Guadalupe Johnson" (1864); ibid., book 4, entries no. 521 "Santiago Johnson" (1866), and 1445 "María del Carmen Anselma Johnson" (1869).

36. For evidence of their relationship, see LAPC, Baptisms, book 2, entries no. 1355 "María Luisa" (1856), and 1844 "Manuela" (1858).

37. For evidence of their relationship and four children, see LAPC, Baptisms, book 4, entries no. 599 "Santiago Bracamontes" (1867), and 1154 "María Bracamontes" (1868); ibid., book 5, entries no. 766 "José Bracamontes" (1874), and 2586 "Castulo Bracamontes" (1879).

38. For more on Rhodes, see LAACR-DC, case no. 282 *Harvey Rhodes v. Juan Domingo* (1855). For their six children, see LAPC, Baptisms, book 3, entry no. 948 "Juan Rhodes" (1861); ibid., entry no. 1593 "María Genoveba Rhodes" (1863); ibid., entry no. 1594 "María Juana Raquel Rhodes" (1863); ibid., book 4, entry no. 281 "María Serafina Rhodes" (1866); ibid., book 4, entry no. 1004 "María Cipriana Rhodes" (1868); and ibid., entry no. 2045 "George Rhodes" (1871).

39. For more on Lyons, see Newmark, *Sixty Years in Southern California*, 194–95; for evidence of Lyons and Triunfo's children, see LAPC, Baptisms, book 2, entry no. 1807 "José Enrique Lionis [*sic*]" (1858); ibid., book 3, entries no. 579 "Carlos Sires [*sic*]" (1860), and 1720 "Alberto Lyons" (1864). For evidence of Lyons and Espinoza, see LAPC, Baptisms, book 3, entry no. 1768 "Eleonor Lyons" (1864); and for his marriage to Cota, see Clary, *Los Angeles County Marriages*, book 4, 335 (October 21, 1876).

40. The records fail to indicate whether any Indian women eventually married their partners in the southern California region. They may have married elsewhere. On "extended engagements," see Twinam, *Public Lives, Private Secrets*, 82–86.

41. For evidence of their marriage, see LAPC, Baptisms, book 3 Entries No. 937 "José Luis Gervasio Stowe [*sic*]" (1861), and 1590 "Luis Eduardo Stone" (1863). The latter has a marginal note that reads "*legitimado por matrimonio*" (legitimized through marriage).

42. LAPC, Baptisms, book 3, entry no. 1534 "María Josefa de los Angeles Miranda" (1863).

43. LAPC, Baptisms, book 2, entry no. 1813 "Julia Marcelina Dávalos" (1858).

44. For the birth of Verdugo and Apodaca's child, see LAPC, Baptisms, book 2, entry no. 1322 "José Francisco Apodaca" (1856); for evidence of their impoverishment and her flight, see Los Angeles County Records, Probate Court, Seaver Center for Western History, Natural History Museum, "Guardianship of Navarro Children" (1852).

45. For evidence of Elias's inability to support her, see LAACR-DC, case no. 1668 *Andrés Elias v Gumecinda Cruz de Elias* (1870); for their three children, see LAPC, Baptisms, book 3, entry no. 583 "Concepción Reyes" (1866); ibid., book 4, entries no. 1264 "Antonio Salomon Reyes" (1868), and 2157 "Juan Wenceslao Reyes" (1871).

46. For evidence of abandonment, see LAACR-DC, case no. 1623 *Tomasa Cosio de Journeaux v. Antonio Journeaux* (1870); for their six children, see LAPC, Baptisms, book 3, entry no. 1503 "Ramón Antonio Young [*sic*]" (1863); ibid., book 4, entries no. 600 "Ramona E. Younge [*sic*]" (1867), 1574 "Carlos Francisco Yong [*sic*]" (1869), and 2192

"Adolfo Francisco Young [*sic*]" (1871); ibid., book 5, entries no. 462 "Carlos Francisco Younge [*sic*]" (1873), and 1934 "Adolfo Manuel Younge [*sic*]" (1877). For more on Junge, see Newmark, *Sixty Years in Southern California*, 290–91, 367.

47. Antonia I. Castañeda makes a similar finding for Monterey in Spanish California. See "'*Presidarias y pobladoras*,'" 269–70.

48. California law barred marriages between "white persons" and "Negroes or mulattoes" but apparently not between "white persons" and native peoples. See *California Statutes* 140 (1850), sec. 3, 424; *Civil Code*, sec. 60, 24. For more on "miscegenation," or interracial marriage, see Pascoe, "Race, Gender, and the Privileges of Property," 215–30. I thank Natalia Molina for bringing this issue to my attention.

49. Castañeda identifies a similar trend in Monterey, see "*Presidarias y pobladoras*," 239, 251, 261. "Spanish-mestizo men in California," Castañeda writes, "seldom formalized their sexual relations with non-white women. . . . [M]arriage to Amerindian [native] women brought [Spanish-mestizo soldiers] few economic and no political rewards."

50. Wells, "Illegitimacy and Bridal Pregnancy in Colonial America," 354–55; and Smith, "The Long Cycle in American Illegitimacy," 371–75. According to these authors, findings for colonial New England are based on scattered evidence, biased toward rural New England towns, and incomplete, especially for the nineteenth century.

51. Twinam, *Public Lives, Private Secrets*, 11.

52. Griswold del Castillo, *Los Angeles Barrio*, 61.

53. Laslett, "Household Structure on an American Frontier," 118–21. For more on the nature of the transient population, see Newmark, *Sixty Years in Southern California*, 94–95.

54. Newmark and Newmark, *Census of the City and County of Los Angeles*.

55. Newmark, *Sixty Years in Southern California*, 19–21.

56. Rohrbough, "No Boy's Play," 23.

57. For more on the cultural and racial diversity of those going to the mines, see Chan, "A People of Exceptional Character," 44–85. For another thoroughly detailed account of the social, cultural, ethnic, and sexual relations in the gold rush, see Johnson, *Roaring Camp*.

58. The exact number of Sonorans who went to the gold mines is unclear. For the figure of 10,000, see Standart, "The Sonora Migration to California," 337. For a much higher figure, 25,000, see Griswold del Castillo, *La Familia*, 57.

59. Woolsey, "Crime and Punishment," 479.

60. Chan, "Exceptional People," 25, 65–66. For more on agricultural and livestock production and the availability of land, see chapter 5.

61. Population figures are cited in chapter 5, note 46.

62. David J. Weber, "Failure of a Frontier Institution," 126. Much of the discussion on the inability of the church to tend to the spiritual needs of the flock is drawn from ibid.; Francis J. Weber, *The Writings of Francisco García Diego y Moreno*; Francis J. Weber, *California's Reluctant Prelate*; Neri, "Hispanic Catholicism in Transitional California"; and Burns, "The Mexican American Catholic Community in California."

63. García Diego y Moreno to Minister of Justice, Mexico, Santa Bárbara, October 17, 1843, in Weber, *The Writings of Francisco García Diego y Moreno*, 139–41. For more on the

shortage of priests in California, see, for example, García Diego y Moreno to Antonio Sunol, Santa Bárbara, December 1, 1842, ibid., 126; and García Diego y Moreno to Jesús María Vazquez del Mercado, Santa Bárbara, December 1, 1842, ibid., 127. On the inability to collect funds, see García Diego y Moreno to Lucas Alaman, Santa Bárbara, September 12, 1843, ibid., 137–38.

64. Weber, "Failure of a Frontier Institution," 130.

65. Neri, "Hispanic Catholicism in Transitional California," 149.

66. Cited in Weber, "Failure of a Frontier Institution," 134.

67. Ibid., 136; García Diego y Moreno to Minister of Justice, Mexico, Santa Bárbara, October 17, 1843, in Weber, *The Writings of Francisco García Diego y Moreno*, 139–41. By 1869, the Church had reintroduced stole fees. The source of this information comes from personal communication with Michael Engh.

68. For more on the Mexican government's failure to restore the mission property to the neophytes, see chapter 3.

69. Tomás Esténega to Abel Stearns, San Gabriel, June 6, 1846, box 24, SC.

70. Neri, "Hispanic Catholicism in Transitional California," 88, 99. Neri reports that in 1846, the region had fifteen priests, two of whom died by 1848. Rubio managed to obtain several more, and by 1851, there were thirty-one priests in California.

71. Weber, "Failure of a Frontier Institution," 137. Weber reports that one Catholic layman said the priests were "very old, others very ignorant, and others again, I am sorry to say it but it is true, very bad." Cited in ibid, 137–38.

72. On Sorrentini, see Neri, "Hispanic Catholicism in Transitional California," 155. For more on the morality of priests, see Sánchez, *Telling Identities*, 316, n. 6; ibid., 317, n. 30; Bouvier, *Women and the Conquest of California*, 134–35, 137–38; and Bancroft, *The Works of Hubert Howe Bancroft*, vol. 18, 446, n. 40; and ibid., vol. 19, 456–69. Bancroft writes that in 1793, after having lived for two years in California, Father Mariano Rubí was expelled from the College of San Fernando, Mexico City, for having contracted a disease that was "probably venereal in nature." Agustín Fernández de San Vicente, the canon of the Durango Cathedral who was sent to California to report on its status, Bancroft notes, scandalized other friars with his gambling and fondness for wine and women.

73. Weber, "The Failure of a Frontier Institution," 136.

74. Neri, "Hispanic Catholicism in Transitional California," 86.

75. Ibid., 130; Weber, "Reluctant Prelate," 30.

76. Pitt, *The Decline of the Californios*, 219.

77. Ibid.

78. Ibid., 220.

79. *El Clamor Público*, December 25, 1855, 2.

80. Ibid.

81. Ibid., January 19, 1856, 2.

82. Pitt, *Decline of the Californios*, 219.

83. For Alemany's attempt to impose the tithe, see Pitt, *Decline of the Californios*, 219. Personal communication with Michael Engh.

84. Pitt, *Decline of the Californios*, 215.

85. Neri, "Hispanic Catholicism in Transitional California," 139. For more on the conformity of the Catholic Church, see Pitt, *Decline of the Californios*, 217.

86. Neri, "Hispanic Catholicism in Transitional California," 153.

87. Ibid.

88. Amat, *Constitutiones*, 9–11, 24, 26, 28. In the 1862 regulations, Amat also restricted traditional practices at burials, such as the use of fireworks, firearms, and *velorios* (wakes, all-night vigils). Once again, I thank Michael Engh for bringing this information to my attention.

89. Ibid.

90. Neri, "Hispanic Catholicism in Transitional California," 110.

91. Ibid.; Burns, "Mexican American Catholic Community," 257.

92. Quotation cited in Neri, "Hispanic Catholicism in Transitional California," 149.

93. Ibid., 145.

94. Ibid., 139, 166–68; and Weber, *Reluctant Prelate*, 56.

95. Neri, "Hispanic Catholicism in Transitional California," 149.

96. Ibid., 169. For evidence that the friars begged—a practice dating back to the origins of the Franciscans in the thirteenth century—in the Mexican period, see García Diego y Moreno to Minister of Justice, Mexico, Santa Bárbara, October 27, 1843, in Weber, *The Writings of Francisco García Diego y Moreno*, pp. 139–41.

97. Quotation cited in Weber, *Reluctant Prelate*, 195.

98. González, *Refusing the Favor*, 82–86.

99. Quotation cited in Neri, "Hispanic Catholicism in Transitional California," 173.

100. For more on these celebrations, see Pitt, *Decline of the Californios*, 218; and Newmark, *Sixty Years in Southern California*, 98.

101. Pitt, *Decline of the Californios*, 264.

102. On the construction and purpose of the cathedral, see Weber, *Reluctant Prelate*, 162–65; on the spiritual isolation of Mexicans, see Burns, "Mexican American Catholic Community," 258–60; and on the increasing numbers of Mexicans who married before justices of the peace, see Castillo, *La Familia*, 91.

103. Weber, *Reluctant Prelate*, 63–97.

104. For first-hand accounts of the difficulties facing Native Americans, see Caughey, *The Indians of Southern California*.

105. California, State Supreme Court, case no. 2132 *Manuelita Williams v. Francisca A. [Williams de] McDougal*, May 24, 1870.

106. Arrom, *Women of Mexico City*, 69–70.

107. For evidence of single mothers begging and stealing, see chapter 3 and ACR.

108. Arrom, *Women of Mexico City*, 57–77; and Twinam, "Honor, Sexuality, and Illegitimacy," 124; Gutiérrez, *When Jesus Came, the Corn Mothers Went Away*, 199–200.

109. For the findings on New Mexico, see ibid., 199.

110. For more on the double sexual standard in Mexican and American Catholic culture, see chapter 2; and Twinam, *Public Lives, Private Secrets*, chap. 4.

111. SGM, Baptisms, book 3, entry no. 6846 "Manuel Silverio Elizalde" (1822).

112. SGM, Baptisms, book 3, entry no. 6825 "María del Carmen Moreno" (1822). For more on Guillen, see Northrop, *Spanish-Mexican Families*, vol. 2, 117.

113. For Machado's child, see LAPC, Baptisms, book 3, entry no. 919 "Herminda R. Machado" (1868); and for Vaquez's child, see LAPC, Baptisms, book 5, entry no. 658 "Lisando Vasquez" (1874).

114. These findings come from my analysis of the baptismal records.

115. LAPC, Baptisms, book 1, entry no. 1909 "María Manuela del Sacramento Rubio" (1848).

116. SGM, Baptisms, book 6, entry no. 1632 "José Eusebio Odignot" (1878).

117. LAACR-DC, case no. 1751 *Whitehorne [sic] v. Reyes* (1870).

118. For more on Cruz, see chapter 4.

Legacies

1. Ruiz de Burton, *The Squatter and the Don.*

2. Ibid., 176. Emphasis added.

3. Ibid., 359; for an extended analysis of Ruiz's novel, see Sánchez and Pita, "Introduction," in ibid., 5–51; and Haas, *Conquests and Historical Identities,* 77–81.

Glossary

alcahueta. A procurer or pimp.

alcalde. Judge and town council member.

amasia. A mistress or lover.

amo. An employer or master.

ayuntamiento. Town council.

bienes gananciales. Community property; property jointly owned by husband and wife.

bienes parafernales. Personal property; property owned by an individual.

casa de honor. Honorable home.

casta. Racially mixed individual.

conquista. Conquest.

comisionado. A Spanish colonial official with authority over local governmental affairs.

depósito. Seclusion, usually in a *casa de honor* or some other safehouse, designed to guard a woman's virtue and person.

ejido. Land held in common.

españoles, españolas. Spanish men or women.

gente de razón. Spanish-speaking colonists as distinguished from the native peoples of California.

gentiles. Non-Christian or "pagan" native peoples.

hijo natural. Child born to unmarried parents, who are eligible to marry.

hijo espurio. Child born as a result of adultery.

hombre bueno. A referee or arbitrator, who acted as an advisor to the local court.

huerta. Vegetable garden or orchard.

indígenas. Native peoples.

indio, india. Native man, woman, or member of an North American indigenous people.

joyas. A practice found among some indigenous groups in which a person of one sex, usually male, takes on the social role of the opposite sex, usually female.

llavera. A matron who held the keys to the women's *monjerios* in the missions.

mala vida. Literally, bad life; more generally, chronic mistreatment; also a label used to identify women who led "sinful lives," that is, whose sexual behavior was deemed antisocial.

monjerio. Nunnery, or a room at a mission where only unmarried females slept, as a way to "guard" sexual virtue.

mulato, mulata. Man or woman of Spanish-African ancestry.

neófito, neófita. Christianized native man or woman.

padrón. Census.

patria potestas. Patria potestad, or paternal authority vested in fathers and husbands.

pobladores, pobladoras. Male or female settlers of pueblos.

prefectura. A system imposed from 1839 to 1844 by the Mexican central government after it abolished ayuntamientos. The three prefectures of Los Angeles, Santa Bárbara, and San Francisco each had prefects, who were directly responsible to the governor, and first courts (for civil and criminal proceedings) in major towns.

presidio. Military garrison or fort.

ranchería. Term used by Europeans to refer to Indian settlements.

sitio. 1 square league, about 6.78 square miles or roughly 4,440 acres.

solar. Land for building a home.

suerte. Land for agriculture.

vergüenza. Shame related to corporal matters.

Bibliography

Archives and Manuscript Collections

Bancroft Library, Berkeley, California
Archivo General de la Nación, Californias, vol. 2
California Archives
Department of State Papers, vols. 1–63
Prefecturas y juzgados, vol. 35
United States District Court. Private Land Grant Cases, Southern District, 1852–1880

California State Archives, Sacramento
Spanish Archives. Spanish-Mexican Land Grant Records, 1784–1846, vols. 1–19

Family History Center, Church of Jesus Christ of Latter Day Saints,
Davis, California
Los Angeles Plaza Church, Los Angeles, California. Baptisms, books 1–5, 1826–1920
Misión San Gabriel, San Gabriel, California, Baptisms, books 1–3, 6 (1771–1855, 1868–1908)
Misión San Gabriel, San Gabriel, California, Marriages, book 1 (1774–1855)

Henry E. Huntington Library, San Marino, California
Abel Stearns Collection
De la Guerra y Noriega Collection
Henry Dalton Collection
Los Angeles Area Court Records, District Court, 1851–1880
Los Angeles Area Court Records, Criminal Court, 1851–1880
Plan de colonización estrangera [*sic*] para los territorios de la alta y de la baja California propuesto por la junta de fomento de aquella peninsular de orden especial del gobierno (Mexico City, 1827)
Reglamento a que debe sujetarsela colonización de los territorios de ambas Californias, en cumplimiento de la ley de 18 de Agosto de 1824, formado por la junta de fomento de los mismo, de superior orden de 5 de Abril de 1825 (Mexico City, 1827)

Los Angeles City Archives, Records Management Division
    Deeds from City of Los Angeles. 1849–1883. Vols. 1–3
    Deeds from City of Los Angeles. Index to Vols. 1–3. 1849–1883
    Los Angeles City Archives. Index to Vols. Vols. 1–7
    Los Angeles City Archives / City Council. 1827–1871. Vols. 1–7
    Los Angeles City Council (Minutes). 1850–1874. Vols. 1–7
    Los Angeles City Council (Minutes). Index to Vols. 1–7
    Los Angeles Prefecture Records. 1830–1850. Vols. 1–3
    Padrónes, 1836, 1844. Vol. 3, pp. 666–801
    Revised Ordinances to the City of Los Angeles, 1855, 1860, 1873
Seaver Center for Western History, Natural History Museum of Los Angeles County,
   Los Angeles
    Alcalde Court Records. 1830–1850. Vols. 1–9
    Avila Family Papers
    Coronel Collection
    Delinquent Tax List for the County of Los Angeles. 1864
    Del Valle Collection
    First Judicial District. District Court: Probate. 1850–1860
    Los Angeles County Court. Court of Sessions: Criminal. 1850–1860
    Patents to Land in Los Angeles County. 1837–1890
    Prudhomme Collection
    Sepúlveda-Mott Collection
    Thomas Workman Temple Collection
UCLA Special Collections, University Research Library
    Bandini Collection

Newspapers

El Clamor Público
Los Angeles Star / La Estrella
Los Angeles Times

Primary Sources

Amat, Thaddaeo. *Constitutiones.* San Francisco, CA: Vincentii Torras, 1862.

Asisara, Lorenzo. "The Assasination of Padre Andrés Quintana by the Indians of Mission Santa Cruz in 1812: The Narrative of Lorenzo Asisara." Ed. Edward D. Castillo. *California History* 68 (1989): 117–25, 150–52.

Bell, Horace. *Reminiscences of a Ranger; or, Early Times in Southern California.* Los Angeles: Yarnell, Caystile, and Mathes, 1881.

Bolton, Herbert E. *Anza's California Expeditions.* Vols. 1–5. Berkeley: University of California Press, 1930.

——, trans. and ed. *Font's Complete Diary: A Chronicle of the Founding of San Francisco.* Berkeley: University of California Press, 1933.

Boscana, Gerónimo. *A Historical Account of the Beliefs, Usages, Customs, and Extravagan-cies of the Indians of this Mission of San Juan Capistrano, called the Acágchemem tribe.* Trans. Alfred Robinson. New York: Wiley and Putnam, 1846.

Bucareli y Ursúa, Antonio María de. Instrucción que debe observer el Comandante nombrado para los Establecimientos de San Diego y Monterey, 1773, ms.

California. *Reports of Cases Determined in the Supreme Court.* Vols. 1–55. San Jose, San Francisco, and Sacramento: State Printers, 1850–1880.

——. *Statutes and Amendments to the Codes of California, Passed at the First Session to the Twenty-Third Session of the Legislature.* San Jose, San Francisco, and Sacramento: State Printers, 1850–1880.

Clary, Jeanne B., comp. *Los Angeles County Marriages, 1851–1877.* Vols. 1–4. Burbank, CA: Southern California Genealogical Society, 1985.

Deering, James H., ed. *Civil Code of the State of California, As Enacted in 1872 . . .* San Francisco, CA: Bancroft-Whitney, 1903.

Diaz del Castillo, Bernal. *Historia verdadera de la conquista de la Nueva España.* Mexico City: Editorial Porrúa, 1942.

Fages, Pedro. *A Historical, Political, and Natural Description of California by Pedro Fages, Written for the Viceroy in 1775.* Trans. by Herbert Ingram Priestly. Ramona, CA: Ballena Press, 1972.

Geiger, Maynard. "Instructions Concerning the Occupation of California, 1769." *scq* 47 (June 1965): 209–15.

——, trans. and ed. *As the Padres Saw Them: California Indian Life and Customs as Reported by the Franciscan Missionaries, 1813–1815.* Santa Barbara: Santa Barbara Mission Archive, 1976.

——, trans. and ed. *Letter of Luís Jayme, O.F.M: San Diego, October 17, 1772.* Los Angeles: Dawson's Book Shop, 1970.

——, trans. and ed. "Six Census Records of Los Angeles and Its Immediate Area between 1804 and 1823." *scq* 54 (Winter 1972): 313–352.

Layne, J. Gregg, ed. "The First Census of the Los Angeles District [1836]." *hsscq* 18 (September–December 1936): 81–99. With facsimile, 1–54.

Lugo, José del Carmen. "*Vida de un ranchero* (Life of a Rancher)." Trans. Helen Pruitt Beattie. *hsscq* 32 (September 1950): 185–236.

Neve, Felipe de. *Reglamento para el gobierno de la provincia de californias.* Mexico, 1784.

Newmark, Maurice, and Marco Newmark, comps. and eds. *Census of the City and County of Los Angeles, California for the Year 1850.* Los Angeles: Times-Mirror Press, 1929.

Northrop, Marie E. "The Los Angeles Padrón of 1844, as Copied from the *Los Angeles City Archives.*" *scq* 42 (December 1960): 360–417.

——, trans. and ed. "Padrón (Census) of Los Angeles, 1790." *scq* 41 (June 1959): 181–82.

Osio, Antonio María. *The History of Alta California: A Memoir of Mexican California.* Trans. and ed. Rose Marie Beebe and Robert M. Senkewicz. Madison: University of Wisconsin Press, 1996.

Prudon, Victor. "Vigilantes de Los Angeles, 1836." Ms. in Bancroft Library, Berkeley, California.

Recopilación de leyes de los reynos de las indias, mandadas imprimir y publicar por la magestad Católica del Rey Don Carlos II. Vol. 1. Madrid: Viuda de Ibarra, 1791.

Robinson, W. W. "The Indians of Los Angeles, As Revealed by the Los Angeles City Archives." *HSSCQ* 20 (December 1938): 156–72.

Ruiz de Burton, María Amparo. *The Squatter and the Don: A Novel Descriptive of Contemporary Occurrences in California*, ed. Rosaura Sánchez and Beatrice Pita. Houston: Arte Público Press, 1992.

Sánchez, Rosaura, Beatrice Pita, and Bárbara Reyes, eds. "Eulalia Pérez, Una Vieja y sus Recuerdos Dictados . . . a la Edad Avanzada de 139 años, San Gabriel, California, 1877." *Critica* (Spring 1994): 31–44.

——. "*Memorias* de doña Apolinaria Lorenzana 'La Beata' dictadas por ella en Santa Bárbara en marzo de 1878 a Thomas Savage, Bancroft Library 1878." *Critica* (Spring 1994): 1–14.

Teggart, Frederick J., ed. *The Portolá Expedition of 1769–1770: Diary of Miguel Costanso*. Publications of the Academy of Pacific Coast History, vol. 2. Berkeley: University of California Press, 1911.

Tibesar, Antonine, ed. and trans. *Writings of Junípero Serra*. 4 vols. Academy of American Franciscan Historical Documentary Series, nos. 4–7. Washington, DC: Academy of American Franciscan History, 1955–66.

United States. *An Act to Ascertain and Settle the Private Land Claims in the State of California. Statutes at Large and Treaties*. Vol. 9 (1862): 631–34.

——. *Population Schedules of the Eighth Census of the United States, 1860*. Washington, DC: National Archives, 1965. Textfiche.

——. *Population Schedules of the Ninth Census of the United States, 1870*. Washington, DC: National Archives, 1965. Textfiche.

——. *Population Schedules of the Tenth Census of the United States, 1880*. Washington, DC: National Archives, 1965. Textfiche.

United States Congress. House. *Report on the Laws and Regulations Relative to Grants or Sales of Public Lands in California, by Henry W. Halleck, March 1, 1849*. 31st Cong., 1st sess., House Exec. Doc. 17, App. 5. Washington, DC, 1849.

United States Congress. Senate. 29th Cong., 2nd Sess., Senate Executive Document 1, Serial No. 493, 644–45. Washington, DC, 1850.

Weber, Francis. J., ed. and trans. *The Writings of Francisco García Diego y Moreno, Obispo de Ambas Californias*. Hong Kong: Libra Press Ltd., 1976.

Secondary Sources

Alarcón, Norma. "Chicana's Feminist Literature: A Re-Vision through Malintzin/or Malinche: Putting Flesh Back on the Object." In *This Bridge Called My Back: Writings by Radical Women of Color*, ed. Cherríe Moraga and Gloria Anzaldúa, 182–90. New York: Kitchen Table, Women of Color Press, 1983.

Arrom, Sylvia M. *The Women of Mexico City, 1790–1857*. Stanford: Stanford University Press, 1985.

August, Ray. "The Spread of Community-Property Law to the Far West." *Western Legal History* 3 (Winter/Spring 1990): 35–66.

Avilez, Alexander. *Population Increases in Alta California in the Spanish Period, 1769–1821*. San Francisco, CA: R & E Research Associates, 1974.

Baker, Charles C. "Mexican Land Grants in California." *HSSCQ* 9 (1914): 236–43.

Bancroft, Hubert Howe. *Register of Pioneer Inhabitants of California, 1542 to 1848*. Los Angeles: Dawson's Book Shop, 1964 [1886].

———. *The Works of Hubert Howe Bancroft*. Vols. 18–22: *History of California*. San Francisco, CA: A. L. Bancroft & Co., 1884–86.

Bannon, John Francis, ed. *The Spanish Borderlands Frontier, 1513–1821*. New York: Holt, Rhinehart and Winston, 1970.

Basch, Norma. *Framing American Divorce: From the Revolutionary Generation to the Victorians*. Berkeley: University of California Press, 1999.

———. *In the Eyes of the Law: Women, Marriage, and Property in Nineteenth-Century New York*. Ithaca, NY: Cornell University Press, 1982.

Becker, Robert H. *Diseños of California Ranchos: Maps of Thirty-Seven Land Grants, 1822–1846*. San Francisco, CA: Grabhorn Press, 1964.

Beilharz, Edwin A. *Felipe de Neve: First Governor of California*. San Francisco, CA: California Historical Society, 1971.

Bernal de Bugeda, Beatríz. "Situación Jurídica de la Mujer en las Indias Occidentales." In *Condición Jurídica de la Mujer en México*, ed. Facultad de Derecho, 21–40. Mexico City: Editorial de la Universidad Autónoma de Mexico, 1975.

Black, Esther Boulton. *Rancho Cucamonga and Doña Merced*. Redlands, CA: San Bernardino County Museum Association, 1975.

Borah, Woodrow, and Sherburne F. Cook. "Marriage and Legitimacy in Mexican Culture: Mexico and California." *California Law Review* 54 (May 1966): 960–1004.

Bouvier, Virginia M. *Women and the Conquest of California, 1542–1840: Codes of Silence*. Tucson: University of Arizona Press, 2000.

Bowman, J. N. "Prominent Women of Provincial California." *HSSCQ* 39 (September 1957): 149–66.

Boyer, Richard. "Women, La Mala Vida, and the Politics of Marriage." In *Sexuality and Marriage*, ed. Asunción Lavrin, 252–86. Lincoln: University of Nebraska Press, 1989.

Bradfute, Richard W. *The Court of Private Land Claims: The Adjudication of Spanish and Mexican Land Grant Titles, 1891–1904*. Albuquerque: University of New Mexico Press, 1975.

Brown, Kathleen. *Good Wives, Nasty Wenches, and Anxious Patriarchs: Gender, Race, and Power in Colonial Virginia*. Chapel Hill: University of North Carolina Press, 1997.

Burkett, Elinor C. "In Dubious Sisterhood: Class and Sex in Spanish South America." *Latin American Perspectives* 4 (Winter–Spring 1977): 18–26.

Burns, Jeffrey M. "The Mexican American Catholic Community in California, 1850–1980." In *Religion and Society in the American West*, ed. Carl Guarneri and David Alvarez, 255–73. New York: University Press of America, 1987.

Camarillo, Albert. *Chicanos in a Changing Society: From Mexican Pueblos to American Barrios in Santa Barbara and Southern California, 1848–1930*. Cambridge, MA: Harvard University Press, 1979.

Campbell, Leon. "The First Californios: Presidial Society in Spanish California, 1769–1822." *Journal of the West* 7 (October 1972): 583–95.

Candelaria, Cordelia. "La Malinche, Feminist Prototype." *Frontiers* 5 (1980): 1–6.

Carrico, Richard L. "Sociopolitical Aspects of the 1775 Revolt at Mission San Diego de Alcalá." *Journal of San Diego History* 43 (Summer 1997): 142–57.

Castañeda, Antonia I. "The Political Economy of Nineteenth Century Stereotypes of Californianas." In *Between Borders: Essays on Mexicana/Chicana History*, ed. Adelaida Del Castillo, 213–36. Encino, CA: Floricanto Press, 1990.

——. "*Presidarias y pobladoras*: Spanish-Mexican Women in Frontier Monterey, Alta California, 1770–1821." Ph.D. diss., Stanford University, 1990.

——. "Sexual Violence in the Politics and Policies of Conquest: Amerindian Women and the Spanish Conquest of Alta California." In *Building with Our Hands: New Directions in Chicana Studies*, ed. Adela de la Torre and Beatriz M. Pesquera, 15–33. Berkeley: University of California Press, 1993.

——. "Women of Color and the Re-writing of Western History: The Discourse, Politics and Decolonization of History." *Pacific Historical Review* 61 (November 1992): 501–33.

Caughey, John W., ed., *The Indians of Southern California in 1852: The B.D. Wilson Report* Lincoln: University of Nebraska Press, 1995.

Chan, Sucheng. "A People of Exceptional Character: Ethnic Diversity, Nativism, and Racism in the California Gold Rush." In *Rooted in Barbarous Soil: People, Culture, and Community in Gold Rush California*, ed. Kevin Starr and Richard J. Orsi, 44–85. Berkeley: University of California Press, 2000.

Cleland, Robert Glass. *Cattle on a Thousand Hills: Southern California, 1850–1870*. San Marino, CA: Huntington Library, 1941.

Cook, Sherburne F. *The Conflict between the California Indian and White Civilization*. Berkeley: University of California Press, 1976.

——. "Historical Demography." In *The Handbook of North.*

American Indians, vol. 8: *California*, ed. Robert F. Heizer, 91–98. Washington, DC: Smithsonian Institution, 1978.

——. *The Population of the California Indians, 1769–1970*. Berkeley: University of California Press, 1976.

Costo, Rupert, and Jeannette Henry Costo, eds. "Interview with Francis F. Guest." In *The Missions of California: A Legacy of Genocide*, ed. Costo and Costo. San Francisco, CA: Indian History Press, 1987.

Cott, Nancy F. "Eighteenth-Century Family and Social Life Revealed in Massachusetts Divorce Records." In *A Heritage of Her Own: Toward a New Social History of American Women*, ed. Nancy F. Cott and Elizabeth H. Pleck, 107–35. New York: Simon and Schuster, 1979.

Cowan, Robert G. *Ranchos of California: A List of Spanish Concessions, 1775–1822, and Mexican Grants, 1822–1846*. Fresno: Academy Library Guild, 1956.

Cutter, Charles R. *The Legal Culture of Northern New Spain, 1710–1810*. Albuquerque: University of New Mexico Press, 1995.

Dakin, Sussana Bryant. *A Scotch Paisano in Old Los Angeles: Hugo Reid's Life in California, 1832–1852: Derived From His Correspondence*. Berkeley: University of California Press, 1939.

Del Castillo, Adelaida. "Malintzin Tenépal: A Preliminary Look into a New Perspective." In *Essays on La Mujer*, ed. Rosaura Sánchez, 124–49. Los Angeles: Chicano Studies Research Center Publications, 1977.

De Funiak, William Q. *Principles of Community Property.* Chicago: Callahan and Co., 1943.

De la Torre, Adela and Beatriz Pesquera, eds. *Building with Our Hands: New Directions in Chicana Studies.* Berkeley: University of California Press, 1993.

Dwinelle, John W. *The Colonial History of the City of San Francisco.* San Francisco: Towne & Bacon, 1863.

Ellison, William H. "The Federal Indian Policy in California, 1846–1860." *Mississippi Valley Historical Review* 9 (June 1922–March 1923): 37–67.

Engelhardt, Zephyrin. *San Gabriel Mission and the Beginnings of Los Angeles.* San Gabriel: Mission San Gabriel, 1927.

Engh, Michael E. *Frontier Faiths: Church, Temple, and Synagogue in Los Angeles, 1846–1888.* Albuquerque: University of New Mexico Press, 1992.

Engstrand, Iris H. W. "California Ranchos: Their Hispanic Heritage." *SCQ* 67 (Fall 1985): 282–86.

——. "The Legal Heritage of Spanish California." *SCQ* 75 (Fall/Winter 1993): 205–36.

Erickson, Amy Louise. *Women and Property in Early Modern England.* London: Routledge, 1993.

Eversole, Robert Wayne. "Towns in Mexican Alta California: A Social History of Monterey, San José, Santa Bárbara, and Los Angeles, 1822–1846." Ph.D. diss., University of California, San Diego, 1986.

Fairchilds, Cissie. "Female Sexual Attitudes and the Rise of Illegitimacy: A Case Study." *Journal of Interdisciplinary History* 8 (Spring 1978): 627–67.

Fernández, Ferdinand F. "Except a California Indian: A Study of Legal Discrimination." *SCQ* 50 (June 1968): 161–75.

Fogelson, Robert M. *The Fragmented Metropolis: Los Angeles, 1850–1930.* 2d. ed. Berkeley: University of California Press, 1993.

Forbes, Jack D. *Native Americans of California and Nevada.* Healdsburgh, CA: Naturegraph, 1969.

——. *Warriors of the Colorado: The Yumas of the Quechan Nation and Their Neighbors.* Norman: University of Oklahoma Press, 1965.

Ford, Bonnie. "Women, Marriage, and Divorce in California, 1849–1872." Ph.D. diss., University of California, Davis, 1985.

Garr, Daniel J. "A Rare and Desolate Land: Population and Race in Hispanic California." *WHQ* 6 (April 1975): 134–48.

Gates, Paul W. "The California Land Act of 1851." *California Historical Quarterly* 50 (December 1971): 95–130.

Gauderman, Kymm. "Father Fiction: The Construction of Gender in England, Spain, and the Andes." *UCLA Historical Journal* 12 (1992): 122–51.

Góngora, Mario. *Studies in the Colonial History of Spanish America.* Trans. Richard Southern. Cambridge: Cambridge University Press, 1975.

González, Deena J. *Refusing the Favor: The Spanish-Mexican Women of Santa Fe, 1820–1880.* New York: Oxford University Press, 1999.

González, Michael J. "Searching for the Feathered Serpent: Exploring the Origins of Mexican Culture in Los Angeles, 1830–1850." Ph.D. diss., University of California, Berkeley, 1992.

González, Sylvia A. "La Chicana: Guadalupe or Malinche." In *Comparative Perspectives of Third World Women: The Impact of Race, Sex, and Class*, ed. Beverly Lindsay, 229–50. New York: Praeger, 1980.

Goodman, Dena. "Public Sphere and Private Life: Toward a Synthesis of Current Historiographical Approaches to the Old Regime." *History and Theory* 31 (1991): 1–20.

Griswold, Robert L. *Family and Divorce in California, 1850–1890: Victorian Illusions and Everyday Realities*. Albany: State University of New York Press, 1982.

Griswold del Castillo, Richard. *La Familia: Chicano Families in the Urban Southwest, 1848 to the Present*. Notre Dame, IN: Notre Dame University Press, 1984.

——. *The Los Angeles Barrio, 1850–1890: A Social History*. Berkeley: University of California Press, 1980.

——. "Patriarchy and the Status of Women in the Late Nineteenth-Century Southwest." In *The Mexican and Mexican American Experience in the Nineteenth Century*, ed. Jaime E. Rodriguez, 85–99. Tempe, AZ: Bilingual Press, 1989.

——. *The Treaty of Guadalupe-Hidalgo: A Legacy of Conflict*. Norman: University of Oklahoma Press, 1990.

Grivas, Theodore. "Alcalde Rule: The Nature of Local Government in Spanish and Mexican California." *California Historical Society Quarterly* 40 (March 1961): 11–19.

Guest, Francis F. "An Inquiry into the Role of the Discipline in California Mission Life." *SCQ* 71 (Spring 1989): 1–67.

——. "Municipal Government in Spanish California." *California Historical Society Quarterly* 46 (December 1967): 307–35.

Guinn, J. M. *A History of California and an Extended History of Los Angeles and Environs*. Vols. 1–3. Los Angeles: Historic Record Co., 1915.

Gutiérrez, Ramón A. "Chicano History: Paradigm Shifts and Shifting Boundaries." In *Voices of a New Chicana/o History*, ed. Refugio Rochin and Dennis N. Valdes, 91–114. East Lansing: Michigan State University Press, 1999.

——. "Unraveling America's Hispanic Past: Internal Stratification and Class Boundaries." *Aztlán* 17 (Spring 1986): 79–101.

——. *When Jesus Came, the Corn Mothers Went Away: Marriage, Sexuality, and Power in New Mexico, 1500–1836*. Stanford: Stanford University Press, 1990.

Gutiérrez, Ramón A., and Genaro Padilla, eds. *Recovering the U.S. Hispanic Literary Heritage*. Houston: Arte Público Press, 1993.

Haas, Lisbeth. *Conquests and Historical Identities in California, 1769–1936*. Berkeley: University of California Press, 1995.

——. "War in California, 1846–1848." In *Contested Eden: California before the Gold Rush*, ed. Ramón A. Gutiérrez and Richard J. Orsi, 331–55. Berkeley: University of California Press, 1998.

Haring, Clarence Henry. *The Spanish Empire in America*. New York: Oxford University Press, 1947.

Harlow, Neal. *California Conquered: The Annexation of a Mexican Province, 1846–1850.* Berkeley: University of California Press, 1982.

———. *Maps and Surveys of the Pueblo Lands of Los Angeles.* Los Angeles: Dawson's Book Shop, 1976.

Horsman, Reginald. *Race and Manifest Destiny: The Origins of Racial Anglo-Saxonism.* Cambridge, MA: Harvard University Press, 1981.

Hunter, Burton L. *The Evolution of Municipal Organization and Administrative Practice in the City of Los Angeles.* Los Angeles: Parker, Stone, and Baird, 1933.

Hurtado, Albert L. *Indian Survival on the California Frontier.* New York: Yale University Press, 1988.

———. *Intimate Frontiers: Sex, Gender, and Culture in Old California.* Albuquerque: University of New Mexico Press, 1999.

Hutchinson, Cecil A. *Frontier Settlement in Mexican California: The Hijar-Padres Colony and Its Origins, 1769–1835.* New Haven: Yale University Press, 1969.

Iduarte, Marta Morinueau. "Condición Jurídica de la Mujer en el México del siglo XIX." In *La Condición Jurídica de la Mujer en México,* ed. Dirección General de Publicaciones (UAM), 41–54. Mexico City: Universidad Autónoma de México, 1975.

Jackson, Helen Hunt. *Ramona: A Story.* With an introduction by Michael Dorris. New York: Penguin, 1988.

Jackson, Robert H. *Indian Population Decline: The Missions of Northwestern New Spain, 1687–1840.* Albuquerque: University of New Mexico Press, 1994.

Jackson, Robert H., and Edward Castillo. *Indians, Franciscans, and Spanish Colonization: The Impact of the Mission System on California Indians.* Albuquerque: University of New Mexico Press, 1995.

Johnson, Susan L. " 'A Memory Sweet to Soldiers': The Significance of Gender in the History of the 'American West.' " *WHQ* 24 (November 1993): 495–517.

———. *Roaring Camp: The Social World of the California Gold Rush.* New York: W. W. Norton, 2000.

Kartunnen, Frances. "Rethinking Malinche." In *Indian Women of Early Mexico,* ed. Susan Schroeder, Stephanie Wood, and Robert Haskett, 291–312. Norman: University of Oklahoma Press, 1997.

Kierner, Cynthia A. *Beyond the Household: Women's Place in the Early South, 1700–1835.* Ithaca: Cornell University Press, 1998.

Kuznesof, Elizabeth, and Robert Oppenheimer. "The Family and Society in Nineteenth-Century Latin America: An Historiographical Introduction." *Journal of Family History* 10 (Fall 1985): 215–234.

Ladd, Doris. *The Mexican Nobility at Independence, 1780–1826.* Austin: University of Texas Press, 1976.

Langum, David J. "Californios and the Image of Indolence." *WHQ* 9 (April 1978): 181–196.

———. "*Californio* Women and the Image of Virtue." *SCQ* 59 (Fall 1977): 245–250.

———. *Law and Community on the Mexican California Frontier: Anglo-American Expatriates and the Clash of Legal Traditions, 1821–1846.* Norman: University of Oklahoma Press, 1987.

——. "Sin, Sex, and Separation in Mexican California: Her Domestic Relations Law." *The Californians* 5 (May/June 1987): 44–50.

Laslett, Barbara. "Household Structure on an American Frontier: Los Angeles, California, in 1850." *American Journal of Sociology* 81 (1975): 109–28.

——. "Social Change and the Family: Los Angeles, California, 1850–1870." *American Sociological Review* 42 (April 1977): 268–90.

Laslett, Peter, Karla Oosterveen, and Richard M. Smith, eds. *Bastardy and Its Comparative History.* London: Edward Arnold Pub., 1980.

Lavrin, Asunción. *Sexuality and Marriage in Colonial Latin America.* Lincoln: University of Nebraska Press, 1989.

Lavrin, Asunción, and Edith Couturier. "Dowries and Wills: A View of Women's Socio-economic Role in Colonial Guadalajara and Puebla, 1640–1790." *Hispanic American Historical Review* 59 (May 1970): 280–304.

Lerner, Gerda. *The Creation of Patriarchy.* New York: Oxford University Press, 1986.

Livingston, M. M. "Earliest Spanish Land Grants in California." HSSCQ 9 (1914): 195–99.

Lockhart, James, and Stuart B. Schwartz. *Early Latin America: A History of Colonial Spanish America and Brazil.* Cambridge, MA: Harvard University Press, 1985.

Lockhart, Katherine Meyer. "A Demographic Profile of an Alta California Pueblo: San José de Guadalupe, 1777–1850." Ph.D. diss., University of Colorado, 1986.

Lothrop, Gloria Ricci. "Rancheras and the Land: Women and Property Rights in Hispanic California." SCQ 76 (Spring 1994): 59–84.

Lummis, Charles, trans. "Felipe de Neve, Regulations and Instructions for California." HSSCQ 15 (1931): 156–88.

Luna, Guadalupe T. " 'This Land Belongs to Me': Chicanas, Land Grant Adjudication, and the Treaty of Guadalupe Hidalgo." *Harvard Latino Law Review* 3 (Fall 1999): 115–62.

MacLachlan, Colin M. *Criminal Justice in Eighteenth Century Mexico: A Study of the Tribunal of the Acordada.* Berkeley: University of California Press, 1974.

Martínez-Alier, Verena. *Marriage, Class and Colour in Nineteenth-Century Cuba.* 2d. ed. Ann Arbor: University of Michigan Press, 1989.

Mason, William M. *The Census of 1790: A Demographic History of Colonial California.* Novato, CA: Ballona Press, 1998.

——. "Indian-Mexican Cultural Exchange in the Los Angeles Area, 1781–1834." *Aztlán* 15 (Spring 1984): 123–44.

McAlister, Lyle N. *The "Fuero" Militar in New Spain, 1764–1800.* Gainesville, FL: University of Florida Press, 1952.

McKnight, Joseph W. "Law Books on the Hispanic Frontier." *Journal of the West* 27 (July 1988): 74–84.

——. "Law without Lawyers on the Hispano-Mexican Frontier." *West Texas Historical Association Year Book* 66 (1990): 51–65.

McMurray, Orrin K. "The Beginnings of the Community Property System in California and the Adoption of the Common Law." *California Law Review* 3 (July 1915): 359–80.

Meyer, Michael C. *Water in the Hispanic Southwest: A Social and Legal History, 1550–1850.* Tucson: University of Arizona Press, 1984.

Miranda, Gloria E. "Hispano-Mexican Childrearing Practices in Pre-American Santa Barbara." *SCQ* 65 (Winter 1983): 307–20.

Monroy, Douglas. "'They Didn't Call Them 'Padre' for Nothing': Patriarchy in Hispanic California." In *Between Borders: Essays on Mexicana/Chicana History,* ed. Adelaida Del Castillo, 443–46. Encino, CA: Floricanto Press, 1990.

——. *Thrown among Strangers: The Making of Mexican Culture in Frontier California.* Berkeley: University of California Press, 1990.

Montoya, María E. *Translating Property: The Maxwell Land Grant and the Conflict over Land in the American West, 1840–1900.* Berkeley: University of California Press, 2002.

Moorehead, Max L. *The Presidio: Bastion of the Spanish Borderlands.* Norman: University of Oklahoma Press, 1975.

Murray, Mary. *The Law of the Father? Patriarchy in the Transition from Feudalism to Capitalism.* London: Routledge, 1995.

Nelson, Howard. "The Two Pueblos of Los Angeles: Agricultural Village and Embryo Town." *SCQ* 59 (Spring 1977): 1–11.

Nelson, Kjerstie. *Marriage and Divorce Practices in Native California.* Berkeley: Archeological Research Facility, 1975.

Neri, Michael C. "Hispanic Catholicism in Transitional California: The Life of José González Rubio, O.F.M." Ph.D. diss., University of California, Berkeley, 1974.

Newmark, Harris. *Sixty Years in Southern California, 1853–1913.* 3d. ed. Boston: Houghton Mifflin, 1930.

Nizza Da Silva, María Beatriz. "Divorce in Colonial Brazil: The Case of São Paulo." In *Sexuality and Marriage in Colonial Latin America,* ed. Asunción Lavrin, 331–40. Lincoln: University of Nebraska Press, 1989.

Northrop, Marie F. *Spanish-Mexican Families of Early California, 1769–1850.* 2 vols. Burbank: Southern California Genealogical Society, 1984–87.

Osburn, Katherine M. B. "'Dear Friend and Ex-Husband': Marriage, Divorce, and Women's Property Rights on the Southern Ute Reservation, 1887–1930." In *Negotiators of Change,* ed. Nancy Shoemaker, 157–75. New York: Routledge, 1995.

Pascoe, Peggy. "Race, Gender, and the Privileges of Property: On the Significance of Miscegenation Law in the U.S. West." In *Over the Edge: Remapping the American West,* ed. Valerie J. Matsumoto and Blake Almendinger, 215–30. Berkeley: University of California Press, 1999.

Pateman, Carole. *The Sexual Contract.* Stanford: Stanford University Press, 1988.

Paz, Octavio. *The Labyrinth of Solitude: Life and Thought in Mexico.* Trans. Lysander Kemp. New York: Grove Press, 1961.

Penyak, Lee M. "Safe Harbors and Compulsory Custody: *Casas de Depósito* in Mexico, 1750–1865." *Hispanic American Historical Review* 79 (1999): 83–99.

Pérez, Crisostomo. *Land Grants in Alta California: A Compilation of Spanish and Mexican Private Land Claims in the State of California.* Rancho Cordova, CA: Landmark, 1996.

Pérez, Emma. *The Decolonial Imaginary: Writing Chicanas into History.* Bloomington: Indiana University Press, 1999.

Pescatello, Ann. *Power and Pawn: The Female in Iberian Families, Societies, and Cultures.* Westport Conn.: Greenwood Press, 1976.

———, ed. *Female and Male in Latin America.* Pittsburgh: University Press, 1973.

Phelan, John Leddy. "Authority and Flexibility in the Spanish Imperial Bureaucracy." *Administrative Science Quarterly* 5 (1960): 47–65.

Phillips, George H. *Chiefs and Challengers: Indian Resistance and Cooperation in Southern California.* Berkeley: University of California Press, 1975.

———. *The Enduring Struggle: Indians in California History.* San Francisco: Boyd & Frasier, 1981.

———. "Indians in Los Angeles, 1781–1875: Economic Integration and Social Disintegration. *PHR* 49 (August 1980): 427–51.

Phillips, Rachel. "Marina / Malinche: Masks and Shadows." In *Women in Hispanic Literature: Icons and Fallen Idols,* ed. Beth Miller, 97–114. Berkeley: University of California Press, 1983.

Pitt, Leonard. *The Decline of the Californios: A Social History of the Spanish-Speaking Californians, 1846–1890.* Berkeley: University of California Press, 1966.

Prager, Susan Westerberg. "The Persistence of Separate Property Concepts in California's Community Property System, 1849–1975." *UCLA Law Review* 24 (October 1976): 1–48.

Riley, Glenda. *Building and Breaking Families in the American West.* Albuquerque: University of New Mexico Press, 1996.

———. *Divorce: An American Tradition.* New York: Oxford, 1991.

Ríos-Bustamante, Antonio Rios, and Pedro Castillo. *An Illustrated History of Mexican Los Angeles, 1781–1985.* Los Angeles: Chicano Studies Research Center Publications, 1986.

Robinson, W. W. *Land in California.* Berkeley: University of California Press, 1948.

———. *Lawyers of Los Angeles.* Los Angeles: Bar Association, 1959.

———. *The Malibu: Rancho Topanga Malibu Sequit, An Historical Approach.* Los Angeles: Ward Ritchie Press, 1958.

———. *Tarnished Angels: Paradisiacal Turpitude in Los Angeles.* Los Angeles: Ward Ritchie Press, 1964.

Rohrbough, Malcolm. "No Boy's Play: Migration and Settlement in Early Gold Rush California." In *Rooted in Barbarous Soil: People, Culture, and Community in Gold Rush California,* ed. Kevin Starr and Richard J. Orsi, 25–43. Berkeley: University of California Press, 2000.

Ryan, Mary P. *Women in Public: Between Banners and Ballots, 1825–1880.* Baltimore: John Hopkins University Press, 1990.

Salmon, Marylynn. *Women and the Law of Property in Early America.* Chapel Hill: University of North Carolina Press, 1986.

Sánchez, George J. *Adaptation to Conquest: The Mexican Community of San José, 1845–1880.* Working Paper Series No. 4. Stanford: Stanford Center for Chicano Research, Stanford University, 1984.

Sánchez, Rosaura. *Telling Identities: The Californio Testimonios.* Minneapolis: University of Minnesota Press, 1995.

Saunders, Myra K. "An Examination of the Legal Transformation of California from a Mexican Province to a United States State, 1846–1850." (Unpublished paper).

Schuele, Donna C. "Community Property Law and the Politics of Married Women's Rights in Nineteenth-Century California." *Western Legal History* 7 (Summer/Fall 1994): 245–81.

Scott, Joan W. "Gender: A Useful Category of Historical Analysis." *American Historical Review* 91 (December 1986): 1053–75.

———. *Gender and the Politics of History.* New York: Columbia University Press, 1988.

———, ed. *Feminism and History.* New York: Oxford University Press, 1996.

Seed, Patricia. *To Love, Honor, and Obey in Colonial Mexico: Conflicts over Marriage Choice, 1574–1821.* Stanford: Stanford University Press, 1988.

Shoemaker, Nancy, ed. *Negotiators of Change: Historical Perspectives on Native American Women.* New York: Routledge, 1995.

Smith, Daniel Scott. "The Long Cycle in American Illegitimacy and Prenuptial Pregnancy." In *Bastardy and Its Comparative History*, ed. Peter Laslett, Karla Oosterveen, and Richard M. Smith, 362–78. London: Edward Arnold Publishers, 1980.

Soto, Shirlene. "Tres modelos culturales: La Virgen Guadalupe, La Malinche y la Llorona." *Feminist Studies* 10 (October–November 1986): 13–16.

Standart, Sister M. Collette. "The Sonora Migration to California, 1848–1856: A Study in Prejudice." *SCQ* 58 (1976): 333–58.

Stern, Steve J. *The Secret History of Gender: Women, Men, and Power in Late Colonial Mexico.* Chapel Hill: University of North Carolina Press, 1995.

Temple, Thomas W., II. "Se fundaron un pueblo de españoles." *HSSCQ* 15 (1931): 69–98.

———. "Soldiers and Settlers of the Expedition of 1781." *HSSCQ* 15 (1931): 99–116.

———. "Toypurina the Witch and the Indian Uprising at San Gabriel." *Masterkey* 32 (1958): 136–52.

Tilly, Louise A., Joan W. Scott, and Miriam Cohen. "Women's Work and European Fertility Patterns." *JIDH* 6 (Winter 1976): 447–76.

Trexler, Richard C. *Sex and Conquest: Gendered Violence, Political Order, and the European Conquest of the Americas.* Ithaca, NY: Cornell University Press, 1995.

Twinam, Ann. "Honor, Sexuality, and Illegitimacy in Colonial Spanish America." In *Sexuality and Marriage*, ed. Asunción Lavrin, 118–55. Lincoln: University of Nebraska Press, 1989.

———. *Public Lives, Private Secrets: Gender, Honor, Sexuality, and Illegitimacy in Colonial Spanish America.* Stanford: Stanford University Press, 1999.

Van Young, Eric. *Hacienda and Market in Eighteenth-Century Mexico: The Rural Economy of the Guadalajara Region, 1675–1820.* Berkeley: University of California Press, 1981.

Vorspan, Max, and Lloyd P. Gartner. *History of the Jews of Los Angeles.* San Marino, CA: Huntington Library, 1970.

Weber, David J. "Failure of a Frontier Institution: The Secular Church in the Borderlands under Independent Mexico, 1821–1846." *WHQ* 12 (April 1981): 125–43.

———. *The Spanish Frontier in North America.* New Haven: Yale University Press, 1992.

Weber, Francis J. *California's Reluctant Prelate: The Life and Times of Wright Reverend Thaddeus Amat, C.M.* Los Angeles: Dawson's Book Store, 1964.

Wells, Robert V. "Illegitimacy and Bridal Pregnancy in Colonial America." In *Bastardy and Its Comparative History*, ed. Peter Laslett, Karla Oosterveen, and Richard M. Smith, 349–61. London: Edward Arnold Pub., 1980.

White, Richard. *"It's Your Misfortune and None of My Own": A New History of the American West*. Norman: University of Oklahoma Press, 1991.

Wittenberg, Sister Mary Ste. Therese. *The Machados and Rancho La Ballona*. Los Angeles: Dawson's Book Shop, 1973.

Woolsey, Ronald C. "Crime and Punishment: Los Angeles County, 1850–1856." In *Crime and Justice in American History*, vol. 4: *The Frontier*, ed. Erick Monkonnen. London: Meckler Publishing, 1991.

Index

abortion, 11, 15
absolute divorce, 91–92
abuelas, 177
Aguilar, José María, 36–39
Alamar, Don Mariano, 174
Alanis, Raimundo, 36–38
alcahueta, 31
alcalde, 25–26, 55–56
Alemany, Joseph Sadoc, 165
Alexander, David W., 133
alimony, 100
Alipas, Asención, 35
Alipas, Gervasio, 43–45
almudes, 72
Alvarado, Francisco Javier, 22
Alvarado, Josefa, 69–71, 83–85
Alvarado, Juan Bautista, 52–53, 57–58, 66–67, 129
Alvarado, Ramona, 157
Alvitre, Sebastián, 3–4
Amador, María Ignacia, 22
amasia, 30–31
a mensa et thoro, 91
amonestaciones, 66–67
anti-assimilationist mentality, 161
Antonio, José, 58–59
Antonio, Manuel, 60–61
Apis, María Antonia, 50
Apodaca, José, 159

aranceles, 164
Argüello, Luis, 63
Argüello, María de los Angeles, 157
Argüello, Santiago, 33
Arias, Ygnacia, 158
Armenta, María, 147
Arnaz, José, 70–72
Arrillaga, José Joaquín de, 136–38
Articles 8 and 9, 123
Arús, Domingo, 17
Arzaga, Manuel, 41–42, 50
Austin, Stephen, 79 81
Avila, Asención, 57–58, 78
Avila, Francisca, 71, 74–75
Avila, Francisco, 3–4
Avila, Hilaria, 46
Avila, José, 36–38
Avila, Juan, 78
Avila, María Andrea, 71
Avila, María Francisca, 119–20
a vinculo a matrimonii, 91–92
ayuntamiento, 43–45, 55–56

Ballestreros, Juana, 84–85
Baltz, Angelica, 108–9
Bandini, Arcadia, 33
Bandini, Margarita, 112 (fig.)
barbareño, 73–74
Barter, Sarah, 120

Bautista de Anza, Juan, 15–16
Bear Flag Republic: declaration of, 80–81
Beaudry, Prudent, 117–18
bed-and-board divorce, 91
Bell, Horace, 154
Benavides, Julia, 120–121
Bermudez, Antonio, 164
bienes gananciales, 54
bienes parafernales, 106–9
Bilderrain, Jesús, 157
bisabuelas, 177
Bojorquez, Luisa, 158
Bore, Santiago. *See* Burke, James
Boronda, Josefa, 42–43
Botello, Narciso, 55
Bouchet, Luis, 55
boundary disputes, 63–64
Bouvier, Virginia Mayo, xv
Bridger, Joseph, 113
Bucareli y Ursúa, Antonio, 4, 8
Buelna, Dolores, 148
Buelna, Encarnación, 148
Bureau of Indian Affairs, 93
Burke, James, 42–43
Butrón, Manuel, 17

Californio-Mexicans: alienation from church, 169; illegitimacy rate among, 159–60
callejon de los negros, 149
Cambón, Pedro, 8
Carpenter, Samuel, 66–67
Carreaga, Nicolasa, 30–31, 48–49, 73, 148
carretas, 69
Carrillo, José Antonio, 55, 119–20, 129
Carrillo, José Clemente, 111–13
Carrillo, Mariano, 3–4
Carrillo, Rafaela, 100
Carrión, Casimiro, 74
casa de cuna, 18–19
casa de honor, 29
casta, 5
Castañeda, Antonia I., xv
Castro, José, 129

Catholic, Spanish, 15
Catholic Church, 163; and alienation of Californio-Mexicans and Native Americans, 169; Americanization of, 165; colonization of California and, 13; priests in, 11; Spanish Crown and, 6; weakening of, 159–60
Celia, María, 16
Celís, Eulogio de, 82–85
census, 46, 67–69
Chapman, John, 107–8, 148
Charles III, 5
Chávez, Julian, 83–85, 148–49
Church of England, 92
church-state struggle, 163–64
Civil Code of 1872, 93, 98–99, 102, 157
class biases, 39
clergy: views on sexual relations, 27–28
Cohn, Bernard "Bernardo," 151–52
colonists: indígenas and, 23
colonization: attempts to encourage, 18–19
comadre, 120
Comcrabit, Victoria, 76–77, 97, 134–35
comisionado, 45–46, 73–74
common-law marriage, 156–57
companionate marriage, 92
Coronel, Antonio Francisco, 128
Coronel, María Antonia, 104
Cortés, Hernán, xiii
Cosio, Tomasa, 159
Cota, Guillermo, 58–59
Cota, Josefa, 65–67, 71, 83–85
Cota, Matilda, 72
Cota, Ynéz, 158
Council of the Indies, 5
Court of First Instance, 29, 56
Court of Second Instance, 29
Crisanta, María, 157–58
Croix, Teodoro de, 4, 18
Cruz, Gumecinda, 116, 159, 172
Cuba: illegitimacy rate in, 47
culture, 5

Dalton, Guadalupe Zamorano de, 105 (fig.)
Dalton, Henry "Enrique," 70–72, 82–85, 139
Dana, Richard Henry, 79
Dávalos, José María, 158
death rates, 153
dehesas, 56
depósito, 33
Dias, Rosario, 109–10
Diego y Moreno, Francisco García, 33, 163
Diocese of Sonora, 163
Dios Rendon, Juana de, 83–85
diputación, 129–30
discrimination: ethnic, 60; gender, 51, 60
diseases: sexually transmitted, 12
divorce, 89–122; ethnicity and, 97–98; personal property and, 106–9; right to, 123
D'Oliveira, Manuel, 76–77
Dolores, Maria, 7–8
Domingo, José, 131
Domingo, Juan, 78
Domínguez, Hilaria, 157
Domínguez, Josefa, 49
Domínguez, Luisa, 30
Domínguez, Margarita, 17
Domínguez, María Antonia, 71, 107–8
Domínguez, María Antonia Gastelum de, 117–18
donation system, 140–41
doncellas, 21
double standard: sexual, 23–24, 48–49, 116, 170–71, 175
Duarte, Andrés, 130–31
Duarte, Martín, 114–15
Duarte, Ramón, 34
Durán, Narciso, 41–42

Easton, María Antonia R. de, 103–4
ecclesiastical taxation, 6
Echeandía, José Maria de, 58–59
Echeveste Regalmento, 14–15

economic independence, 52–85
ejidos, 18, 56, 139
El Clamor Público (newspaper), 91, 135, 165
Elias, Andrés, 116, 159
Elizalde, Antonio, 171
Elizalde, María, 89–90
Elizalde, Ygnacia, 36–38
Enrique, José, 158
Escobar, Anselma, 158
Escolástica, 157–58
escribanos, 55
Espinosa, Gregoria, 73
Espinoza, Luisa, 158
estado, 40–41
Esténega, Tomás Eleuterio, 32–33, 41 42, 57–58, 62, 76–77, 164
ethnic composition: Los Angeles City and, 143
ethnic discrimination, 60
ethnicity, 5, 39
Euro-Americans: population of, 154–55
Eusebio, José, 172
execution, public, 43–45
expedientes, 125

Fages, Pedro, 8, 12 13, 15, 58–59
family, 15, 52–85; women's power in, 123
Felch, Noah, 117–18
Félix, Domingo, 43–45
Féliz, José Antonio, 130
Féliz, Juan, 58–59, 129–30
female-headed households: increase in, 156
Ferris, Alfred, 121
Ferris, Maria G., 121
Figueroa, José, 76–77
Figueroa, Luz, 31–32
Figueroa, María, 70–72
Finley, Ella, 120
Flores, José María, 80–81
Flugge, Charles, 82–85
Foley, D.J., 120
Forster, John "Juan," 60

Fort Tejón, 155
Foster, Stephen "Esteban," 172
Fraijo, Gregorio, 113
Francisco de Croix, Carlos, 5
Frémont, John C., 80–81
frijoles, 69

Gadsden Purchase, 81
gálico, 12
Galindo Navarro, Pedro, 4
Gallardo, Rafael, 71
Gálvez, José de, 5
García, Marina, 30–31, 158
Garfias, Manuel, 133–34
gender, xvi, 5, 39
gender discrimination, 51, 60
General Land Office, 125
gente-de-razón, xiv, 53
gentiles, xiv
Gift, Fannie, 101
Gillespie, Archibald, 82–85
Godey, Alexis, 104
Godey, María Antonia Coronel de, 105
    (fig.)
gold rush of 1849, 162
Gómez, Juana, 41–42, 50
González, Deena, xvi, 177
Goycoechea, Felipe, 136–38
Grabs, Charlotte, 118–19
Gracia, María de, 17
Guerra, Pablo de la, 94–95, 167
Guerra y Noriega, José de la, 45–46, 73–
    74
Guillen, Ysidro, 171
Guirado, Carmen, 157
Guirado, Rafael, 147
Gwin, William M., 124
Gwin Act of 1851, 140
Gwin's Act to Ascertain Land Claims. *See*
    Land Act of 1851

haciendas, 67
Hancock, Henry, 140–41
Hayes, Benjamin, 95

healing practices, 11
Higuera, Victoria, 69–71
Hijar-Pádres expedition, 19
hijos espurios, 28, 47, 170
hijos naturales, 28, 46, 47, 50, 170
Hill, Daniel, 168
Hollenbeck, J.E., 148
hombre bueno, 29
Homestead Act, 126
honor, 27
Hope, Alejandro, 84–85
huertas, 72
humiliation: public, 46

Ibarra, Desiderio, 73
illegitimacy, 151–78; among Californio-
    Mexicans, 159–60
independence: economic, 123–50
Indian problem: eradicating the, 153–54
Indian reservations, 155
indias, 12
indígenas: colonists and, 23
infanticide, 11, 15, 40–41
Institución Caritativa, 120

jacales, 68
Jayme, Luis, 9
Jesús, María de, 50
Jesús, Serafin de, 134
Joaquín, Emilio, 62
Johnson, Francisco, 157
Johnson, James "Santiago," 157
José, Juan, 58–59
José, Matias Bernardo, 151–52
José, Nicolás, 10–11
Josefa, Felicita: daughter of, 132 (fig.)
Journeaux, Antonio, 159
joyas, 15
juez de campo, 57–58
juez de paz, 29
juicio de concilio, 29
Junge, Adolfo "Younge," 159
junta defensora de la seguridad publica, 43–
    45

juzgado de primera instancia, 29
juzgado de segunda instancia, 29

Kartunnen, Frances, xiv
Kearny, Stephen Watts, 81
Keller, Matthew, 138

labor relations: nature of, 67–69
La Estrella (newspaper), 94
Lamoreau, Louis, 148
Lamy, Jean Baptiste, 167
Land Act of 1851, 124–25, 138, 140
La Soledad *ranchería*, 3
laws, state and local: abusive, 154
Leandry, Juan Bautista, 52–53, 69
Leobijilda "Jilda," 177
Lestrade, Jaime, 165
leve, 29
Leyes de Toro, 28, 54
Limón, Francisco, 30–31
llaveras, 21
López, Cornelio, 36–38
López, Esteban, 41
López, José, 46
López, Pedro, 133
López de Santa Anna, Antonio, 79–81
Lorenzana, Apolinaria, 12, 21, 22
Lorenzana, María Jesús, 73
Los Angeles Plaza, 70 (fig.)
Los Angeles Plaza Church, 165, 168; illegitimacy rates, 160 (table)
Los Angeles Star (newspaper), 94
Lugo, Antonio María, 60
Lugo, José del Carmen, 68–69
Lugo, María Antonia, 49, 60
Lugo, María Merced, 133–34, 172
Lyons, Cyrus "Cy," 158

Machado, Bárbara, 72
Machado, Francisco, 171
Machado, Luisa, 148–49
madrina, 171
mala vida, malas vidas (MV), 30, 46, 48
Malintzin, xiii–xiv

Manifest Destiny, 79
Maria, Antonio, 58–59
Mariner, Juan, 65
marital status: women and, 53
Martin, Montgomery, 143
Mather, Cotton, 92
McLoughlin, Ben "Vincente," 157
Mellus, Francis, 133
Méndez, María Francisca, 113
mestizas, xiv
mexicanas, 122
Mexican Independence, 56
Mexico City: illegitimacy rate in, 47
Micheltorena, Manuel, 57–58, 60, 62, 129–30
Miranda, Ramón, 158
Misión San Carlos de Borromeo, 11
Misión San Gabriel, 8–12, 9 (fig.); illegitimacy rates, 160 (table)
monjerios, 21
Moreno, Gertrudis, 171
mulatas, xiv
MV. *See* mala vida

Native Americans, 176
Navarro, Carmen, 75
Navarro, José Antonio, 19
Navarro, María Presentación, 40–41
Navarro, Teodoro, 159
Negro Alley, 149
Nelson, Alexandro, 158
neófitas, xiv, 5, 61 (fig.)
Neve, Felipe de, 3–4, 17–18
Newmark, Harris, 162
Nieto, Antonio María, 66–67
Nieto, Manuela, 58–59
Nieto, Manuel Pérez, 58–59
Nieto, María Cleofas, 63–64
nuevomexicana, 50

O'Campo, Francisco, 131
Ochoba, Gerónimo, 157–58
Odignot, Luis, 172
Olivas, Domingo, 38–39

Olivera, María J., 114–15
Olvera, Agustín, 94–95
Olvera, Martín, 172
Ord, E.O.C., 140
Ordaz, Blas, 62–63
Orduño, Ramón, 130
Osa, Vicente de la, 62–63, 74–75

Paco, Ramón, 157
padre no conocido, 171
padrinos, 166
padrónes, 46
Palma, María, 158
Palomares, Ygnacio, 139
Pañuelas de Féliz, Antonia, 16
Parker, Charlotte, 120
parteras, 23
paternal authority, 28
patria potestas, 28
patriarchal authority: defiance of, 45–46
patriarchal ideology, xix, 5, 26
patronage, 6
patronato real, 5–6
Pegui, María, 42-43
Pérez, Emma, xvii
Pérez, Eulália, 21, 22 (fig.), 65
Pérez, Francisca, 25–26, 30–31
Pérez, José, 65, 133–34
Pérez, Manuel Nieto, 66–67
personal property: divorce and, 106–9;
    loss of, 123–50
Pico, Isidora, 60
Pico, Pío, 60, 61, 64–65, 71, 76–77, 80–
    81, 131
Pico, Tomasa, 71
pinole, 69
Pious Fund, 164
Plan de Pitic, 54
pobladoras, 17–18
Polk, James, 80–81
Pollorena, Ángel, 30
Pollorena, María, 70–72
polygamy, 15
population: of Euro-Americans, 154–55;

Los Angeles City and, 143 (table); re-
    production of, 23
pozolera, 21
prefectura, 33
presidio, 4
prisoners: auctioning of, 154
property, 52–85
property holders: Los Angeles City and,
    145 (table)
property values: of Californio-Mexicans,
    147 (table); by gender and ethnicity,
    148 (table); Los Angeles City and, 144
    (table); Los Angeles County and, 135
    (table), 141–42
propíos, 56, 139
Protestant Orphan Asylum, 121
Provincias Internas, 4
Prudhomme, Leon Victor, 55, 136–38
public execution, 43–45
public humiliation, 46
Pueblo de los Angeles, 140
pueblos, 17–18
Puritans: divorce and, 92
puta, 31

Rains, Cornelia, 111–13, 120
Ramírez, Francisco, 135, 165
Ramírez, José Antonio, 45–46
ranchería, 3
rancheros, 67; struggles of, 139
rape, 4–5, 36–38
real-estate speculation, 142, 144
Recopilación de los reynos las leyes de las in-
    dias, 5, 54, 124
Regalmento para el gobierno de las provin-
    cias de Californias, 17–18
Regulacion para el gobierno de las ambas
    californias, 75
Reid, Hugo, 76–77, 97, 134–135
Reid, Victoria, 139
Reina, Antonio, 40–41
Rendon, Juana, 83–85
Reyes, Ignacio, 116
Reyes, María Lugarda, 172

Reyes, Marta, 30–31
Reyes, Martin, 16
Reyes, Ygnacio, 159, 172
Rheim, Felipe, 109–10
Rhodes, Harvey, 158
Riera, Juan, 32
Rivera y Moncada, Fernando, 7, 15
Robinson, John, 92
Roland, John "Juan," 59–60
Royal Pragmatic on Marriage, 32–33
Rubio, Andrés, 89–90
Rubio, Lugarda, 172
Ruiz, Catarina, 63–64
Ruiz, Joaquín, 64
Ruiz, Maria, 23
Ruiz, Romualdo, 23
Ruiz de Burton, María Amparo, 174

Saint Charles Seminary, 166
Saint Vibiana's, 168
Saiz, Teodacia, 47
San Antonio (ship), 7
San Carlos (ship), 7
San Carlos Borromeo de Monterey, 7
Sánchez, José Antonio, 47
Sánchez, Vicente, 69–71
San José (ship), 7
Santiago (ship), 14–15
Scott, Jonathon, 147
Sepúlveda, Bernardo, 49
Sepúlveda, Casilda, 34, 41–42
Sepúlveda, Diego, 89–90
Sepúlveda, Encarnación, 74–75
Sepúlveda, Enrique, 32–33, 65
Sepúlveda, Francisca, 119–20
Sepúlveda, Francisco, 59
Sepúlveda, José Andrés, 119–20
Sepúlveda, Ramona, 71
Sepúlveda, Vincenta, 64–65, 71, 128
Seraphina, María, 17
Serra, Junípero, 4–5
Serrano, María Ramona, 59
Seventh Provincial Council of Baltimore,
    165

sexual attacks, 4–5, 23, 35–38
sexuality: double standard and, 23–24,
    48–49, 116, 170–71, 175
sexually transmitted diseases, 12
sexual violence, 8–14
sexual virtue, 27
shame, 27
Shrugg, Ester Caroline, 110
Sierra, Altgracia, 157
Siete Partidas, 5, 28, 54
Silvas, María Guadalupe, 23, 25–26
Sisters of Charity, 120
Sloat, John Drake, 80–81, 124
smallpox epidemic, 155
social dislocation, xxiii, 151–78
socio-sexual codes of behavior, 51, 175
solares, 18, 56, 139
sole trader, 126
Somera, Ángel, 8
Sorrentini, Cajetan, 165
Soto, Casilda, 57–58, 70–72
Soto, Luis, 157
Soto y Rodríguez, María, 19
Southern Pacific Railroad, 146
Spanish Catholics: family life of, 15
Squatter and the Don (book), 174
Stearns, Abel, 33, 70–72, 82–85, 128,
    130–31, 164
Stockton, Robert F., 128
stole fees, 164
Stone, Pedro, 158
suerte, 18, 56, 91, 139
Superior Tribunal, 36–38, 43–45, 56, 63
Sutter's Mill, 162
Swigart, Swena, 117
Swigart, Thomas, 117
syphilis, 12

Talamantes, Ysidora, 171
Tapia, Jesús, 157
Tapia, José Bartolomé, 136–38
Tapia, María Antonia, 147
Tapia de Prudhomme, María Merced,
    136–38, 137 (fig.)

Taraval, Sebastián, 7–8
Temple, John "Juan," 43–45, 70–72, 84–85, 143
terrenos, 135
testimony: Native Americans and, 93
Thompson, James, 120
tithes, 6, 164
Torba, Antonio, 17
Toypurina, 10–11
Treaty of Cahuenga, 80–81, 84–85
Treaty of Guadalupe Hidalgo, 78, 81, 84–85, 123, 152, 174
Triunfo, Nicolasa, 158
Trujillo, Matilda, 32–33, 34
Two Years Before the Mast (Dana), 79

uniones libres, 157
Uribes, Francisca, 69
Uriste, Nicolasa, 59–60
U.S. Act of 1851. *See* Land Act of 1851
U.S. Indian Service, 93
Urquides, Dolores, 84–85
Urquides, Tomás, 31

vagrancy law, 154
Valdez, Luciano, 52–53
Valdez, María Rita, 52–53, 128
valdio, 65
Valencia, Antonio, 41
Valencia, Eugenia, 48–49, 73
Valenzuela, Cesaría, 120
Valenzuela, Dolores, 31
Valenzuela, Estanislao, 40–41
Valenzuela, Felipe, 172
Valenzuela, Luisa, 171
Valenzuela, María Antonia, 171
varas, 60
Varela, Hilario, 47
Varela, Petra, 41, 74
Varelas, Cayetano, 46
Varelas, Delfina, 151–52
Varelas, Dolores, 46
Varelas, Ygnacio, 38–39
Vasquez, Carlos, 171

Vejar, Emidio, 52–53
Vejar, Josefa, 75
Vejar, Juan Cristóbal, 36–38
Vejar, Ramona, 31
Vejar, Ricardo, 52–53
venereal diseases, 12
Verdugo, Julio, 49
Verdugo, María Catalina, 71, 139, 159
Verdugo, Mariano de la Luz, 73
Verdugo, María Ygnacia, 58–59, 129–30, 138
Verger, Rafael, 8
vergüenza, 27, 172
Victoria, Manuel, 12
vigilante, 43–45
Villa, Manuela, 30–31, 73
Villa, María del Rosario, 43–45
Villalobos, María Francisca, 55, 83–85
Villareal, Guadalupe, 120
viñas, 72
violentíssimos, 13

Weber, Francis J., 167
White, Michael, 131, 134
Whitehouse, George, 172
Williams, Francisca, 112 (fig.)
Williams, Isaac "Julian," 50, 60
Williams, María Merced, 111–13, 112 (fig.), 120
Wilson, Benjamin D., 143, 155
Wolfskill, William, 139
Workman, William "Julian," 59–60

Ybarra, Gil, 41–42
Ybarra, Timotea, 157
Ygnacio de Soto, Matheo, 3–4
Yorba, Bernardo, 64–65
Yorba, José Antonio, 64–65
Yorba, Teodosio, 49, 68
Yorba, Tomás Antonio, 64–65, 128

Zamorano, Agustín, 58–59
Zúñiga, Anastacia, 45–46

About the Author

Miroslava Chávez-García is an associate professor of Chicana/o History in the Chicana/o Studies Program at the University of California, Davis. She received her doctorate in History from the University of California, Los Angeles, and she has published articles on gender, patriarchy, and the law in nineteenth-century California and on the historic and contemporary relationship between Chicana Studies and Women's Studies. She teaches courses on Chicana/o history, Latina/o history, U.S.–Mexico border relations, and Chicana politics and community activism. Her current research interests focus on youth, race, science, and juvenile delinquency in the late nineteenth and early twentieth centuries.